John Clark Murray

The Ballads and Songs of Scotland

In View of their Influence on the Character of the People

John Clark Murray

The Ballads and Songs of Scotland
In View of their Influence on the Character of the People

ISBN/EAN: 9783744782128

Printed in Europe, USA, Canada, Australia, Japan

Cover: Foto ©Thomas Meinert / pixelio.de

More available books at **www.hansebooks.com**

THE
BALLADS AND SONGS OF SCOTLAND.

THE BALLADS AND SONGS

OF

SCOTLAND,

IN VIEW OF THEIR INFLUENCE ON THE CHARACTER OF THE PEOPLE.

BY

J. CLARK MURRAY, LL.D.,

*Professor of Mental and Moral Philosophy in McGill College, Montreal;
Author of "An Outline of Sir William Hamilton's Philosophy."*

> " Songs of my native land,
>   To me how dear!
> Songs of my infancy,
>   Sweet to my ear!
> Entwined with my youthful days,
> Wi' the bonny banks and braes,
> Where the winding burnie strays,
>   Murmuring near."
>   THE BARONESS NAIRNE.

London:
MACMILLAN AND CO.
1874.

[The Right of Translation and Reproduction is reserved.]

LONDON
R. CLAY, SONS, AND TAYLOR, PRINTERS,
BREAD STREET HILL.

PREFATORY NOTICE.

THE following Essay was awarded a Prize offered by the St. Andrew's Society of Glasgow. By the terms of competition the copyright of the essay remained with the author; and as it was written with a view to publication, it is now given to the world with such alterations and additions as have been suggested on revision. The essay represents the fruit of studies in which the author has been accustomed to find relief from severer professional work; and his object in its publication will be attained, if it afford to his readers any of the recreation which its studies have brought to himself, while it may not be without service even to the student of the literature which it reviews. All other necessary information with regard to the general object and plan of the work will be found in the Introduction.

MONTREAL, *March* 1874.

CONTENTS.

INTRODUCTION ix

CHAPTER I.

PAGE
LEGENDARY BALLADS AND SONGS . . 1

CHAPTER II.

SOCIAL BALLADS AND SONGS . . 50
   § 1. Love Songs and Ballads . . 50
   § 2. Domestic Songs and Ballads . . . 82
   § 3. Lyrics of general Social Relations 108

CHAPTER III.

ROMANTIC BALLADS AND SONGS 127

CHAPTER IV.

HISTORICAL BALLADS AND SONGS . . 135
   § 1. The War of Independence . . . 136
   § 2. The Border Feuds 141
   § 3. The Reformation Period 157
   § 4. The Jacobite Struggle 163

CHAPTER V.

	PAGE
GENERAL INFLUENCE OF THE BALLADS AND SONGS	167
§ 1. Their Poetical Character	168
§ 2. Extent of their Popularity	178
INDEX	199
GLOSSARY	203

INTRODUCTION.

"I knew a very wise man that believed that if a' man were permitted to make all the ballads, he need not care who should make the laws of a nation."—FLETCHER OF SALTOUN, in a *Letter to the Marquis of Montrose*, etc.

IT is desirable that the reader of the following essay should notice the precise subject to which it is limited. The essay is simply an investigation of the influence which the ballads and songs of Scotland may be shown to have exerted on the character of the Scottish people. It makes no pretension, therefore, to be a satisfactory treatment of these lyrical productions in any other aspect. It is impossible, indeed, to discuss the effect of these or of any other productions of the Scottish mind on the development of Scottish character, without indicating more or less definitely the character of the productions themselves; and, consequently, this essay contains a large number of historical and critical observations on the ballads and songs of Scotland. The extent to which such observations were required to elucidate the main question of the essay, will be differently determined by different persons; and possibly a rigid criticism would exclude as irrelevant a considerable amount of what is contained in the following pages. But the reader must meet with disappointment, who opens these pages with the expectation of finding in them an exhaustive treatment of the Scottish ballads and songs in general, or in any particular aspect other than that to which the essay is definitely limited by its title.

Even the special inquiry, however, to which we are thus confined, raises certain preliminary questions which cannot be accurately answered with ease. It involves, to some extent, an inquiry into the national character of the Scottish people, and into the agencies by which that character has been produced and modified. Both of these inquiries may be ranked among the most perplexing of those intricate problems which the science of human nature encounters at every step of its progress.

The former of these—the inquiry into national character—will, if answered at all by those who apprehend it clearly, be answered only with diffidence and by an indefinite outline; for the phenomena, on which an answer must be founded, are so subtle as often to elude the keenest observation, so intricate as to baffle the most searching analysis, so manifold as to exceed the grasp of the most comprehensive understanding. By means of the spectrum we can now analyse the constitution of a world at immeasurable distance in space; but what agent of decomposition can unfold with certainty the character of a nation, or even of an individual? A remarkable instance of the difficulty involved in estimating even one's own character is furnished by the fact, that Goethe attached more importance to his scientific insight than to his poetical power; and, in summing up the results of his life, declared that as it had been the mission of Luther to dispel the darkness of the Papacy, so it had been his to overturn the Newtonian theory of colours![1]

The other inquiry—that, namely, into the agencies by which a nation's character is developed, or into the precise influence which any particular agency may have exerted on its development—is even more difficult than the preceding. Here all the machinery of philosophical induction breaks down under the difficulty of making sufficiently accurate and sufficiently extensive observations, and the collateral difficulty of arranging the data which observation yields with a view to legitimate inference.

Now, if we had to serve merely the purposes of popular declamation, it would be easy enough, concealing the difficulty of all such inquiries, to assert a number of questionable platitudes on the Scottish character and on the influences by which it has been formed. The aim in the following essay has been to avoid all asser-

[1] Eckermann's "Conversations of Goethe," vol. i., p. 162. Compare Lewes' "Life of Goethe," vol. ii., p. 124.

tions with reference to national character and the causes at work in its development, except in so far as such assertions are implied in the solution of the main problem with which we have to deal.

This problem is in reality twofold. It involves two questions: (1), whether any influence at all has been exerted on the character of the Scottish people by their ballads and songs; and (2), if so, what that influence has been. The preliminary inquiry, which forms the first of these two questions, may be disposed of easily in a general way. The character of a nation, as well as of an individual, is moulded by *all* the influences in the midst of which the nation or the individual lives. It is generally, indeed, impossible to determine with certainty the comparative importance of the influences at work; and often the most insignificant in appearance are the most powerful in reality. In the early years of the Roman Empire, for example, no man could have thought of seeking, among the villages of Galilee, the events from which were to issue the most valuable forces of subsequent history; and biographical records, especially of the religious life, have made us familiar with the fact, that the most efficient cause in shaping an individual's character has often been an incident which was externally of the most trivial nature. But however slight in appearance or in reality, *every* influence, working upon the people of a country in general, will contribute something to the national character, though some influences may be so slight as to be incapable of being traced. The only question, therefore, which really remains for answer, is whether we can discover, in the Scottish character, any trace of an influence exerted by the Scottish ballads and songs.

Before proceeding to the detailed examination of the ballads and songs with a view to the solution of this question, it may be well to remark, that it is exceedingly difficult to pitch on any feature of the Scottish character, and say, without hesitation, *that* is due to the influence of the ballads and songs alone. For it is not enough to prove that the ballads and songs are capable of producing such an effect: numerous instances will occur to anyone, in which the perplexity of a problem is precisely to discover, among several phenomena all capable of producing a certain effect, *which* has actually been the cause. Moreover, the agencies at work in human nature, as well as in external nature, are often thwarted, counteracted, in fact completely neutralized, by others; and this circumstance creates one of the main difficulties of all scientific inquiry. In addition to this, there is a peculiar difficulty attaching to inquiries concerning the agencies which go to form social character; for every such agency is alternately cause and effect. A certain type of character in a people cannot be due, for example, to the agency of the people's songs alone; for the people's songs are, in the first instance, due to its character. Every manifestation of character is thus at once evidence of the existence of a certain tendency, and a contribution to the force of the tendency from which it has sprung.

The presence, therefore, of a certain agency is not sufficient to prove that it has produced a certain effect which it is capable of producing, till it has been shown that the effect has not been produced by some other coexisting cause. How, then, must we proceed in our endeavour to trace in the Scottish character some features which are due to the Scottish ballads and songs?

The method adopted in the following essay is the only method allowed by the nature of the inquiry, and the only method of arriving at reliable results. The object has been, after arranging the ballads and songs into groups, to elicit some of the features by which each group is distinguished, to point out the effects which such features are calculated to produce, and to trace these effects in Scottish life. The proof in each detail, taken by itself, is not expected to be convincing; but when the line of argument is comprehended as a whole, it must be evident that the people of Scotland cannot have continued, from generation to generation, singing certain kinds of lyrics, without the distinctive features of these lyrics being stamped, more or less clearly, on the character of that people.

Following, then, the method thus indicated, we must start with some classification of the ballads and songs. In doing so, a sentence or two may not be out place, to define the precise sense in which the terms *ballad* and *song* are severally employed.

1. Without going into a history of the various uses of the former term, it may be defined as denoting *a lyrical narrative, unguided by conscious art, of any event, real or imaginary, which is calculated to excite emotion.* It need only be added, that, by this definition, our review is limited to the *genuine ballad,* and that therefore its modern imitations are excluded. In a critical investigation there may be doubt as to the genuineness of particular ballads; but for our purposes the question of genuineness may be left out of view altogether.

2. A song is *a lyrical utterance of an emotion.* It is not always possible, therefore, to distinguish precisely between a ballad and a song; for songs are often, perhaps commonly, founded on an event, imaginary if not real. But when the narrative of the event predominates over the mere utterance of the emotion which the event calls forth, the lyric becomes in propriety a ballad; and *vice versâ.* Still, some lyrics may, without impropriety, be classed either among ballads or among songs, and are consequently found in collections of both. *Barbara Allan,* commonly met with in song-books, partakes more of the nature of a ballad; while *Helen of Kirconnell* and *The Lament of the Border Widow,* as well as some other lyrics generally included in our books of ballads, are more correctly regarded as songs. The *Song of Moses*[1] is a splendid specimen of lyrical narrative, borne on by such an impetuous tide of emotion,

[1] Exodus, chap. xv.

swelling at a great national crisis, that it is difficult to say whether the narrative or the emotional element prevails.

It is impossible to suggest a perfectly logical classification of the ballads and songs, or of any other literary works whatever. The following must justify itself simply by its convenience for our purposes:—

1. *Legendary* ballads and songs—those in which a supernatural element, embodying the superstitions of a less scientific age, comes into play.

2. *Social* ballads and songs—those to which the social affections or the events of social life furnish a theme.

3. *Romantic* ballads and songs—those in which the subject is an imaginary, or at least an uncertain event.

4. *Historical* ballads and songs—those which contain a poetical narrative of, or reference to, some known event of history.

THE BALLADS AND SONGS OF SCOTLAND.

CHAPTER I.

LEGENDARY BALLADS AND SONGS.

" There must thou wake perforce thy Doric quill;
   'Tis fancy's land to which thou sett'st thy feet
   Where still, 'tis said, the fairy people meet,
Beneath each birken shade, on mead or hill.
There each trim lass, that skims the milky store,
   To the swart tribes their creamy bowls allots;
By night they sip it round the cottage door,
   While airy minstrels warble jocund notes.
There every herd, by sad experience, knows
   How, winged with fate, their elf-shot arrows fly,
When the sick ewe her summer food forgoes,
   Or, stretched on earth, the heart-smit heifers lie.
Such airy beings awe the untutored swain:
   Nor thou, though learned, his homelier thoughts neglect;
Let thy sweet Muse the rural faith sustain;
   These are the themes of simple, sure effect,
That add new conquests to her boundless reign,
And fill, with double force, her heart-commanding strain."

   COLLINS' *Ode on the Superstitions of the Scottish Highlands.*

THE poems comprehended under this designation, are those which involve a belief in forms of agency incompatible with the known laws of nature. Such a belief arises spontaneously in any mind unacquainted with the uniformity of type which modern science has detected in the innumerable varieties of being, and with the uniformity of sequence which we have been taught to trace through all the various processes by which Nature reaches her ends. In order to study the legendary lyrics with profit, we must, therefore, carry ourselves by imagination back into those old times, when the convictions of science found as yet no place in the culture of men,—when no shock was given to ordinary human beliefs by the idea of creatures which violated every principle of anatomical structure,—when an extraordinary event, instead of being laboriously referred to some recognized agency of nature, was at once explained as the work of some of those supernatural beings which peopled the fancy of our ancestors.

Most of the superstitious conceptions thus originated, which we come upon in the legendary songs and ballads, have been handed down from an exceedingly remote period, and, in the course of tradition, have gathered numerous features by which their original shape is more or less concealed. In fact, nearly all those superstitions of modern Europe, which have a title to be called *popular*, on the ground of their acceptance among a people at large, and not merely among isolated individuals or isolated sections of a community, still bear traces of their descent from heathen times. The recent researches of comparative mythology have put into our hands the clue by which we can already track many of the legendary beliefs, of the Aryan nations at least, to their common Eastern home; and in studying the poems which come under review in the present chapter, several opportunities will occur for observing the various shapes which the same primitive legend has assumed under the various influences to which it has been subjected at the different points where it has been deposited along the stream of Aryan migration.

The most universal agency in modifying Aryan mythology among the Western nations has been the introduction of Christianity. The mass of beliefs and practices which formed the religious faith and worship of the pre-Christian Teutons, in whom we find our ancestry, did not at once yield to the force of Christian teaching. As Roman Christianity became tainted by numerous symbols and festivals of the paganism it supplanted, so the Teutonic tribes, long after their conversion, clung to the old beliefs which in fact entered into all their forms of thought and speech about the world, as well as to the observances which had, in many cases, woven themselves into the habits of their daily lives. The influence, indeed, of the new religion on these Teutonic superstitions was various. Those which were clearly incompatible with essential principles of Christian thought and life, were, of course, ultimately compelled to give way, though the struggle of the Church with even these was protracted longer than might have been anticipated, and isolated remains of heathen cultus may still be discovered by the antiquary, in various retired districts throughout Europe.[1] In some

[1] See some instances in Sir John Lubbock's "Origin of Civilization," chap. v. But the whole subject of such survivals of an earlier culture in a later has been recently investigated, with great learning, in Tylor's "Primitive Culture," vol. i. chapters iii. and iv.

cases, however, the Church was forced to content itself with a compromise, throwing what is often a very thin veil of Christianity over ideas and practices of Teutonic heathenism. An instance or two of this kind may be worthy of attention, as introducing us to some of the Scottish ballads.

In studying the intellectual progress of modern Europe, we are met by no fact more mournful than the prolonged hold, even over educated minds, of the belief in witches and witchcraft. In its essential nature this savage superstition takes us back to that rudimentary faith in supernatural power, designated by the historians of religion *fetichism*, which is found among tribes at the lowest stage of civilization.[1] Springing from essential tendencies of human thought, it crops out in places which are separated by all the earth's diameter, and distinguished by every variety in the manners of life; while it survives among us still in minds which have yet been scarcely affected by the scientific spirit of modern times. Though the culture of the past three half centuries has taught us to view this faith as wholly alien to Christian civilization, yet even the revolting results which it exercised on judicial practice did not exclude it, till recent times, from the realm of Christian thought. The reason of this is evidently the fact, that it found a point of attachment in a certain cycle of Christian dogma,—the doctrine of a devil, and a world

---

[1] It is just possible that, in Britain, there may have been a slim thread of historical connection between ancient Druidism and modern witchcraft, some of the Druids, whose individual personality has come down to us, having been women. See Burton's "History of Scotland," vol. i. pp. 222-4.

of demons over which he rules. It must not be supposed, indeed, that the malignant features of witchcraft were first stamped upon it by being dragged into the service of a Christian dogma, or—to speak perhaps more truly—by dragging a Christian dogma into its service;[1] but the result of this alliance was to obliterate all the mitigating features of the primitive superstition, reducing it to a scheme of pure diabolism. This fact is worth referring to as illustrating one of the effects upon heathen superstitions resulting from their contact with Christian ideas; but for our more immediate purpose witchcraft might almost have been passed without mention. For it cannot but strike one as remarkable, that a superstition which was so universally prevalent, which, by its fascinating horror, must have seized such a hold on the popular imagination and entered so extensively into popular thought and language, should yet have influenced so slightly the songs and ballads, even of a people over whom it appears to have exercised a more unrestricted tyranny than over any other.[2] I shall not attempt to account for this circumstance, except by suggesting the unpoetical nature of the materials furnished by such a superstition; for the essential object of poetry

---

[1] There is abundant evidence, from the laws of Rome, both under the Republic and under the pagan Empire, that the magic of ancient paganism was believed to be employed for malicious purposes (Lecky's "History of Rationalism," vol. i. pp. 42-4, Amer. edit.); while Simrock has pointed out beliefs in Teutonic heathenism which have probably given to witchcraft the malignant aspect exclusively developed in Christendom ("Deutsche Mythologie," § 129).

[2] "In other lands the superstition was at least mixed with much of imposture; in Scotland it appears to have been entirely undiluted."—Lecky's *History of Rationalism*, vol. i. p. 144, Amer. edit.

—the production of an intellectual pleasure—could hardly be attained by any treatment of a faith so grossly unspiritual, and suggestive of no ideas which can be imagined without unmitigated pain.

In the very few ballads into which witchcraft enters as an essential motive in the development of the plot, the superstition appears in its more ancient form, and rises to that aspect of sublimer horror which has been noticed as a prominent characteristic imparted to it by the sterner features of Scottish scenery acting on the Scottish mind.[1] The ballad of *Willie's Ladye* may be taken in illustration. Its theme is a common property of the Aryan nations. Sir Walter Scott refers to its occurrence in ancient Greek mythology, in the *Golden Ass* of Apuleius, and in a mediæval legend;[2] while Professor Child notices Danish and Swedish ballads founded on the same story.[3] In the Scottish ballad, the witch-mother of Willie, fired into malicious resolution by his marrying against her will, tortures his wife by working a spell, similar to that by which, in the Greek myth,

[1] Buckle, referring to the influence which the physical features of Scotland have exerted on its superstitions, says: "Even the belief in witchcraft . . . . has been affected by these peculiarities; and it has been well observed, that while, according to the old English creed, the witch was a miserable and decrepit hag, the slave rather than the mistress of the demons which haunted her, she, in Scotland, rose to the dignity of a potent sorcerer, who mastered the evil spirit, and, forcing it to do her will, spread among the people a far deeper and more lasting terror."—*History of Civilization*, vol. ii. p. 148, Amer. edit. See also the numerous authorities he adduces in a note to this passage; and I may add one authority more recent, Burton's "History of Scotland," vol. vii. p. 382.

[2] Scott's "Border Minstrelsy," vol. iii. pp. 168-9.

[3] Child's "English and Scottish Ballads," vol. i. p. 162.

Hera took revenge on Alcmena, when the latter had won the erratic affections of Zeus.

> "Of her young bairn she's ne'er be lighter,
> Nor in her bower to shine the brighter;
> But she shall die and turn to clay,
> And you shall wed another may."

But the good office which was performed for Alcmena by a stratagem of her maid Galanthis, is here accomplished, in a similar manner, by the ingenuity of a good spirit named *Billy Blind*, who, in his kindly services to men, resembles the homely *Brownie*, for

> "He spak aye in good time."

Instructed by this propitious familiar, Willie pretends that his child is born, and invites his mother to the christening. Surprised by the trick, the hag demands to know who has revealed the secret of her spell?

> "O wha has loosed the nine witch knots,
> That were amang that ladye's locks?
> And wha's ta'en out the kames o' care,
> That were amang that ladye's hair?
> And wha's ta'en down that bush o' woodbine,
> That hung between her bour and mine?
> And wha has killed the master kid,
> That ran beneath that ladye's bed?
> And wha has loosed her left foot shee,
> And let that ladye lighter be?"

The elaborate charm, the explanation of which has been thus elicited from the witch herself, is soon dissolved by Willie:—

> "And now he has gotten a bonny son,
> And meikle grace be him upon!"

The ballad of *Alison Gross*[1] ought also to be mentioned in this connection. Though the theme of this ballad does not recall, so definitely as that of *Willie's Ladye*, similar stories current in different countries, yet the germ of it is contained in the fancy, which we meet under different forms in all literatures, of supernatural beings seeking and winning the love of mortals. Here, indeed, it is not the more common story of a male of higher race coming down to one of the daughters of men; but the legend is one which would not startle a Greek familiar with the mythical amours of Aphrodite. The ballad is a monologue, the speaker of which is wooed by one who, in the outline of her features and in her manner of action, resembles one of the Valkyrs of the old mythology more than the vulgar witch of later times.

> "O Alison Gross, that lives in yon tower,
>   The ugliest witch in the North Countrie,
> Has trysted me ae day up till her bower,
>   And mony fair speeches she made to me.
>
> "She straiked my head, and she kembed my hair,
>   And she set me down saftly on her knee,
> Says, 'Gin ye will be my lemman sae true,
>   Sae mony braw things as I would you gie.'"

[1] Obtained by Jamieson from the recitation of Mrs. Brown of Falkland. (See his "Popular Ballads and Songs," vol. ii. p. 187.) *Willie's Ladye* was taken by Scott from Mrs. Brown's MS. To the excellent memory of this lady we owe apparently the preservation of much popular poetry. (See Jamieson's *Advertisement* prefixed to his collection.) It would be unfair, however, to Mr. Chambers not to acknowledge that there is a certain mystery about Mrs. Brown's memory and MS., which is not easily explained. (See Chambers' "Popular Rhymes of Scotland," Note prefixed to edit. 1870.)

But, whether it was owing to an eery shudder at her uncanny nature, or to her want of personal attractions, the fair speeches and caresses of Alison Gross failed to produce any impression, even though strengthened by successive offers of "mony braw things." Still the language in which her solicitations were repelled, was certainly unwise when addressed to one whose malice it was so undesirable to provoke.

> "Awa, awa, ye ugly witch,
>   Haud far awa, and lat me be;
> For I wadna kiss your ugly mouth
>   For a' the gifts that ye could gie."

Stimulated by these words to the exercise of her supernatural powers,

> "She's turned her richt and round about,
>   And thrice she blew on a grass-green horn;
> And she sware by the moon and the stars aboon,
>   That she'd gar me rue the day I was born.
>
> "Then out she has ta'en a silver wand,
>   And she's turned her three times round and round;
> She's muttered sic words, that my strength it failed,
>   And I fell down senseless on the ground.
>
> "She's turned me into an ugly worm,[1]
>   And gar'd me toddle about the tree."

It chanced, however, that the night was near, on which all the supernatural beings of the old heathendom were believed to ride forth for festive celebrations,[2] and which

---

[1] *Worm* is here used, in its old general sense, for a *reptile*.

[2]   "The night it is good Hallowe'en,
             When fairy folk will ride."
                                    The Young Tamlane.

the Church has therefore constituted into the Feast of All the Saints. On this auspicious night the Queen of the "Seely Court"[1] fortunately lighted down not far from the tree where the victim of the witch's revenge had been doomed to toddle.

> "She took me up in her milkwhite hand,
>   And she straiked me three times o'er her knee;
> She changed me again to my ain proper shape,
>   And I nae mair maun toddle about the tree."

It is thus seen that in both of these ballads, while the witchcraft on which they are founded has not yet contracted its later vulgar characteristics, the horror of the story is mitigated, and thus rendered more poetical, in consequence of the witch's spell being broken by one of those more beneficent creatures of the fancy, who will be described presently as occupying a more pleasing niche in the Pantheon of the Teutons. In no other Scottish ballads that I remember does witchcraft obtrude itself into notice as guiding the course of the story; and the subject may, therefore, be dismissed with

---

[1] *Seely* is identical with the Old English *sely*, modern *silly*, which originally, like the German *selig*, expressed the idea of *blessed* or *happy*. It seems that, of all the designations by which the fairies were known, that of *the seely wichts* was the one preferred by themselves.

> "Gin ye ca' me imp or elf,
> I rede ye look weel to yourself;
> Gin ye ca' me fairy,
> I'll work ye muckle tarrie;
> Gin guid neibour ye ca' me,
> Then guid neibour I will be;
> But gin ye ca' me seelie wicht,
> I'll be your freend baith day and nicht."

(See Chambers' "Popular Rhymes of Scotland," p. 324.)

the remark, that if, in seeking to find out what influence the ballads and songs of Scotland *have* exerted, we shall be aided by knowing what they have *not* done, it may be worth while to observe that they cannot be charged with directly fostering the degrading belief in the vulgar witchcraft of later times.

Witchcraft, as we have seen, retained its place among the beliefs of Christendom from its unfortunately finding a point of attachment in a dogma of the Church, with which it was made to harmonize. We now come to a prettier and pleasanter world of imaginary beings, which has retained its hold on the Christian mind mainly from there being no doctrine of Christianity with which it came into manifest conflict. The Elves, Fairies, Brownies, Mermaids, Kelpies, and that whole class of variously designated creations, could all live in the Christian mind outside the world of peculiarly Christian thought; and they have continued to hold their ground in popular belief for a much longer time and in a less altered form than any other fiction of ancient mythologies. For the deities of a more civilized heathendom suffered the same fate as the fetich of the savage: the heathen, unable to think, like the Hebrew Paul,[1] of an idol as nothing, was content, after his conversion, to admit the existence of his old gods, but degraded them from the Pantheon to the Pandemonium. Thus Thor and his fellows of the Northern Asgard were sent packing to the same dismal limbo, to which the Fathers of the Church, with Milton[2] after them, had banished the gods of Olympus and the East. In like manner the

---

[1] See 1 Cor. viii. 4.   [2] "Paradise Lost," Book I.

beings of the elfin world could not be ousted from the thought of the Teuton by the new religion; but though the anathemas of ecclesiastical authority would have consigned them heartily to the doom of their superiors, the only change in their position consisted in their being clothed with some less pleasing attributes than they seem to have originally possessed. The primitive elf, as the apparent connection of the name with the root of *albus*[1] seems to imply, is essentially a being of light; and though the Edda, elder as well as younger,[2] distinguishes from the elves of light another species as elves of darkness, yet these seem to be named rather from their dwelling underground than from any malevolence of disposition. The beings of the elfin world, therefore, continued, even in Christian times, to be regarded as, if not positively benevolent, often extremely useful, and generally harmless; while the harm at times attributed to them arose either from the freakishness of a nature without moral characteristics, or from the connection into which the Church sought to bring them with the ecclesiastical world of devils. The fairy of the nursery tale, in any "dignus vindice nodus," is often called in to counteract the harmful doings of the witch; and in the two ballads cited above, the witch's charm is detected and broken,—in the one, by the good genius *Billy Blind;* in the other, by the Queen of the Fairies herself. It would seem, therefore, that the earth of Teutonic

---

[1] See Grimm's "Deutsches Wörterbuch," under the word *Alb*.
[2] See, in the former, the fifth song of the gods, *Hrafnagaldr Odhins*, and, in the latter, *Gylfaginning*, 17. Compare Simrock's "Deutsche Mythologie," § 124.

heathendom—its woods and mountains, its lakes and streams—were peopled by a race of fanciful beings, perhaps as beautiful in their conception as the nymphs of the ancient Greek world;[1] and it must be admitted that, on the whole, this superstition tended to soften the savage influence of the belief in witches, imparting to nature a happier aspect,—more of that Hellenic aspect, over the disappearance of which, under the dissolving processes of modern science, Schiller sings his celebrated dirge in the *Götter Griechenlands*.[2]

These observations may suffice to indicate the origin and general character of the superstitions which enter into Scottish ballad literature. Before proceeding to examine more closely the influence which these superstitions have exerted, through that literature, on the character of the Scottish people, it may be worth while to notice the value of the ballads as sources of information with reference to the superstitions, and the changes which these have undergone from the progress of civilization. An extremely interesting illustration may be found in the comparison of several ballads, in all of which the general outline of the legend is identical. It would lead too far into unnecessary details, to notice the numerous varieties of this legend in the literatures

---

[1] The fairies have in fact been often identified, or more properly confounded, with the fictions of Greek and Latin mythology; and this confusion is among the influences which have modified the superstition. See Scott's well-known and still valuable Essay on the Fairies in the "Border Minstrelsy," vol. ii. pp. 279-291.

[2] "Schöne Welt, wo bist du? Kehre wieder,
  Holdes Blüthenalter der Natur!
 Ach, nur in dem Feenland der Lieder
  Lebt noch deine fabelhafte Spur."—Verse 12.

even of the Teutonic nations.[1] In many of these varieties there is a prominent feature, in which most readers will recognize a likeness to the familiar *Bluebeard* of household story. Of the Scotch series of ballads on this legend, *The Water o' Wearie's Well*[2] may be placed at the commencement. Here in a mysterious manner,—a manner the mystery of which is apparently enhanced by some imperfection in the opening verses,—there is all at once ushered in a vaguely defined personage, gifted with extraordinary skill in the use of the harp, by which he soothes to sleep all his hearers, and charms a king's daughter on to his steed behind himself.

> "There cam a bird out o' a bush,
>   On water for to dine;
> And sighing sair, says the King's daughter,
>   'O wae's this heart o' mine.'
>
> "He's ta'en a harp into his hand,
>   He's harped them all asleep;
> Except it was the King's daughter,
>   Who ae wink couldna get.
>
> "He's luppen on his berry-brown steed,
>   Ta'en her on behind himsell;
> Then baith rade down to that water,
>   That they ca' Wearie's Well."

---

[1] An enumeration of similar legends, with a reference to sources of more detailed information, will be found in Child's "English and Scottish Ballads," vol. i. pp. 195 and 198; and vol. ii. pp. 271-3. Compare Jamieson's "Popular Ballads and Songs," vol. i. pp. 208-224. Are not all these legends perhaps merely separate rills which have trickled from the same primeval source, out of which has flowed the story of Paris and Helen?

[2] Buchan's "Ballads of the North of Scotland," vol. ii. p. 201.

Gradually, amid much trepidation, she is led ever further into the water, till "she stepped to the chin," when her mysterious charmer tells her:—

"Seven King's-daughters have I drowned there
  In the water o' Wearie's Well;
And I'll mak you the eight o' them,
  And ring the common bell."

The narrative, with which the ballad closes, of the courage and presence of mind by which the princess escaped from the doom intended for her, is exceedingly spirited. On her asking for "ae kiss of his comely mouth,"

"He louted him ower his saddle bow,
  To kiss her cheek and chin;
She's ta'en him in her arms twa,
  And thrown him headlong in.

"'Sin' seven King's-daughters ye've drowned there,
  In the water o' Wearie's Well,
I'll mak you bridegroom to them a',
  And ring the bell mysell.'"

This ballad may be taken as representing the pre-Christian form of the legend it relates; and the same antiquity may be ascribed to the legend as it appears in *Lady Isabel and the Elf-Knight*, otherwise entitled *The Gowans sae Gay*,[1] the difference between the two ballads being, that, in the former, the charmer is evidently a spirit of the waters,—a kelpie or merman,[2]—while, in

---

[1] Buchan's "Ballads of the North of Scotland," vol. i. p. 22.
[2] A fine Danish ballad on the same subject, *The Merman and Marstig's Daughter*, is translated into Scotch by Jamieson in his "Popular Ballads and Songs," vol. i. p. 210. Further on will be noticed those legends, according to which a man is allured into the waters by a mermaid.

the latter, he is a knight of the elfin world. In *The Demon Lover*[1] we recognize a later development of the legend from a reference to a well-known feature of the vulgar mediæval devil, discovered by the unfortunate princess in the mysterious wooer.

> "They hadna sailed a league, a league,
> A league but barely three,
> Until she espied *his cloven foot*,
> And she wept right bitterlie."

It is not surprising, from the treatment which the creations of heathen fancy generally received at the hands of the Church, that the legend should have undergone this transformation of an elf of heathenism into the devil of Christianity. It seems, however, as if the advance of culture had rendered incredible the action of the demon introduced into this ballad; and accordingly in *James Herries*[2] the fatal charmer becomes

---

[1] Scott's "Border Minstrelsy," vol. iii. p. 194.

[2] Buchan's "Ballads of the North of Scotland," vol. i. p. 214. The appearance of the ghost of a lover, whom the false fair one had "killed under trust," and who leads her to destruction much in the same way as the charmer in the above ballads, forms the subject of the imperfect but impressive ballad *Sir Roland*, preserved in Motherwell's "Minstrelsy, Ancient and Modern," vol. i. p. 273, Amer. edit. Though Professor Child unhesitatingly pronounces this to be a modern composition, yet, even if this be the case, the author is evidently not the creator of his story, which is merely a modification of the legend we are considering. Motherwell suggests to the "sanguine antiquarian" the identity of *Sir Roland* with the ballad from which Shakspere quotes:

> "Child Rowland to the dark tower came,
> His word was still."
> *King Lear*, Act III. Sc. 4.

But Jamieson has hit on the most probable source of this quotation, which belongs perhaps to the same cycle of ballads as those mentioned in the text ("Popular Ballads and Songs," vol. i. p. 217).

the ghost of a former lover: while, as if to laugh modern spiritualism out of countenance, even this superstition gives way, among the ballad-singers themselves and at last in *May Colvin*,[1] though there is a vanishing trace of the legendary features of its original, the supernatural character of the lover wholly disappears in the vulgar seducer and murderer of ordinary life.

What, then, has been the result of the legendary ballads in Scottish life? Undoubtedly they have contributed, with other causes, to quicken the feeling awakened in the presence of objects which, from the mystery enshrouding them, appear to be preternatural. That this feeling is peculiarly prominent in the Scottish mind will be made evident, in the sequel, from the multiform legends which it has strewn around every hill and glen and stream in Scotland, as well as from the developments of Scottish character in the national history; but a significant indication of its prominence is afforded by the fact, that the Scottish dialect contains a term whose precise use is the expression of this feeling. The import of this fact will be felt in attempting to translate the word *eery* by an English equivalent. The word, indeed, expresses a great variety of emotions. From the faint tremor in the presence of what is felt to be uncanny on account of its uncommonness and our consequent ignorance as to its possible operation, eeriness ranges the whole gamut of emotions excited by what is mysterious, up to the subduing dread with which the soul is smitten by the appearance of supernatural power. Let us trace some of the principal

[1] Herd's "Scottish Songs," vol. i. p. 93 (Glasgow reprint, 1869).

varieties of this feeling, as they are represented in different ballads of Scotland.

As expressive of that vague eeriness without positive fear, which forms the faintest stage of the feeling, *The Wee Wee Man*[1] may be cited,—a ballad in which we seem to hear an indistinct echo, dying in some far-off nook among the Aryan settlements, of the primeval fancy which is repeated in the ancient Greek legends of Philytas, who had to wear lead on his shoes lest the wind should blow him away, and of Archestratus, who weighed only an obolus,[2] as well as in the numerous modern versions of the German *Däumling* (Thumbling), our own Tom Thumb.[3] The hero of this ballad, though his legs were "scant a shathmont's length," resembled the dwarfs of most legendary stories in the superhuman power with which he was endowed.

> "He has tane up a meikle stane,
> And flang 't as far as I could see;
> Ein though I had been Wallace wicht,
> I dought na lift it to my knee."

Like Tom Thumb, moreover, this mysterious little man was on terms of familiar intercourse with the fairy world. For the minstrel and he, riding on together, light at last upon a "bonny green," such as the fairies are known to choose for their revels; and there comes forth "a lady

---

[1] First given to the world, I believe, in Herd's "Scottish Songs."

[2] See Grimm's "Kinder und Hausmärchen," vol. iii. p. 71.

[3] It is a curious circumstance, that Sir Walter Scott found *The Wee Wee Man* introduced in one version of *The Young Tamlane*—a ballad the legend of which, as we shall afterwards find, is of the same origin with that of *Thumbling* ("Border Minstrelsy," vol. ii. p. 334).

sheen" with four-and-twenty others in her train, all clad in "glistening green,"—the orthodox hue of fairy costume. On passed, with a pleasing wonder, the cheery procession, till they reached "a bonny ha," the roof of which was of "the beaten gowd," and the floor of crystal. Here burst upon the view a scene of elfin revelry; but it is well known that the fairies shrink from exposing their festivities to mortal eye, and that, whenever they become aware of mortal presence, they vanish from sight in some mysterious way. This was the result upon the advent of the mortal minstrel with his unearthly little guide.

> "When we cam there, wi' wee wee knichts
> Were ladies dancing, jimp and sma';
> But in the twinkling of an eie
> Baith green and ha war clein awa." [1]

As expressing eeriness of a similar mild form, *The Elfin Knight*[2] may be adduced. Opening in a manner that recalls the ballad of *Lady Isabel and the Elf-Knight* mentioned above, it introduces us to a knight of the fairy world, who, by some preternatural motion, is brought to a maiden's side by her mere wish.

> "The Elfin Knight sits on yon hill;
> He blaws his horn baith loud and shrill.

---

[1] The *dénouement* in Motherwell's version is different, and connects *The Wee Wee Man* perhaps more definitely with the legend of *Thumbling*, and with that of *Thomlin* or *Tamlane*, which is to be afterwards described.

> "There were pipers playing in every neuk,
> And ladies dancing, jimp and sma';
> And aye the owreturn o' their tune
> Was, 'Our wee wee man has been lang awa!'"

[2] Child's "English and Scottish Ballads," vol. i. pp. 129 and 277.

> "He blaws it east, he blaws it west,
> He blaws it where he liketh best.
>
> "'I wish that horn were in my kist,
> Yea, and that Knight in my arms neist.'
>
> "She had no sooner these words said,
> Than the Knight came to her bed."

The maiden, however, is considered by the knight "ower young" to be married at once; and there arises, accordingly, a lively bandying of impossible demands, the inability to perform which results in the retirement of the knight discomfited, the ballad concluding with a verse which sounds like the chorus of some old song:—

> "My plaid awa, my plaid awa,
> And owre the hills and far awa,
> And far awa to Norowa;
> My plaid shall not be blown awa."

In the ballad just cited there is much to remind one of the sportive, half-meaningless rhymes of the nursery. *The Earl of Mar's Daughter*,[1] again, is a pleasing play of fancy, which readily recalls the myth of Eros and Psyche, as well as the burden of many a nursery tale. The heroine of this ballad, amusing herself one day "below a green aik tree," is attracted by "a sprightly doo," which she induces to come down to her under the promise of "a cage o' guid red gowd." On being taken home to her bower, the dove turns out to be a beautiful prince who has been transformed into this shape; and the prettiness of the story is enhanced by the fact that

---

[1] Buchan's "Ancient Ballads and Songs of the North of Scotland," vol. i. p. 49. One cannot but join in Professor Child's regret, that this ballad has not been preserved in an older form.

the transformation is ascribed, not to the malice of a stepdame or witch, but to the kindly magic of the prince's own mother, whose ambition has been to render him thus a more potent charm to maidens.

> "My mither lives in foreign isles,
>   She has nae mair but me;
> She is a queen o' wealth and state,
>   And birth and high degree.
>
> "Likewise well skilled in magic spells,
>   As ye may plainly see;
> And she transformed me to yon shape,
>   To charm such maids as thee.
>
> "I am a doo the live lang day,
>   A sprightly youth at night;
> This aye gars me appear mair fair
>   In a fair maiden's sight."

Of a more exciting nature are the ballads which relate deliverances from the enchantments of superhuman power, such as form the theme of popular fictions in all lands. In the ballad which has just been described, as well as in several others already noticed, there is a reference to such enchantments; but the ballads of which I now speak, are those in which, not the enchantment itself, but the deliverance from it, constitutes the plot of the story. Scottish literature possesses at least one fine specimen of these ballads in *Kempion*,[1] or *Kemp Owyne*, as it is called in Buchan's

---

[1] First published by Scott from Mrs. Brown's MS. in "Border Minstrelsy," vol. iii. p. 230. *Kempion* resembles a very popular Border ballad, *The Laidley Worm of Spindleston-heugh*, ascribed, either in whole or in part, to the Rev. Mr. Lamb, of Norham. The reader may find some interest in comparing Mr. Morris' tale, *The Lady of the Land*, in "The Earthly Paradise," in which the would-be deliverer, feebler in nerve than Kempion, quails at the sight of the lips he is required to kiss.

and Motherwell's versions. Scott has referred to the frequency of similar fictions in mediæval romance. Norse literature is also full of them: in fact, Mr. Child sees in the word *Kemp* (*Champion*) a monument of the relation of our ballads to the *Koempeviser*. Mr. Motherwell holds that the name Owyne connects this ballad with the Celtic hero Ewain or Owain ap Urien, King of Strathclyde; while the legend of enchantment and deliverance will probably recall to many some of the fascinating and luxuriant fancies in the tales of

> "the golden prime
> Of good Haroun Alraschid."

Kempion opens with the utterance against a maiden of a doom which transforms her into a dragon's shape.

> "'Cum heir, cum heir, ye freely feed,
>   And lay your head low on my knee
> The heaviest weird I will you read,
>   That ever was read to gay ladye.
>
> "'O meikle dolour sall ye dree,
>   And aye the salt seas o'er ye swim;
> And far mair dolour sall ye dree
>   On Estmere crags, when ye them climb.
>
> "'I weird ye to a fiery beast,
>   And relieved sall ye never be,
> Till Kempion, the Kingis son,
>   Cum to the crag, and thrice kiss thee.'"

The event, however, which the sorceress has set as a presumed impossibility in the way of her victim's disenchantment, actually takes place. Kempion hears of the dragon's presence, and, with his brother Segramour, chivalrously sets out to rid the land of its ravages. On coming within sight of the monster, he challenges her to quit the land, or he will send a shaft at her head from his "arblast bow."

> "'O out of my stythe I winna rise,
>   (And it is not for the awe o' thee,)
> Till Kempion, the Kingis son,
>   Cum to the crag, and thrice kiss me.'
>
> "He has louted him o'er the dizzy crag,
>   And gien the monster kisses ane;
> Awa she gaed, and again she cam,
>   The fieryest beast that ever was seen."

Twice again she returns to announce the same condition, on which alone she will quit her place, receiving, the second time, two kisses,—the third time, three; and at the three kisses the spell breaks,—she is restored to her own shape :—

> "The loveliest ladye e'er could be!"
>
> "'O was it warwolf in the wood?
>   Or was it mermaid in the sea?
> Or was it man or vile woman,
>   My ain true love, that mishapęd thee?'
>
> "'It wasna warwolf in the wood,
>   Nor was it mermaid in the sea;
> But it was my wicked stepmother,
>   And wae and weary may she be!'
>
> "'O, a heavier weird shall light her on,
>   Than ever fell on vile woman;
> Her hair shall grow rough, and her teeth grow lang,
>   And on her four feet shall she gang.

None shall take pity her upon
In Wormeswood aye shall she be won;
And relieved shall she never be,
Till St. Mungo come over the sea.'

"And sighing said that weary wight,
'I doubt that day I'll never see.'"[1]

More definitely eery still is the emotion excited by those ballads which refer to a return from the dead. Death is, under any circumstances, an irresistible stimulus of eery feeling, from the consciousness that it brings us to a limit of the natural world, and the irrepressible surmise, that there the beings of a preternatural world may possibly disclose themselves to mortal ken. The hope,—the belief,—is thus originated, that the soul, which has passed beyond the limits of earthly life, may yet not only take an interest in the fate of former friends, but even reveal itself to their sorrowing, longing eyes; and this belief finds expression, not only in the crude ghost stories of every region, but in numerous fictions throughout the prose and poetical literature of various countries.[2] Of these the ballad poetry of Scotland furnishes not a few examples. The ballads of *James Herries* and *Sir Roland* have already

---

[1] The concluding lines, in the measure of the metrical romances, are exceedingly interesting and valuable, since they can scarcely be explained except as a corrupted snatch of one of the romances, and, therefore, as exhibiting, in its arrested progress, the breaking down of one of those old poems of the high-born into a ballad of the people. See Scott's "Border Minstrelsy," vol. iii. p. 230.

[2] The investigation of these legends has become a favourite inquiry in the *Animism* of recent archæologists; and the reader will find an extraordinary collection of interesting information on the subject in Tylor's "Primitive Culture."

been referred to, as describing the ghost of a dead lover revisiting the object of his earthly passion; and the ballad of *Clerk Saunders*,[1] which relates a similar imagination, may also be noticed here. In the two former ballads, however, the return from the dead does not form the principal theme; and the most affecting part of *Clerk Saunders* is the scene of the hero's assassination, while the account of the ghostly visit is marred by horrid details of the grave, confounding the dim imagination of the disembodied spirit's mysterious home with pictures of the charnel-house in which the body corrupts.

The best examples of ballads on this subject are to be found in the beautiful fragment, *The Wife of Usher's Well*, and in the more complete, but apparently composite poem, *The Clerk's twa Sons o' Owsenford*.

The former of these coincides so completely with the second part of the latter that there can be no doubt of the original identity of the two poems. The opening verses of the former, however, from their evident deficiency, afford just such an indication of the previous history of the two sons as stimulates curiosity to learn more; and it is probable that the first part of the latter is an originally independent ballad tacked on to the other, as a satisfaction to this curiosity.[2] The independence of this ballad is further confirmed by the circumstance that it is evidently of English origin. It is a tragic

---

[1] Scott's "Border Minstrelsy," vol. iii. p. 175.
[2] Mr. Chambers, less probably, regards the former ballad as an imperfectly preserved fragment of the latter ("Scottish Ballads," p. 345). Professor Child and others point out, that we have a similar combination of two originally distinct ballads in *Clerk Saunders*.

story of two sons of an Oxford clerk, who fall in love each with a daughter of the Mayor of the parish in which they are ordained, and are sentenced to death by the Mayor for the shame which they bring upon his house. The father of the two sons, on hearing that they are "bound in prison strang," hastens to effect their pardon; and the second part of the ballad opens with a picture of their mother waiting for his return:—

> " His lady sat on her castle wa',
>   Beholding dale and doun;
> And there she saw her ain gude lord
>   Come walking to the toun.
>
> "'Ye're welcome, ye're welcome, my ain gude lord,
>   Ye're welcome hame to me;
> But where away are my twa sons?
>   Ye suld hae brought them wi' ye.'
>
> "'O they are putten to a deeper lear,
>   And to a higher scule:
> You ain twa sons will no be hame
>   Till the hallow days o' Yule.'
>
> "'O sorrow, sorrow, come mak my bed;
>   And, dule, come lay me doun;
> For I will neither eat nor drink,
>   Nor set a fit on groun'!'
>
> " The hallow days o' Yule were come,
>   And the nights were lang and mirk,[1]

---

[1] "It fell about the Martinmas,
   When nights are lang and mirk."
                    The Wife of Usher's Well.

When in and cam her ain twa sons,
    And their hats made o' the birk.[1]

"It neither grew in syke nor ditch,
    Nor yet in ony sheuch;
But at the gates o' Paradise
    That birk grew fair eneuch.

"'Blow up the fire now, maidens mine,
    Bring water from the well;
For a' my house shall feast this night,
    Since my twa sons are well.

"'O eat and drink, my merry men a',
    The better shall ye fare;
For my twa sons they are come hame
    To me for evermair.'

"And she has gane and made their bed,
    She's made it saft and fine;
And she's happit[2] them wi' her gray mantil,
    Because they were her ain.

"Up then crew the red, red cock,
    And up and crew the gray;[3]

---

[1]
    "Ane young man stert into that steid,
      Als cant as ony colt,
    Ane birken hat upon his heid,
      With ane bow and ane bolt."
              Peblis to the Play, verse vi.

[2] "Can the English reader catch the strange tenderness and pathos of the word *happed*? It is one of the dearest to a Scottish ear, recalling infancy and the thousand instances of a mother's heart, and the unwearied care of a mother's hand.... *Happed* is the nursery word in Scotland, expressing the care with which the bed-clothes are laid upon the little forms, and carefully tucked in about the round sleeping cheeks."—Alexander Smith, in the *Edinburgh Essays*, p. 218.

[3] So in *Clerk Saunders*:—
    "Then up and crew the milkwhite cock,
      And up and crew the grey."

The eldest to the youngest said,
  "'Tis time we were away.

" The cock, he hadna crawed but once,
  And clapped his wings at a',
When the youngest to the eldest said,
  'Brother, we must awa.

"' The cock doth craw, the day doth daw,
  The channerin' worm doth chide;
Gin we be mist out o' our place,
  A sair pain we maun bide.[1]

" 'Fare ye weel, my mother dear!
  Fareweel to barn and byre!
And fare ye weel, the bonny lass
  That kindles my mother's fire.'"[2]

The eeriest ballads, however, are probably those which penetrate the interior of the elfin world, and reveal the stratagems by which its unearthly inhabitants gratify their well-known fondness for human beings. Reference has already been made to ballads in which an elfin knight or a spirit of the waters is described as wooing a woman to destruction; and the effect of progressive civilization was illustrated in eliminating the supernatural elements of the legend. There are also some ballads relating the endeavours of female elves to wile

---

[1] "O, cocks are crowing a merry midnight,
    I wot the wildfowl are boding day;
  The psalms of heaven will soon be sung,
    And I, ere now, will be missed away."
                                    Clerk Saunders.

[2] The last four verses are taken from *The Wife of Usher's Well*, as being finer than the corresponding verses in *The Clerk's two Sons o' Owsenford*.

men to their mysterious dwelling-place. Legends of both these kinds are numerous in the early literature of the Teutonic nations; and, indeed, tales of an essentially identical import are scattered throughout all Aryan mythology, possibly traceable to a primeval metaphor, which spoke, on the one hand, of the Day being charmed by the awful beauty of the Night away to her invisible home, and, on the other hand, of the Night or the Dawn disappearing in the embrace of the Day.[1] Let us take an example of the legends in which the charmer is a mermaid. In all these the plot is essentially similar. The hero is fascinated by the glance or gesture or song of the mermaid, and dies or is lured into the water, while a shout of elfin revelry is heard, or some other sign of elfin merriment is observed, over the success of her charm. Herd has preserved an imperfect specimen in *Clerk Colvill, or the Mermaid;* and another, entitled *The Mermaid*, of more poetical merit, though of more modern appearance, was obtained by Finlay from the recitation of a lady, who informed him that it had once been popular on the Carrick coast.[2] It is worth quoting:—

> "To yon fause stream, that near the sea
>   Hides mony an elf an' plum,
> And rives wi' fearfu' din the stanes,
>   A witless knicht did come.
>
> "The day shines clear,—far in he's gane
>   Whar shells are silver bright,

---

[1] See Cox's "Mythology of the Aryan Nations," vol. i. pp. 394-415.
[2] Finlay's "Scottish Ballads," vol. ii. p. 81.

    Fishes war loupin' a' aroun',
        And sparklin' to the light:

" Whan as he laved, sounds cam sae sweet
        Frae ilka rock an' tree,
The brief was out, 'twas him it doomed
        The mermaid's face to see.

" Frae 'neath a rock, sune, sune she rose,
        And stately on she swam,
Stopped in the midst, an' becked an' sang
        To him to stretch his haun'.

" Gowden glist the yellow links,
        That round her neck she'd twine;
Her een war o' the skyie blue,
        Her lips did mock the wine:

" The smile upon her bonnie cheek
        Was sweeter than the bee;
Her voice excelled the birdies' sang
        Upon the birchen tree.

" Sae couthie, couthie did she look,
        And meikle had she flecched;
Out shot his hand, alas, alas!
        Fast in the swirl he screeched.

" The mermaid leuch, her brief was gane,
        And kelpie's blast was blawin',
Fu' low she duked, ne'er raise again,
        For deep, deep was she fawin'.

" Aboon the stream his wraith was seen,
        Warlocks toiled lang at gloamin';
That e'en was coarse, the blast blew hoarse,
        E'er lang the waves war foamin'."

Another and more familiar ballad, which relates the disappearance of a man to the elfin world, is *Thomas the Rhymer*,[1] in which the Queen of the Fairies herself plays the charmer's part. The hero of this ballad, as is well known, occupies a distinguished place in the legendary history and literature of Scotland. Gifted, in popular tradition, not only with the power of the poet, but with the insight of the prophet, he was believed to have attained his superhuman knowledge by a daring intrigue with the Fairy Queen, as the legend of the pious Numa Pompilius attributed to his intercourse with the nymph Egeria the suggestion of the religious institutions which were traced to his reign. As True Thomas lay on the fairy-haunted Huntly Bank,[2]—so runs the legend,—he saw a bright lady in raiment of "grass green silk," with innumerable silver bells tinkling at her horse's mane. Warned that if he kiss her lips she will become mistress of his fate, he cries—

> "'Betide me weal, betide me woe,
>   That weird shall never daunton me.'
> Syne he has kissed her rosy lips,
>   All underneath the Eildon Tree.

---

[1] Scott's "Border Minstrelsy," vol. iv. p. 117. The reader will find it interesting to compare the English ballad on the same subject given by Jamieson ("Popular Ballads and Songs," vol. ii. p. 11). This ballad is preserved, with variations, in three MSS., which are collated by Jamieson. A beautiful Danish ballad on a similar legend, *Sir Olaf and the Elf King's Daughter*, has been translated into Scotch by the same writer (Ibid. vol. i. p. 219).

[2] This spot in the neighbourhood of Melrose was purchased by Sir Walter Scott, at probably fifty per cent. above its real value, that it might be included in the Abbotsford estate.

"'Now, ye maun go wi' me,' she said;
  'True Thomas, ye maun go wi' me;
And ye maun serve me seven years,
  Through weal or woe as may chance to be.'

"She mounted on her milkwhite steed;
  She's ta'en true Thomas up behind:
And aye, whene'er her bridle rung,
  The steed flew swifter than the wind."

So sped on the elfin steed with elfin velocity, till they reached a wide desert, where "living land was left behind." Here they lighted down, and while True Thomas rests his head upon the Fairy Queen's knee, she shows him three wonders. First, she reveals to him the narrow road of righteousness, beset with thorns and briars; then "the braid, braid road" of wickedness that lies across a lawn of lilies; and last of all, she points to a "bonny road that winds about the fernie brae," as the road to fair Elf-land, by which they must go. Again they mount the elfin steed, which flies on as before:—

"O they rade on, and farther on,
  And they waded through rivers aboon the knee,
And they saw neither sun nor moon,
  But they heard the roaring of the sea.

"It was mirk mirk night, and there was nae stern light,
  And they waded through red blude to the knee;
For a' the blude that's shed on earth
  Runs through the springs o' that countrie.

"Syne they came to a garden green,
  And she pu'd an apple frae a tree,—
'Take this for thy wages, true Thomas;
  It will give thee the tongue that can never lie.'

"'My tongue is my ain,' true Thomas said;
  'A gudely gift ye wad gie to me!
I neither dought to buy nor sell,
  At fair or tryst where I may be.

"'I dought neither speak to prince or peer,
  Nor ask of grace from fair ladye.'
'Now hold thy peace!' the lady said,
  'For as I say, so must it be.'

"He has gotten a coat of the even cloth,
  And a pair of shoes of velvet green;
And till seven years were gane and past,
  True Thomas on earth was never seen."

The gift of the Fairy Queen from the fruits of fairy-land, which True Thomas seeks, with amusing *naïveté*, to decline, is evidently connected with his alleged prophetic powers. Indeed, this ballad appears, from other sources,[1] to be merely an introduction to a larger poem on the prophecies attributed to the hero.[2] The legend further tells, that although Thomas was allowed to revisit the earth and there deliver his prophecies, yet he continued under an obligation to return to fairyland whenever the Queen of the Fairies should intimate her wish. "Accordingly, while Thomas was making merry with his friends in the Tower of Ercildoune, a person came running in and told, with marks of fear and astonishment, that a hart and hind had left the neighbouring forest, and were, composedly and slowly, parading the street of the village. The prophet instantly

---

[1] See the English ballad above referred to as given by Jamieson.

[2] His prophecies will be found, with interesting historical comments, in Chambers' "Popular Rhymes of Scotland," pp. 210–224.

arose, left his habitation, and followed the wonderful animals to the forest, whence he was never seen to return. According to the popular belief, he still 'drees his weird' in fairyland, and is one day expected to revisit the earth.'[1]

There is one element in the development of this legend, which has dropt out of the above ballad; I refer to the reason why the hero was restored to the earth after seven years' residence in fairyland. This element, which we are able to supply from the English ballad on the subject,[2] is founded on one point of the creed about fairies, which looks almost like a satisfaction to Christian dogma for allowing the existence of such beings. Though they belonged to no limbo in the peculiar world of Christian thought, it was believed that they required every seven years to pay a "teind" or "kane"[3] to hell, similar to that which the Athenians, in the myth of Theseus and Ariadne, used to pay to the

---

[1] Scott's "Border Minstrelsy," vol. iv. pp. 114-15.

[2] "To morne of helle the foulle fende
  Among these folke shall chese his fee;
 Thou art a fayre man and a hende,
  Fful wele I wot he wil chese the.

"Ffore all the golde that ever myght be
  Ffro heven unto the worldys ende,
 Thou bese never betrayede for me;
  Therefore with me I rede the wende.

"She broght hym agayn to the Eldyntre,
  Underneth the grene wode spray,
 In Huntley Banks ther for to be,
  Ther foulys syng bothe nyght and daye."

[3] *Teind* is technical Scotch for *tenth*, English *tithe*. *Kane*, *Cane*, or *Kain* is a duty paid in kind by a tenant to a landlord.

Minotaur of Crete; and this was supposed to explain that dreaded hankering of the elfin world's inhabitants after human beings, which moved them to spirit away a beautiful bride or bridegroom on the eve of a wedding, or to rob the cradle of a chubby little infant, leaving in its place a hideous, withered changeling of their own.

In the legend of *Thomas the Rhymer* the Fairy Queen appears under the same amiable aspect which is given to the large-hearted Zee by the author of "The Coming Race,"—that of a mistress who disinterestedly saves her alien lover from the doom to which he would have been consigned by her own people. There are other legends, however, in which the hero achieves his restoration to earth in defiance of the fairy powers; and the ballad now to be described derives its fascinating terror from the account of the elfin stratagems set at work to prevent the recovery of the hero from the fairy world.

The Young Tamlane will probably be acknowledged by most critics to be the finest of the legendary ballads of Scotland. The hero is known under considerable variations in his name, among which it is worth while to compare Tamlane, Tamlene, Tam-a-line, Tam o' the Linn, Tom Linn, Thom of Lynn, Thomalin, and Thomlin. Amid these varieties none can hesitate to pronounce an original identity; and methods of research, which our modern comparative mythologists have already followed to valuable results, enable us, without much difficulty, to trace the name, with the main features of the legend gathering round it, to the same source which has given to the nursery the numerous tales of *Thumbling* or *Tom*

Thumb, and of *Jack the Giant-killer*.[1] Everyone acquainted with the science of nursery stories knows that Thumbling, whatever degradation he may have suffered in his later history, was originally no other than the god Thor, who, in his wandering from Asgard, the home of the Aesir, to Utgard, the home of the Giants, put up one night in the glove of the Giant Skrymir, which he mistook for a house, and, on being frightened by a seeming earthquake, sought refuge in what he supposed to be an adjoining building, but which turned out to be the thumb (German *Däumling*) of the glove. This is not the place to follow the myth of Thor, from this incident of his lodging in the thumb of Giant Skrymir's glove, through all the transformations he has undergone in the popular literature of Europe. Probably no branch of that literature presents, among the later offshoots of the Thor-myth, such a luxuriant outgrowth as the Scottish ballad of *The Young Tamlane*. The hero is, indeed, a favourite in Scottish verse. He

---

[1] The original identity of *Thumbling* and *Tamlane* does not seem to have been surmised by our collectors of ballads. It was asserted, however, so long ago as in the *Quarterly Review* for January 1819, p. 100, in an article on the "Antiquities of Nursery Literature," to which my attention was drawn by the eulogistic language in which it is spoken of by Grimm ("Kindermährchen," vol. iii. p. 315). "Among the popular heroes of romance enumerated in the introduction to the history of *Tom Thumbe* (London, 1621, bl. letter), occurs 'Tom a Lin, the devil's supposed bastard.'" (Scott, in the "Border Minstrelsy," vol. i. p. 222.) It would be interesting to know whether there is here indicated any connection between Tom Thumb and Tom a Lin. Simrock, who traces numerous ramifications of the *Däumling* legend ("Deutsche Mythologie," pp. 270-288), does not appear to know of Tamlane. Uhland has a monograph on the *Mythus von Thor* (Stuttgart, 1836), but it has not come in my way; and I cannot therefore say whether he recognizes the connection of Tamlane with his subject.

does not, it is true, always bear the heroic character which he displays in this ballad. He appears in an enigmatical sort of nursery rhyme, as undergoing a series of undignified adventures, in which, if the rhyme be not wholly meaningless, we may still perhaps recognize a few shattered and distorted fragments of the original image of Thor, as well as some resemblance to the mishaps of Tom Thumb.

> "Tam o' the Linn came up the gait
> Wi' twenty puddings on a plate,
> And every pudding had a pin;
> 'We'll eat them a',' quo' Tam o' the Linn.
>
> "Tam o' the Linn had nae breeks to wear,
> He coft him a sheepskin to make him a pair,
> The fleshy side out, the woolly side in;
> 'It's fine summer cleeding,' quo' Tam o' the Linn.
>
> "Tam o' the Linn he had three bairns,
> They fell in the fire in each other's arms;
> 'Oh!' quo' the boonmost, 'I've got a het skin;'
> 'It's hetter below,' quo' Tam o' the Linn.
>
> "Tam o' the Linn gaed to the moss,
> To seek a stable to his horse;
> The moss was open, and Tam fell in;
> 'I've stabled mysel',' quo' Tam o' the Linn."[1]

[1] Chambers' "Popular Rhymes of Scotland," p. 33. In Chambers' "Scottish Songs" (p. 455) occurs a slightly varied version of this rhyme, with the chorus *Fa la, fa la, fa lillie*, between each line, and with the additional opening verse—

> " Tam o' the Lin is no very wise,
> He selt his sow, and boucht a gryce;
> The gryce gaed out, and never cam in·
> 'The deil gae wi' her!' quo' Tam o' the Linn."

In the same spirit appears to be an old English song, the following snatch of which is introduced into "a very merry and pithie comedie," entitled *The longer thou livest, the more Fool thou art* :—

"Tom a Lin and his wife and his wives mother
They went over a bridge all three together,
The bridge was broken and they fell in,
'The devil go with all,' quoth Tom a Lin."[1]

It may be interesting to mention, moreover, that Joanna Baillie has developed, with the fruitfulness of her own fancy, a similar conception of our hero in her song *Tam o' the Lin;* and as this humorous reproduction of an old Teutonic legend is not very generally familiar, it will not be out of place here in connection with the more primitive versions of the same theme :—

"Tam o' the Lin was fu' o' pride,
And his weapon he girt to his valorous side,
A scabbard o' leather wi' deil-hair't within.
'Attack me wha daur!' quo' Tam o' the Lin.

"Tam o' the Lin he bought a mear;
She cost him five shillings, she wasna dear.
Her back stuck up, and her sides fell in.
'A fiery yaud!' quo' Tam o' the Lin.

Tam o' the Lin he courted a may;
She stared at him sourly, and said him nay;
But he stroked down his jerkin and cocked up his chin
'She aims at a laird, then,' quo' Tam o' the Lin.

"Tam o' the Lin he gaed to the fair,
Yet he looked wi' disdain on the chapman's ware;

---

[1] See Ritson's Dissertation prefixed to his "Ancient Songs and Ballads," p lxxxiv.

Then chucked out a sixpence, the sixpence was tin.
'There's coin for the fiddlers,' quo' Tam o' the Lin.

"Tam o' the Lin wad show his lear,
And he scanned o'er the book wi' wise-like stare.
He muttered confusedly, but didna begin.
'This is Dominie's business,' quo' Tam o' the Lin.

"Tam o' the Lin had a cow wi' ae horn,
That likit to feed on his neighbour's corn.
The stanes he threw at her fell short o' the skin;
'She's a lucky auld reiver,' quo' Tam o' the Lin.

"Tam o' the Lin he married a wife,
And she was the torment, the plague o' his life;
She lays sae about her, and maks sic a din,
'She frightens the baby,' quo' Tam o' the Lin.

"Tam o' the Lin grew dourie and douce,
And he sat on a stane at the end o' his house.
'What ails, auld chiel?' He looked haggard and thin.
'I'm no very cheery,' quo' Tam o' the Lin.

"Tam o' the Lin lay down to die,
And his friends whispered softly and woefully—
'We'll buy you some masses to scour away sin.'
'And drink at my lykewake,' quo' Tam o' the Lin."

Whether this conception of our hero originated from the confidence of his great prototype in the sheer force of his hammer Miölnir exposing him to be outwitted at times by the trickery of Utgard's inhabitants, it is unnecessary for us to inquire. In the ballad of *The Young Tamlane* the hero assumes the character of one who has entered an unearthly world, and returned from it victorious over the efforts to retain him within its power. The legend, moreover, has lost its general relations to the mythology of the Teutons, and become thoroughly localized. The hero is not merely what a modern song makes him, "a Scotchman born;" he announces himself definitely to be a son of "Randolph, Earl Murray;" while "Dunbar, Earl March," is named as the father of the maiden whose daring love achieves his recovery from the world of the fairies. The locality also in which the adventure of the ballad takes place, is assigned to Carterhaugh, at the confluence of the Ettrick and the Yarrow above Selkirk. This spot, though naturally pitched upon by the collector of the Border Minstrelsy as the native home of the legend, is evidently, like *Chaster's Wood, Charter Woods*, and *Kerton Ha'*, which occur in other versions, merely a local adaptation and corruption of some original common to all these names.

Tamlane of our ballad has been kidnapped by the fairies; and the manner of his spiriting away is well described, and worth quoting as a type of such adventures :—

> "When I was a boy just turned of nine,
> My uncle sent for me,
> To hunt, and hawk, and ride with him,
> And keep him companie.
>
> "There came a wind out of the north,
> A sharp wind and a snell;
> And a deep sleep came over me,
> And frae my horse I fell.
>
> "The Queen of Fairies keppit me,
> In yon green hill to dwell;
> And I'm a fairy, lythe and limb;
> Fair ladye, view me well."

In this serene land Tamlane would never tire of his new friends, were it not for the dread that his fair and plump appearance may tempt them to use him as a "kane-bairn" for the purpose of paying the next instalment of their tribute to the king of hell. Fortunately, however, he has won at Carterhaugh the dearest tokens of love[1] from an earthly maid, fair Janet, who undertakes, at his instruction, the bold feat of rescuing him from the elfin world.

> "This night is Hallowe'en, Janet,
>   The morn is Hallowday;
> And, gin ye dare your true-love win,
>   Ye hae nae time to stay.
>
> "The night it is good Hallowe'en,
>   When fairy folk will ride;
> And they that wad their true-love win,
>   At Miles Cross they maun bide."

Janet, who is brave enough to undertake the "winning" of her lover, is yet doubtful whether she will be able to recognize him "among so many unearthly knights." Tamlane, accordingly, describes the order of the fairy procession which she must watch, the place which he will occupy in it, the distinctive marks by which he may be recognized; and he warns her against what it seems impossible for mortal nerve to avoid—quailing before the appalling artifices by which the fairies will endeavour

---

[1] There is probably a connection between this part of *The Young Tamlane* and the ballad of *Broomfield Hill* ("Border Minstrelsy," vol. iii. p. 28), as well as the fragment beginning *I'll wager, I'll wager, I'll wager with you*, preserved in Herd's "Scottish Songs." See "Border Minstrelsy," vol. ii. p 334, and vol. iii. p. 28.

to frighten her from her resolution. The emotion of eeriness could scarcely be worked up with greater power than by this collocation of the "elritch" appearances which are to test the courage of fair Janet. The work of the ballad-singer here recalls the mixture of dread ingredients in the hell-broth of Macbeth's witches; or, more appropriately, the frightfully suggestive objects which *Tam o' Shanter* passed on his road from Ayr; or, perhaps more appropriately still, the combination of horrors ranged before his eyes in Alloway Kirk.

> "The first company that passes by,
>   Say na, and let them gae;
> The next company that passes by,
>   Say na, and do right sae;
> The third company that passes by,
>   Then I'll be ane o' thae.
>
> "First let pass the black, Janet,
>   And syne let pass the brown;
> But grip ye to the milk-white steed,
>   And pu' the rider down.
>
> "For I ride on the milk-white steed,
>   And aye nearest the town;
> Because I was a christened knight,
>   They gave me that renown.
>
> "My right hand will be gloved, Janet,
>   My left hand will be bare;
> And these the tokens I gie thee,
>   Nae doubt I will be there.
>
> "They'll turn me in your arms, Janet,
>   An adder and a snake;

But haud me fast, let me not pass,
    Gin ye wad buy me maik.

"They'll turn me in your arms, Janet,
    An adder and an ask;
They'll turn me in your arms, Janet,
    A bale that burns fast.

"They'll turn me in your arms, Janet,
    A red-hot gad o' airn;
But haud me fast, let me not pass,
    For I'll do you no harm.

"First dip me in a stand o' milk,
    And then in a stand o' water;
But haud me fast, let me not pass—
    I'll be your bairn's father.

"And, next, they'll shape me in your arms
    A tod, but and an eel;
But haud me fast, nor let me gang,
    As you do love me weel.

"They'll shape me in your arms, Janet,
    A dove, but and a swan;
And last they'll shape me in your arms
    A mother-naked man:
Cast your green mantle over me—
    I'll be myself again."

Stories are related of others who attempted the achievement of fair Janet, but whose hearts quailed at the first sight of the unearthly procession; so that the whole fairy troop was allowed to pass, and vanish amid shouts of exultant laughter, mingled with the lamentations of the unrecovered mortal.[1] Happily, however, for Tamlane, the courage of his mistress was stout enough to conquer the elfin terrors by which it was assailed.

> "Gloomy, gloomy was the night,
>   And eery was the way,
> As fair Janet, in her green mantle,
>   To Miles Cross she did gae.
>
> "Betwixt the hours of twelve and one
>   A north wind tore the bent;
> And straight she heard strange elritch sounds
>   Upon that wind which went.
>
> "About the dead hour o' the night
>   She heard the bridles ring;
> And Janet was as glad o' that
>   As any earthly thing.
>
> "Will o' the Wisp before them went,
>   Sent forth a twinkling light;
> And soon she saw the fairy bands
>   All riding in her sight.
>
> "And first gaed by the black, black steed,
>   And then gaed by the brown;
> But fast she gript the milk-white steed,
>   And pu'd the rider down.
>
> "She pu'd him frae the milk-white steed,
>   And loot the bridle fa';
> And up there raise an erlish cry—
>   'He's won amang us a'!'"

---

[1] See "Border Minstrelsy," vol. ii. p. 327. Compare No. 7 of the Notes to "Rob Roy."

Then followed the various terrifying transformations of Tamlane, which the fair Janet had been warned to expect, but during which, undaunted, " she held him fast in every shape."

> "They shaped him in her arms at last
> A mother-naked man:
> She wrapt him in her green mantle,
> And sae her true-love wan!"

The fairy troop seemed to be scattered in sheer bewilderment: the voice of the Queen was heard, now in one place, now in another, uttering the bitterness of her chagrin at the successful daring of fair Janet:—

> "Up then spake the Queen o' Fairies
> Out o' a bush o' broom—
> 'She that has borrowed young Tamlane,
> Has gotten a stately groom.'
>
> "Up then spake the Queen o' Fairies
> Out o' a bush o' rye—
> 'She's ta'en awa the bonniest knight
> In a' my companie.
>
> *   *   *   *   *
>
> "'Had I but had the wit yestreen
> That I hae coft the day,
> I'd paid my kane seven times to hell
> Ere you'd been won away.'"

Such is an analysis of the principal legendary ballads of Scotland that have been preserved. It is evident that these ballads at once evince the existence of a certain class of emotions strongly active in the Scottish mind, and must have been perpetually re-invigorating these emotions. To estimate, therefore, the value of those ballads in the building up of the Scottish character, requires an estimate of the value of these emotions as elements of human life. Now, the emotions which manifest themselves under the form of superstition are merely excesses, or rather misdirections, of the feeling, that the meaning of this universe is not exhausted by the scientific arrangement of natural phenomena,—that behind all natural law there is a mystery, which scientific conceptions do not embrace, but the sense of which they cannot banish from the spirit of man. Until there is a mediation, such as has not yet been accomplished even in advanced minds, between the scientific faith in the invariability of natural law and the religious faith in the existence of a world above natural law, the latter faith will continue to appear in a belief that that world reveals itself in operations which are out of Nature's ordinary course. To the great majority of minds this belief is probably the indispensable nutriment and the irresistible outflow of the higher faith; and there are not wanting minds of high culture, to whom a sympathetic realization in fancy of this belief is the only avenue to a poetical view of Nature.[1] In fact, the belief can be neither of unmitigated evil nor of unmitigated good; and the evil, as well

---

[1] See Collins' "Ode on the Superstitions of the Highlands," especially verses 11 and 12; Schiller's "Götter Griechenlands," especially verse 2. Compare Allan Cunningham's "Scottish Songs," vol. i. pp. 128-9.

as the good effects of it,—the superstitious fanaticism, as well as the religious conviction, which it has wrought,—may be traced in bold features of the Scottish character.

Without entering into questionable comparisons with other nations, it may be said with safety, that at all great crises in their modern history the Scottish people have exhibited unconquerable trust in an irresistible Power and an inviolable Order above the things that are seen and temporal. The light of that Divine trust throws a pleasant gleam over the many dark aspects of the Scottish struggle in the seventeenth century. It is not easy to realize the calamity which would have fallen upon Europe if the nations which have suffered for their religious convictions had given way; and it is, therefore, difficult to restrain indignation, impossible to overcome regret, that the courage of the Scottish people in their great struggle should not only have been so cruelly misinterpreted at the time, but continues to be misinterpreted even by those who are enjoying the fruit of their sufferings. But a closer view of the period shows that the faith of the Scots was manifested not only in a trustful struggle against oppression, but in an unreasoning fanaticism which did more perhaps than the political folly and the religious indifference of the enemy to postpone the achievement of toleration. It becomes, consequently, not altogether unintelligible, that cavaliers of cultured, and even of gentle nature, should have viewed their Scotch opponents as a pack of intractable rebels; and that some historical students, even at this distant day, should scarcely be able to see beyond the rant and bickering of the Covenanters into the nobler elements of their character.

It is difficult to refer to the facts of existing society without provoking the antagonistic passions by which its harmony is marred ; and, therefore, any reference to these facts now must be as brief as possible. It is sufficient, however, to remark, that while the Scottish people display an activity of religious feeling which is scarcely to be seen in any other country, there are few, if any, Protestant communities in which that feeling is so unpardonably misdirected to microscopic distinctions of dogma and ecclesiastical polity, which are being constantly exalted into objects of a spurious reverence, wholly unintelligible to minds beyond the infection of passionate controversy.

Apart, then, from all other advantages to be derived from the study of the legendary ballads, they are of value as recalling to us, in its living freshness, a time when the world was still wonderful and awful in the eyes of men ; and they remain worthy of study, if they serve to make us feel anew the mystery which lies before us in "the open secret of the Universe." We need not, in cherishing the feeling of this mystery, oppose the beneficent work of science in revealing to us the "faithfulness" with which the Ruler of the Universe evolves similar results from similar antecedents ; but the work of science would cease to be beneficent if, in dissipating the ruder awe and wonder of an uncultured age, it made us forget that the Universe is awful and wonderful still. "This green, flowery, rock-built earth ; the trees, the mountains, rivers, many-sounding seas; that great deep sea of azure that swims overhead; the winds sweeping through it; the black cloud fashioning itself together, now pouring out fire now hail and rain: what *is* it? Ay, what? At bottom we do not yet know; we can never know at all. It is not by our superior insight that we escape the difficulty; it is by our superior levity, our inattention, our *want* of insight. It is *not* by thinking that we cease to wonder at it. Hardened round us, encasing wholly every notion we form, is a wrappage of traditions, hearsays, mere *words*. We call that fire of the black cloud 'electricity,' and lecture learnedly about it, and grind the like of it out of glass and silk; but *what* is it? Whence comes it? Whither goes it? Science has done much for us; but it is a poor science that would hide from us the great, deep, sacred infinitude of Nescience, whither we can never penetrate, on which all science swims as a mere superficial film. This world, after all our science and sciences, is still a miracle; wonderful, inscrutable, *magical*, and more, to whosoever will *think* of it."[1]

[1] Carlyle's "Lectures on Heroes."

CHAPTER II.

SOCIAL BALLADS AND SONGS.

> " All hail, ye tender feelings dear !
> The smile of love, the friendly tear,
> The sympathetic glow !
> Long since, this world's thorny ways
> Had numbered out my weary days
> Had it not been for you !
> Fate still has blest me with a friend,
> In every care and ill ;
> And oft a more endearing band,
> A tie more tender still."
>   BURNS' *Epistle to Davie.*

UNDER this chapter I include that large group of lyrics to which the events or the affections of social life afford a subject. For the purpose of examination they may be advantageously arranged in three sub-divisions, comprehending severally (1), Love Songs and Ballads ; (2), Domestic Songs and Ballads ; (3), those in which the more general relations of social life form the theme.

§ 1.—*Love Songs and Ballads.*

It is almost impossible to embrace, in a brief sketch like this, a comprehensive survey of the innumerable lyrics coming under this category; but I shall endeavour to point out their leading varieties, with some of the more prominent characteristics of each.

There is, first of all, a whole legion which are merely utterances of amatory passion,—the unwearied twitterings of lovers in the sunshine which their passion gleams over life. This literature, however, is very soon exhausted, as far as real variety is concerned, and therefore as far as it can furnish poetical enjoyment. The most beautiful melody admits of only a limited number of variations with musical effect, even in the hands of the most ingenious composer; and that effect soon fails, if many of the variations are produced by composers of mediocre musical power. For this reason it is scarcely advisable to enter into detailed examination of this class of songs; but for our purpose it is certainly worthy of remark, that a very large proportion of them are the work of persons in very humble grades of society. It is not that poets of higher rank have put into the mouths of imaginary peasants and artisans lyrical expressions of refined sentiment, such as we are familiar with in the antiquated pastorals; but we have the characteristically hearty and often naïve utterances of the peasants and artisans themselves. While this is evidence of a refining sexual affection penetrating the humble life of the people, the existence of such a mass of popular song on the subject has tended to perpetuate the refinement of this affection, and thus to counteract some less gratifying influences which we may yet require to notice.

The history of Scottish literature does not present many poets who have made the love of the sexes so obviously their favourite theme, that they could, with propriety, be called Anacreontic. If we except Alexander Scott—a poet of Queen Mary's time, who has in fact been dubbed the Scottish Anacreon—there is perhaps not a single author who deserves the designation; and Scott himself is to be ranked rather among the poets of culture than among those who have furnished the songs of the people. But no one possessing the most superficial acquaintance with Scottish literature requires to be informed as to the wealth of Anacreontic poetry which it contains. One of the oldest Scottish lyrics which have come down to us in complete form is a love-song—the *Song on Absence*,[1] preserved in the Maitland MS., and ascribed by Pinkerton and Ritson, though without any certainty, to James I. of Scotland. Whoever the poet may have been, he was, for his time, no unskilful handler of an intricate versification.

> "As he that swimmis the moir he ettil fast,
>   And to the schoire intend,
> The moir his febil furie, throw windis blast,
>   Is backwart maid to wend;
>   So wars by day
>   My grief grows ay.
>   The moir I am hurte,
>   The moir I sturte.
> O cruel love, bot deid thow hes none end!"

* * * * *

> "The Day, befoir the suddane Nichtis chaice,
>   Does not so suiftlie go;
> Nor hare, befoir the ernand grewhound's face,
>   With speid is careit so;

[1] See Sibbald's "Chronicle of Scottish Poetry," vol. i. p. 55.

> As I with paine
> For luif of ane,
> Without remeid,
> Rin to the deid.
> O God, gif deid be end of mekil woe!"

The old poet, moreover, was one with the soul of the true singer, who uses the measured language of verse as the natural outlet of his emotions, and finds a solace in " the sad mechanic exercise."

> "He that can plaine
> Dois thoil leist paine.
> Soir ar the hairtis
> But playnt that smartis.
> Silence to dolour is ane nourisching."

From this early song-writer down to those of recent times, the Scottish poets seem to move in their natural element when they enter upon the subject of love. The greatest of them is but the mouthpiece of all, when, referring to his Jean, he describes her influence upon his verse:—

> "Oh how that name inspires my style!
> The words come skelpin', rank and file,
> Amaist before I ken!
> The ready measure rins as fine,
> As Phœbus and the famous Nine,
> Were glowrin' owre my pen."

Burns has expressed several emotions with a happiness of fancy and language which seems to proclaim that they have found their perfect utterance. This may be said of the lyrical expression he has given to those delicious emotions which men owe to the influence of woman; and this lyric has so woven itself into his countrymen's habits of thought, that a Scotchman, expressing himself on the subject, almost instinctively adopts the language of Burns:—

> "Green grow the rashes, O,
>   Green grow the rashes, O;
> The sweetest hours that e'er I spent
>   Were spent amang the lasses, O.
>
> "There's nought but care on every hand
>   In every hour that passes, O;
> What signifies the life o' man,
>   An 'twere na for the lasses, O!
>
> *   *   *   *   *
>
> "Auld Nature swears, the lovely dears
>   Her noblest work she classes, O;
> Her 'prentice-hand she tried on man,
>   And then she made the lasses, O."

Passing from those love-lyrics which are merely expressions of vague sexual affection, we come to those in which there is a love-story more or less explicitly told, in some with a tragic, in others with a comic issue. In the former the pathos varies of course with the nature of its cause, from the bitterness of a disappointment in love to the anguish arising from the death of one who is loved. To anyone familiar with Scottish songs, not a few will readily occur in which the pathos is expressed with irresistible power.

Among those with the most tragic issue, much

prominence is not to be given to ballads, like *Barbara Allan*, in which death is the result of unreciprocated love. There is a weakness of sentiment in these, which is out of unison with a characteristic of Scottish love-songs to be noticed by and by. Where the death arises from less sentimental causes, there is a force of reality in the representation which is immeasurably more affecting. In most of these ballads the effect is due to the simplicity with which the tale of sorrow is told, and could not be felt by the quotation of isolated verses. As an instance may be mentioned *The Lass of Lochroyan*.[1] The story is that of a maiden who has surrendered herself to her lover, and comes to claim at his own home the love he had promised, but is driven from the door by a deceit of his mother, and perishes, with her child, by the wreck of the boat in which she is returning. It is scarcely necessary to mention that it was this ballad which suggested, besides forgotten lyrics by Jamieson and Dr. Wolcott, Burns' beautiful song, *Lord Gregory*. With this ballad may be compared another, *Willie and May Margaret*,[2] in which the hero is the victim of a similar deceit and a similar fate to those which the heroine suffers in the other.

But in love-tragedy the Scottish ballad, which attains the most subduing pathos, is one that carries the imagination away to a Border stream which holds a unique place in Scottish legend and song. The peculiar spell

---

[1] "Border Minstrelsy," vol. iii. p. 199. *Fair Annie of Lochroyan* (Jamieson's "Popular Ballads and Songs," vol. i. p. 37) is, in some passages, a superior version.

[2] Jamieson's "Popular Ballads and Songs," vol. i. p. 135. A completer version, *The Drowned Lovers*, is given by Buchan and by Motherwell.

which the Yarrow wields over the fancy has become a familiar fact to the reader of English poetry as well as of Scotch, from its having been made the theme of three companion poems by the modern poet, whose chief mission has been to teach his countrymen to feel and to understand the influence of natural objects. To any-one at all acquainted with the literature of which this essay treats, the very thought of the Yarrow, even while it remains yet unvisited, is full of "dreams treasured up from early days;" and, when it has been visited, the wonderful scenery through which it flows is felt to be suggestive of a pensive tenderness in unison with the tragic strain of the ballad which is now to be noticed:—

> "And is this—Yarrow?—*This* the stream
>   Of which my fancy cherished,
> So faithfully, a waking dream?
>   An image that hath perished!
> O that some minstrel's harp were near,
>   To utter notes of gladness,
> And chase the silence from the air
>   That fills my heart with sadness!

*   *   *   *   *

> "But thou, that didst appear so fair
>   To fond imagination,
> Dost rival in the light of day
>   Her delicate creation:
> Meek loveliness is round thee spread,
>   A softness mild and holy,
> The grace of forest charms decayed,
>   And pastoral melancholy."

Whether it was this pensive mood that created *The Dowie Dens of Yarrow*[1] as its own interpretation, may perhaps admit of conjecture; but the local tradition refers the ballad to a tragedy which is alleged to have occurred in the district.[2] According to this tradition, the hero was betrothed to the heroine, whose father had promised to give her as a dowry the half of his property. Stung by indignation at the prospect of losing such a large portion of his patrimony, her brother waylaid her betrothed and murdered him, at a spot which is still pointed out on the "dowie banks of Yarrow." In the ballad, however, the combat is a pre-arranged duel; and the hero, on proceeding to the place agreed upon, finds himself met, not by one, but by nine armed men.

Wonderful is the skill with which the old minstrel arrests the interest of his hearers, by rushing at once into the heart of his story:—

"Late at e'en, drinking the wine,
 And ere they paid the lawing,
They set a combat them between,
 To fight it at the dawing."

Our hero, accordingly, visits his mistress to bid her farewell, before setting out for the combat from which he may never return; and, while she "kisses his cheek," and "kaims his hair," and "belts him with his noble brand," earnest are her entreaties that he may stay at home, from the foreboding that he will be betrayed by her "cruel brother." The result of the "unequal marrow"

---

[1] "Border Minstrelsy," vol. iii. p. 147.   [2] Ibid. pp. 144-5.

of nine to one is such as might have been anticipated, and the victim, as he dies, requests the brother to carry tidings of his death to the desolate sister. Meanwhile she sits pining at home, and her yearning after her lover finds vent in a prayer to the southerly wind that is blowing from him to her :—

> "O gentle wind, that bloweth south,
> From where my love repaireth,
> Convey a kiss from his dear mouth,
> And tell me how he fareth."

Her forebodings, moreover, have been intensified by "a doleful dream," that she had been pulling green heather, with her true love, on the banks of the Yarrow; for there is a superstition that it is unlucky to dream of anything green:[1] but her brother, who is approaching with his unhappy tidings, and receives from her an account of her dream, gives it a more pointed interpretation.

---

[1] "It is rather strange that green, the most natural and agreeable of all colours, should have been connected by superstition with calamity and sorrow. It was thought very ominous to be married in a dress of this hue :—

'They that marry in green,
Their sorrow is soon seen.'

To this day, in the North of Scotland, no young woman would wear such attire on her wedding-day. . . . Probably the saying respecting a lady married before her elder sisters, 'that she has given them green stockings,' is connected with this notion."—CHAMBERS' *Popular Rhymes of Scotland*, pp. 341-2. Chambers mentions further, that green was considered a peculiarly unlucky colour to two families, the Lindsays and the Grahams.

> "The Lindsays in green
> Should never be seen."

> "'I'll read your dream, sister,' he says,
>   'I'll read it into sorrow;
> Ye're bidden gae take up your love;
>   He's sleeping sound on Yarrow.'"[1]

The passionate anguish with which the maiden is impelled is expressed by the old singer, in a picture, the horror of which is almost too vivid for poetical effect. Down she speeds to the tragic scene, where she comes upon the lifeless form in which was lost all that had made life dear to her.

> "She kissed his cheek, she kaimed his hair,
>   She searched his wounds all thorough,
> *She kissed them till her lips grew red*
>   On the dowie houms of Yarrow."

The heart smitten by such a grief is like the tree blasted by lightning: never again can it blossom into love; and vain, therefore, are all the consolations addressed to it by friends:—

> "'Now, haud your tongue, my daughter dear,
>   For a' this breeds but sorrow;
> I'll wed you to a better lord,
>   Than him ye lost on Yarrow.'
>
> "'Now, haud your tongue, my father dear,
>   Ye mind me but of sorrow;
> A fairer rose did never bloom
>   Than now lies cropped on Yarrow.'"

Among songs dealing, like these ballads, with the death of one who is loving and loved, everyone will

---

[1] This interesting verse is fortunately preserved in Buchan's version, *The Braes of Yarrow*, though not in Scott's.

remember those, especially *To Mary in Heaven*, inspired by the pathetic fate of Burns' Highland Mary; but there is probably no Scots song in which the anguish produced by such a cause is expressed in more natural or more impassioned language than *Fair Helen of Kirconnell*. The heroine, Helen Irving of Kirconnell, in Dumfriesshire, was wooed by two suitors, one of whom she preferred. As she was walking one evening with her accepted lover on the banks of the river Kirtle, near Kirconnell, she saw his rival, on the opposite side of the stream, level a carabine at the successful object of his jealousy. She threw herself in front of her lover to shield him, received the bullet in her own breast, and died in his arms. The murderer, however, was pursued and cut to pieces by the other. Such is the traditional explanation of the origin of this song,[1] which professes to be an utterance of the survivor's anguish.

The song divides itself into three stages by the threefold repetition, at intervals, of the slightly varied refrain :—

"I wish I were where Helen lies;
Night and day on me she cries:
O that I were where Helen lies
On fair Kirconnell Lee!"

The recurrence of this cry describes, with dramatic vividness, the sufferer's anguish as ebbing and flowing by turns, like all intense emotions—as now subsiding for a little, so as to allow other thoughts to appear, but anon swelling to its full tide and drowning every idea that makes life endurable. At one of those intermis-

[1] See "Border Minstrelsy," vol. iii. pp. 98-9.

sions between the paroxysms of his agony, he reverts to its cause; and an uncontrollable intensity of suffering could not be more powerfully expressed than by the savage exultation, in which he finds relief, over the dreadful revenge he had obtained :—

> "As I went down the water side,
> None but my foe to be my guide,
> None but my foe to be my guide,
> On fair Kirconnell Lee;
>
> "I lighted down my sword to draw,
> I hacked him in pieces sma',
> I hacked him in pieces sma',
> For her sake that died for me."

Of a less tragic nature is the pathos of those songs which express the grief of disappointment in love, whether from separation or from unreciprocated affection. As expressions of the bitterness of separation may be taken some of those songs which arose out of Burns' transient, but, while it lasted, passionate attachment to Mrs. M'Lehose—the *Clarinda* of his correspondence. In *My Nannie's awa*, for example, every verse is a gem of pathetic poetry, the mood of the poet, as (we shall find) is very commonly the case in Scottish love-songs, being brought into apposite relation with the scenes of external nature. Two verses will serve for illustration :—

> "The snawdrap and primrose our woodlands adorn,
> And violets bathe in the weet o' the morn;
> They pain my sad bosom, sae sweetly they blaw,
> They mind me o' Nannie—and Nannie's awa.

> " Thou laverock that springs frae the dews o' the lawn,
> The shepherd to warn o' the gray-breaking dawn ;
> And thou mellow mavis that hails the night-fa',
> Give over for pity—my Nannie's awa."

To the same episode in the poet's life we owe the song *Ae fond kiss, and then we sever.* It is scarcely possible to add to the honour which has been lavished on this song, and especially on the verse beginning " Had we never loved sae kindly."[1] The separation of this verse from the preceding was perhaps unfortunate: the two together tell, in its inner aspect, the whole of the romance which the song celebrates ; and, in doing so, reveal the spirit of all love-stories whose course has been rendered beautiful by their pathos :—

> " I'll ne'er blame my partial fancy,
> Naething could resist my Nancy :
> But to see her was to love her ;
> Love but her, and love for ever.
>
> " Had we never loved sae kindly,
> Had we never loved sae blindly,
> Never met and never parted,
> We had ne'er been broken-hearted."

A deeper pathos still is reached, when, after having surrendered her whole being to her lover, a maiden finds

---

[1] " The fourth stanza Byron put at the head of his poem *The Bride of Abydos.* Scott has remarked that that verse is worth a thousand romances ; and Mrs. Jamieson has elegantly said that not only are these lines what Scott says, 'but in themselves a complete romance. They are,' she adds, 'the alpha and omega of feeling, and contain the essence of an existence of pain and pleasure distilled into one burning drop.'"—CHAMBERS' *Life and Works of Burns,* vol. iii. p. 215.

herself deserted;[1] and such a sorrow is expressed, with affecting simplicity of language and of feeling, in the very old song, *Waly, waly, but Love be bonny*, which appears in the song-books, like many another of equal merit, unclaimed by any author.[2] The introduction of it here will not be unwelcome, even to those who are familiar with it already :—

> " O waly, waly up the bank,
>   And waly, waly down the brae,
> And waly, waly yon burnside,
>   Where I and my love wont to gae.
>
> " I lent my back unto an aik,
>   I thought it was a trusty tree ;
> But first it bowed, and syne it brak,
>   Sae my true love did lichtly me !
>
> " O waly, waly, but love be bonny
>   A little time while it is new ;
> But when 'tis auld, it waxeth cauld,
>   And fades away like the morning dew.
>
> " O wherefore should I busk my head ?
>   Or wherefore should I kame my hair ?
> For my true love has me forsook,
>   And says he'll never love me mair.

[1] There is an old song, *The Murning Maiden*, preserved in the Maitland MS., and probably the same that is referred to in the *Complaint of Scotland* under the title of *Still under the Levis Green*, which contains some pathetic verses, but is spoiled by the maiden comforting herself at the close with another lover. It will be found in Sibbald's " Chronicles of Scottish Poetry," vol. i. p. 201.

[2] The reader will find the song and different versions of the ballad with which it seems connected, as well as all the information he is likely to wish on the circumstance to which it refers, in Child's " English and Scottish Ballads," vol. iv. pp. 132-6 and 287-291.

"Now Arthur-seat shall be my bed,
    The sheets shall ne'er be fyled by me:
Saint Anton's well shall be my drink,
    Since my true love has forsaken me.

"Martinmas wind, when wilt thou blaw,
    And shake the green leaves off the tree?
O gentle death, when wilt thou come?
    For of my life I am weary.

"'Tis not the frost that freezes fell,
    Nor blawing snaw's inclemency;
'Tis not sic cauld that makes me cry,
    But my love's heart grown cauld to me.

"When we came in by Glasgow town,
    We were a comely sight to see;
My love was clad in the black velvet,
    And I mysell in cramasie.

"But had I wist before I kissed,
    That love had been sae ill to win,
I'd locked my heart in a case of gold,
    And pinned it with a silver pin.

"Oh, oh, if my young babe were born,
    And set upon the nurse's knee,
And I mysell were dead and gane!
    For a maid again I'll never be."

Perhaps, however, there is no love-tragedy so overpowering as that of *Auld Robin Gray*, the perfection of which, both in its general conception and in the detailed working out of its plot, makes it a remarkable instance of those efforts in which an author has once risen to the height of poetical creation, but never reached it again.

The authoress belonged to a family who are characterized by an old ballad, in contrast to the strain of her song, as "the Lindsays light and gay." Lady Ann, daughter of James Lindsay, fifth Earl of Balcarras, afterwards married to Sir Andrew Barnard, was accustomed to hear a servant of her father's sing an old Scots song, *The Bridegroom grat when the Sun gaed down.* Wishing to sing the tune, but disliking the words to which it was sung, she set about writing some suitable verses. Her idea was to make the song a "little history of virtuous distress in humble life,"—of a maiden, with her lover at sea, her father and mother oppressed by poverty and sickness, wooed by a wealthy old suitor. A difficulty occurred in the composition; and she applied to her little sister Elizabeth, afterwards Lady Hardwicke, who was the only person in the room beside her. She told her that she was writing a ballad, in which she was overwhelming the heroine with misfortunes. "'I have already sent her Jamie to sea, and broken her father's arm, and made her mother fall sick, and sent her Auld Robin Gray for her lover; but I wish to load her with a fifth sorrow, within the four lines, poor thing! Help me to one.' 'Steal the cow, sister Annie,' said the little Elizabeth. The cow was immediately *lifted* by me, and the song completed."[1]

The song is a perfect embodiment of the finest spirit of tragedy. On the one hand, there is the remorseless tyranny of external circumstances over human affection, in the rapid accumulation of calamities around the path of the heroine, closing her in to a destiny from which all

[1] See the authoress's well-known letter to Sir Walter Scott.

the instincts of her heart shrink back. On the other hand, there is the sublime victory of human will over the tyranny of external events, in the unwavering virtue with which the heroine accepts the obligations of the unkindly destiny to which they had shut her up,—a virtue which appears affectingly in the authoress's own description of the interview with Jamie after his return, but which is obscured in an unhappy popular alteration of the passage—

> "O sair did we greet, and mickle say o' a',
> I gied him ae kiss, and *bade him gang awa'!*"[1]

There are several other touches of nature in the details of the song, which open up additional sources of its power over our feelings. One of these it may be sufficient to point out. The father with his broken arm, and the mother in her sickness, were both anxious that their daughter should accept Auld Robin Gray's proposal to marry him for their sakes; and the contrast in the expression of this anxiety, by the harder nature of the father and the more sympathetic tenderness of the mother, forms a family picture of irresistible pathos :—

> "My father urged me sair[2]: my mither didna speak;
> But she lookit in my face till my heart was like to break."

[1] The popular alteration referred to gives—
> "O sair sair did we greet, and mickle did we say;
> We took but ae kiss, and we tore ourselves away."

[2] A common variation of this passage, which is perhaps an improvement, gives—
> "My faither *argued* sair."

The version given by Herd, in the edition of 1776, presents the father in a

That heart is not to be envied, which, picturing the whole scene with that mother's look, does not feel like to break too.

The popularity of such a song is not astonishing; but the great wave of enthusiasm which swept even over England, and touched the Continent, is almost unprecedented. Not the least significant indication of this popularity is the fact that the fame of the greatest genius among the contemporaries of the authoress was eclipsed in the fashions of the time by a "Robin Gray hat" superseding one that had been named after Goethe's "Werther."[1] The authoress herself gave a happy *résumé* of the various forms of popularity which her song enjoyed on one of those occasions—the source of some capital stories—on which she parried the attempts that were made to surprise her into the acknowledgment, from which she shrank, of having written the song. The secretary of some Antiquarian Society, deputed to inquire into the authorship, was subjecting her to an impertinent cross-examination. "The ballad in question," she replied, "has, in my opinion, met with attention beyond its deserts. It set off with having a very fine tune put to it by a doctor of music; was sung by youth and beauty for five years and more; had a romance composed on it by a man of eminence; was the subject of a play, of an opera, of a panto-

---

more amiable light, referring the persistent pressure of the suit to Auld Robin Gray :—
   "Auld Robin argued sair."

[1] See "The Songstresses of Scotland," by Sarah Tytler and J. L. Watson, vol. i. p. 171.

mime; was sung by the united armies in America, acted by Punch, and afterwards danced by dogs in the street; but never more honoured than by the present investigation!"[1]

One effect, however, of this popularity was unfortunate; it gave rise to a *Continuation of Auld Robin Gray*, which was sung about the streets, and even found its way into magazines, greatly to the annoyance of the authoress. This was probably a chief motive with her in writing the second part, in which the tragic pathos of the original song is wholly dissolved, by Auld Robin being made a martyr to the poetical justice of romance, and yielding his place in his comfortable home to young Jamie by considerately dying soon after his marriage. She may have been influenced partly also by affection for her mother, who used to ask some gratification of her curiosity about the fate of the lovers: "Annie, I wish you would tell me how that unlucky business of Jeanie and Jamie ended."[2] But it was an evil day, for our perfect sympathy with the tragedy, when she abandoned her original conception of the absolute blamelessness of the three main sufferers, and adopted the hint thrown out by the Laird of Dalzell, in an exclamation which he uttered on listening to the first part: "Oh! the villain! Oh! the auld rascal! I ken wha stealt the poor cow—it was Auld Robin Gray himsel'!"[3]

With regard to those songs which refer to the more ordinary disappointment arising from unreciprocated

---

[1] See "The Songstresses of Scotland," vol. ii. pp. 88-9.
[2] Ibid. p. 34.   [3] Ibid. pp. 99, 100.

love, the most and the best are free from a weak Wertherian sentiment. They are mostly the utterances of men and women who have not leisure for such sentiment, to whom love is nothing if it is not a sustaining force in the rough battle of life, and who conquer in life's industry the griefs which conquer the idle. It is pleasing, therefore, to meet in these songs with sentiment of high generosity asserting itself in the midst of painful reminiscences, and of the painful foreboding that these reminiscences will cling to the mind through life. This is finely illustrated in that delicious bit of lyrical composition by Mrs. Grant of Carron, *Roy's Wife of Aldivalloch*, in which the jilted lover cannot choose but doat on the provoking witchery of his mistress's charms, even while he is fretting at her faithlessness. Take the chorus with the last verse:—

> " Roy's wife of Aldivalloch!
> Roy's wife of Aldivalloch!
> Wat ye how she cheated me
> As I cam o'er the braes o' Balloch?

> " Her hair sae fair, her een sae clear,
> Her wee bit mou sae sweet and bonnie.
> To me she ever will be dear,
> Though she's for ever left her Johnnie."

The sentiment, however, finds perfect expression, on the part of a maiden, in an old song, *My Heart's my ain*, which will be quoted in the sequel.

But it is not surprising that the manful feeling which pulsates in these songs of disappointed love should thrill the singer at times with the vigorous indignation of

Locksley Hall, when the heroine has degraded herself in the eyes of her lover, like the Amy of Tennyson's poem, by bartering for wealth the treasure of her young love. The manliest, if not the absolutely best, of Hector Macneill's songs, *Come under my Plaidie*, bears none of the polished sentiment or language of academic culture, by which the poem of the Laureate is distinguished; it takes no reflective flight into the imaginary future of a progressive world, to find there an ideal consolation for the real wrongs of the present: it is simply the unreserved, straightforward, strong—if you will, coarse—utterance of a homely mind, smarting under the endurance of a wrong which crops out in all societies, savage and civilized alike. As in *Roy's Wife of Aldivalloch*, the "Johnnie" of this is simply the typical Scottish peasant-lover. Marion has gone out one evening to meet him at their trysting-place, when she encounters "auld Donald," who wooes her with the powerful inducements which a rich suitor, though old, is always in a position to ply; and the opening of the song, which describes this scene with capital humour, will repay a fresh perusal. The suit is successful; and Johnnie, who has arrived at the spot unobserved, endures the mortification of seeing and hearing her consent to "come under the plaidie" of a lover whom she is glad to find not over "threescore and twa."

" She crap in ayont him, beside the stane wa',
  Whare Johnnie was listenin', and heard her tell a':
The day was appointed; his proud heart it dunted,
  And strack 'gainst his side, as if bursting in twa.

"He wandered hame wearie, the nicht it was drearie,
 And, thowless, he tint his gate 'mang the deep snaw:
 The howlet was screamin', while Johnnie cried,
  'Women
Wad marry auld Nick if he'd keep them aye braw!

"'O the deil's in the lasses! they gang now sae braw,
 They'll lie down wi' auld men o' fourscore and twa;
 The haill o' their marriage is gowd and a carriage,
 Plain love is the cauldest blast now that can blaw.'"

The reader who is curious to know the most passionate utterances of the jilted lover's indignation, may turn up for himself the concluding verse.

Songs of this class form an apt transition to those of a more purely comic character. For several of these lyrics of disappointed love reveal a strong, even if it be at times a somewhat rough, nature, not bursting into the earnest indignation of *Come under my Plaidie*, but playfully turning the disappointment into a source of healthy mirth. There is an old fragment, indeed, preserved by Herd, which is developed by Mr. James Tytler—*Balloon Tytler*, as he was nicknamed from his aëronautic celebrity—into his *I hae laid a Herrin in Saut*, in which the wooer informs his mistress, in a style of very straightforward business, that if she loves him she must tell him at once, for he "canna come ilka day to woo." Allan Ramsay also has given us a couple of songs, which may be regarded as expressing the pure joy of loving, without being so absorbed in one sweetheart that another could not afford equal scope for the gratification of the passion. *Bessie Bell* and *Mary Gray* and the less popular *Gentle Tibby and Sousy Nelly* present exquisite delineations of the amusing swither into which a lover is thrown by the equally irresistible charms of two beauties, between whom he seems as incapable of making a choice as Joannes Baridanus supposed his famous ass would be if placed between two equally attractive bundles of hay.

This heart-whole independence of the lover, before the disposition of the fair one is known, appears also in some songs as retained even after disappointment. It infuses a spirit, for example, into Burns' happy song, *O Tibbie, I hae seen the Day.*

"O Tibbie, I hae seen the day
    Ye wad na been sae shy;
For lack o' gear ye lightly me,
    But, trowth, I care na by.

"Yestreen I met you on the moor,
    Ye spak na, but gaed by like stour;
Ye geck at me because I'm poor,
    But fient a hair care I.

"I doubt na, lass, but ye may think,
    Because ye hae the name o' clink,
That ye can please me at a wink,
    Whene'er ye like to try.

*   *   *   *   *

"But, Tibbie, lass, tak my advice,
    Your daddie's gear maks you sae nice;
The deil a ane wad speer your price,
    Were you as poor as I."

Were it not that the Tibbie of this song seems to be identified with one of the numerous objects that attracted the poet's more transient affections,[1] it might have been supposed that the name was suggested by *Tibbie Fowler o' the Glen*, who is the Scots lyrical representative of the character which Burns intended to ridicule. From a reference in Ramsay's "Tea-Table Miscellany" we gather that there must have been a very old song, with the title *Tibbie Fowler o' the Glen*: it is probably a fragment of this which is preserved by Herd, while a development of it, which first appeared in Johnson's "Museum," is now to be found in most of the more recent collections. The extravagance in the description of the multitudinous suitors by whom the heroine is mobbed is irresistibly laughable; and it may be questioned whether the vulgar attractiveness of a well-dowered maiden has ever been more pithily expressed than in one of the verses of this song :—

> " Tibbie Fowler o' the Glen,
>   There's ower mony wooin' at her;
> Tibbie Fowler o' the Glen,
>   There's ower mony wooin' at her.
>   Wooing at her, pu'in' at her,
>   Courtin' her, and canna get her;
>   Filthy elf, it's for her pelf,
>   That a' the lads are wooin' at her.
>
> " Ten cam east, and ten cam west;
>   Ten cam rowin' ower the water;
>   Twa cam down the lang dyke-side:
>   There's twa and thirty wooin' at her

---

[1] See Chambers' "Life and Works of Burns," vol. i. p. 44.

> "There's seven but, and seven ben,
>   Seven in the pantry wi' her;
> Twenty head about the door:
>   There's ane and forty wooin' at her!

* * * * *

> "Be a lassie e'er sae black,
>   Gin she hae the penny siller,
> Set her up on Tintock tap,
>   The wind will blaw a man till her."[1]

It is due, however, to the Scottish song-writers to notice that they do not represent this heart-whole independence as all on one side; full justice is rendered to the weaker sex in a song mentioned above, *My Heart's my ain*. This old song surpasses those just described in its perfect good-humour; while I have never met anything to equal the cheerful womanly self-respect, made so thoroughly real by the slightest flavour of vanity, from which the song derives a peculiar zest. In every line there smiles a perfectly healthy maiden's soul. It is provoking that we do not know to whom we must accord the honour of this fine lyric; it appears for the first time anonymously in Herd's collection. It deserves to be quoted entire:—

> "'Tis nae very lang sinsyne,
>   That I had a lad o' my ain;
> But now he's awa' to anither,
>   And left me a' my lain.

---

[1] It appears that, in this capital verse, the writer has simply adapted a popular Lanarkshire rhyme. See Chambers' "Popular Rhymes of Scotland," p. 392.

The lass he's courting has siller,
  And I hae nane at a',
And 'tis nought but the love o' the tocher
  That's tane my lad awa.

" But I'm blyth, that my heart's my ain,
  And I'll keep it a' my life,
Until that I meet wi' a lad
  Who has sense to wale a good wife.
For though I say't mysell,
  That should nae say't, 'tis true,
The lad that gets me for a wife,
  He'll ne'er hae occasion to rue.

" I gang aye fou clean and fou tosh,
  As a' the neighbours can tell ;
Though I've seldom a gown on my back,
  But sick as I spin mysell.
And when I'm clad in my curtsey,
  I think mysell as braw
As Susie wi' a' her pearling,
  That's tane my lad awa.

" But I wish they were buckled together,
  And may they live happy for life ;
Though Willie now slights me, and's left me,
  The chield he deserves a good wife.
But O ! I'm blyth that I've missed him,
  As blyth as I weel can be ;
For ane that's sae keen o' the siller
  Will ne'er agree wi' me.

" But as the truth is, I'm hearty,
  I hate to be scrimpit or scant ;
The wee thing I hae, I'll mak use o't,
  And nae ane about me shall want.

For I'm a good guide o' the warld,
  I ken when to haud and to gie ;
For whinging and cringing for siller
  Will ne'er agree wi' me.

" Contentment is better than riches,
  And he wha has that has enough ;
The master is seldom sae happy
  As Robin that drives the plough.
But if a young lad wad cast up,
  To make me his partner for life ;
If the chield has sense to be happy,
  He'll fa' on his feet for a wife."[1]

The wooing of lovers, with all the real pathos which tinges it at times with a deeper earnest, presents its amusing side too, which the Scottish song-writers have not failed to hit ; and there can be few literatures in which all the funny aspects of love-histories are pictured in happier humour. The lyrics of this sort are too numerous to be described in detail ; only a few can be even referred to in general. They commence with Henryson's half-humorous, half-serious ballad, *Robene and Makyne*, which retains its popularity better than most of the old pastorals ; and certainly its natural sentiment and language make this not inexplicable. Henryson belongs to the close of the fifteenth century: next to his *Robene and Makyne*, in the order of time, perhaps contemporaneous with it, may be placed the essentially comic ballad, *The Wowing of Jok and*

---

[1] Ramsay's "Tea-Table Miscellany" contains another old song, *The Country Lass*, expressing, in fresh and simple language, the same heart-whole spirit, while it has been yet untried.

Jynny, which is preserved in the Bannatyne MS., and therefore belongs to a period before 1568. The comedy of this ballad consists in the laughable inventory of articles which the bride and bridegroom respectively contribute to the "plenishing" of their new home, and which may be taken as indicating the limited conveniences and comforts of the Scots peasants in the sixteenth century. On the same theme Allan Ramsay has preserved, in the "Tea-Table Miscellany," two songs, *Maggie's Tocher* and *Muirland Willie*, which, if not quite so old as the above ballad, give quite as lively and perhaps more truthful pictures of the interior of the old Scottish farm; and a more modern, once popular song, *The Wooing of Jock the Weaver and Jenny the Spinner*, which may be compared with these, is preserved by Mr. Chambers.[1] Henryson's ballad is a commentary on the proverb which it puts into the mouth of Makyne: —

> "The man that will not quhen he may,
> Sall haif nocht quhen he wald;"

for she, finding that Robene is deaf to her sighs, rejects his addresses when afterwards he seeks to win her love. In several popular songs of humorous wooing, while the commencement of the courtship is the same as in *Robene and Makyne*, the *dénouement* is reversed. Lady Nairne's *Laird o' Cockpen*, with Burns' *Duncan Gray* and *Last May a Braw Wooer*, would, of themselves, form a literature on this subject. But in the present

---

[1] See his "Scottish Songs," p. 146.

connection it would be unpardonable to pass over Sir Alexander Boswell's *Jenny's Bawbee*, with its happy portraiture of the discomfited suitors, retreating "wi' hinging lugs and faces lang." These songs create, by a few master-touches, a completer picture of human life in its more amusing phases, than many a novel of three volumes: every line in them is the addition of some apposite circumstance, overflowing with irrepressible though kindly laughter.

There is one circumstance, in conclusion, which ought to be noticed in connection with the Scottish love-songs, especially in attempting to estimate their influence on the national character; and that is, the poetical feeling for nature which most of them display. In fact, as was long ago remarked by Cowper, this feature of the Scottish love-songs is often developed to excess, especially by some of our poets. This is the case with regard to most of Tannahill's songs: in *The Braes of Gleniffer*, for example, the love is almost hidden by the luxuriance of poetical description, though the fault is so splendid that one can scarcely wish it removed. It was perhaps a consciousness of a tendency to this excess among the Scottish poets, that led Ramsay to put into the mouth of Peggie a complaint with regard to the Gentle Shepherd's poetical utterance of his love:—

"The scented meadows, birds, and healthy breeze,
For aught I ken, may mair than Peggie please."[1]

Apart, however, from this occasional fault of excess, the Scottish love-songs exhibit in general a remarkable

[1] "Gentle Shepherd," Act ii. Scene 4.

susceptibility to the emotional influences of nature. The loves celebrated in these songs are commonly associated with beautiful scenes; and thus Maxwelton braes and Kelvin grove, Gala Water and the Yarrow, the bonny wood of Craigielea and the birks of Aberfeldy, as well as a hundred other spots, have attained something like a classical fame. But, in addition to this, the varying moods of the passion which these songs express, are brought into correspondence—and often into correspondence of an exceedingly artistic character—with the various objects and the varying aspects of external nature. It is not difficult to point out a cause for this characteristic of Scottish love-songs. The best and most popular are, as has been mentioned, the utterance of persons in the humbler walks of life, whose domestic accommodation seldom affords the daughters the luxury of a room in which they can receive their lovers apart from the rest of the family; and courtship among such is thus of necessity conducted out of doors; so that its pleasures and its pains come to be associated with the sunshine and the gloom, the cheerful and the dreary features of the external world.

"Come, all ye jolly shepherds
  That whistle through the glen,
I'll tell ye of a secret
  That courtiers dinna ken:
What is the greatest bliss
  That the tongue o' man can name?
'Tis to woo a bonny lassie
  When the kye comes hame.

> "'Tis not beneath the coronet,
>   Nor canopy of state;
> 'Tis not on couch of velvet,
>   Nor arbour of the great:
> 'Tis beneath the spreading birk,
>   In the glen without a name,
> Wi' a bonny, bonny lassie,
>   When the kye comes hame."

There is probably, however, a deeper, though less obvious, cause of this association of love with natural scenery. In that feeling for nature which is awakened at the thought of crushing under the plough a "wee modest crimson-tipped flower," and which realizes that

> "The meanest flower on earth can give
> Thoughts that do often lie too deep for tears,"

—in that feeling there is much that is akin to the tenderness of all benevolent affection; and, consequently, the heart which is subdued by the power of woman's beauty becomes more quickly sensitive to the manifold beauties of nature. It is not surprising, therefore, that these love-songs should lead us out to green loans and shady glens, to wimpling burns and bonny knowes, should ring with the notes of laverock and lintie and mavis, should refresh us with the breath of heather and brier and broom. But no one whose attention has not been specially drawn to this circumstance, can have any idea of the extent to which it lends a charm to the love-songs of Scotland. There are few efforts of poetic art higher than that which brings out the mutual reaction of external nature and the moods of the soul; and whether it be in the combination of the various gladness of spring and summer with the joy of the successful lover, or in that of winter's desolation with the dreariness of disappointment, or in the contrast between external sunshine and the gloom of the spirit, the Scottish singer often exhibits a skill which is astonishing when it is seen to be the result of no conscious adherence to any theory of art.

Before passing from the love songs, there is one class of lyrics which cannot be wholly passed over. The prefatory or appended remarks which give value to several collections, occasionally furnish the information that a certain song is a refinement on older verses which are unfit for publication. In an essay like the present, it ought to be explained that the unfitness for publication of many old songs arises simply from the change of manners no longer allowing the freedom of allusion which shocked no one in former times. It is also interesting to mention at present, what will be explained more fully in the fifth chapter, that the poetical taste of successive generations has followed the growing moral refinement in rescuing from their primitive grossness many of the most popular themes in Scottish song. At the same time, in considering the influence of songs on the character of the Scottish people, it is hard to shut out the suspicion that there may perhaps be a connection between these songs, which are no longer admitted into our collections, and a dark feature in the social life, especially of the lower classes of the Scottish people, which has been forced into view by the unsparing statistics of registration.

§ 2.—*Domestic Songs and Ballads.*

Under this section may be noticed, first of all, those songs and ballads which describe the relations of man and wife. Few facts elicited by our inquiry can give more unalloyed satisfaction than the character of these lyrics. We have already observed the evidence which the Scottish love songs furnish of an influence refining sexual relations in the humbler ranks of life. We have also seen that in many of these songs love is felt as a cheering and softening power in the encounter with the sadder and harder realities of existence; and it may be noticed further, in the present connection, that when these songs refer to the prospect of marriage, they become charming with their enthusiastic trust in the sufficiency of love to make up for the want of external luxuries. For, though we have Burns' spirited *Hey! for a Lass wi a Tocher*, and Allan Ramsay's still more spirited *Gie me a Lass wi' a Lump o' Land*,[1] with their laugh at "beauty and wit and virtue in rags," their dislike of meddling with "poortith, though bonny," and their hearty delight over "weel-tochered lasses and jointured widows," yet the extravagance, as well as the authorship of these songs, proves them to be merely ironical satires. The true love song triumphs in its heedlessness about the "warld's gear," all thought of whose value is flooded over by the great wave of delicious emotion which fills the lover's soul. It is, in fact, this childlike, at times childish, unconcern about the hard necessities of exist-

---

[1] Ramsay has tried the same theme in *The Widow*, which is a refinement on an older song, *Wap at the Widow, my Laddie*.

ence, this unthinking trust in the omnipotence of love, that gives the keenest relish to many of these songs. In the old song, *Jamie o' the Glen*, for example, how charmingly is the heroine described as sticking to her choice of penniless Jamie, though her "minnie grat like daft," to induce her to marry "auld Rob, the laird o' muckle land, wi' his owsen, sheep, and kye." Sir Walter Scott never caught the spirit of Scottish song more perfectly than in that lyric, in which the heroine, while courted by the "chief of Errington and lord of Langley Dale," still "aye loot the tears down fa' for *Jock o' Hazeldean*," by whom she was at last carried off in triumph "o'er the Border and awa." The same spirit runs through the beautiful tragic ballad, preserved by Buchan,[1] of *Lord Saltoun and Auchanachie*, in which the friends of Jeanie, by contrasting the poverty of Auchanachie with the wealth of Lord Saltoun, use every effort to induce her to marry the latter; but in vain.

> "Wi' Auchanachie Gordon I would beg my bread
> Before that wi' Saltoun I'd wear gowd on my head;
> Wear gowd on my head or gowns fringed to the knee,
> And I'll die if I getna my love Auchanachie."

This imprudent unworldliness in marriage is sometimes, indeed, carried by the Scottish singers to an extravagance, the relish of which tests the vigour of the reader's palate. Not to dwell again upon the songs, mentioned in the previous section, which amuse by their beggarly inventories of the young couple's possessions, the destitution of *trousseau* and general outfit, which alarms the

---

[1] "Ballads of the North of Scotland," vol. ii. p. 133.

bride in the old song *Wooed and Married and a*,' is startling to the modern reader too. But, fortunately, Joanna Baillie's refinement of this for more delicate tastes is a splendid model for polishing a coarse old song without rubbing off its characteristic points.

> " The bride she is winsome and bonnie,
>   Her hair it is snooded sae sleek ;
> And faithful and kind is her Johnnie,
>   Yet fast fa' the tears on her cheek.
> New pearlings are cause o' her sorrow—
>   New pearlings and plenishing too ;
> The bride that has a' to borrow
>   Has e'en right muckle ado.
>   Wooed and married and a',
>   Wooed and married and a',
>   And is na she very weel aff,
>   To be wooed and married and a'?
>
> " Her mither then hastily spak,
>   ' The lassie is glaikit wi' pride ;
> In my pouches I hadna a plack
>   The day that I was a bride.
> E'en tak to your wheel and be clever,
>   And draw out your thread in the sun ;
> The gear that is gifted, it never
>   Will last like the gear that is won.
>   Wooed and married and a',
>   Tocher and havings sae sma' ;
>   I think ye are very weel aff,
>   To be wooed and married and a'.'
>
> " ' Toot, toot ! ' quo' the grey-headed faither ;
>   ' She's less o' a bride than a bairn ;
> She's taen like a cowt frae the heather,
>   Wi' sense and discretion to learn.

Half husband, I trow, and half daddy,
   As humour inconstantly leans,
A chiel maun be constant and steady,
   That yokes wi' a mate in her teens.
      Kerchief to cover sae neat,
        Locks the winds used to blaw;
      I'm baith like to laugh and to greet,
        When I think o' her married at a'.'

" Then out spak the wily bridegroom,—
   Weel waled were his wordies, I ween,—
'I'm rich, though my coffer be toom,
   Wi' the blinks o' your bonnie blue e'en.
I'm prouder o' thee by my side,
   Though thy ruffles or ribbons be few,
Than if Kate o' the Craft were my bride,
   Wi' purples and pearlings enew.
      Dear and dearest of ony,
        I've wooed and bookit and a';
      And do you think scorn o' your Johnnie,
        And grieve to be married at a'?'

" She turned, and she blushed, and she smiled,
   And she lookit sae bashfully down;
The pride o' her heart was beguiled,
   And she played wi' the sleeve o' her gown;
She twirled the tag o' her lace,
   And she nippit her boddice sae blue;
Syne blinkit sae sweet in his face,
   And aff like a maukin she flew.
      Wooed and married and a',
      Married and carried awa';
      She thinks hersel' very weel aff,
      To be wooed and married and a'."

It is utterly impossible to enumerate all the Scottish songs, in which the worth of love in marriage forms the predominant idea; and we must pass with a bare mention even *Logic o' Buchan* and the delightful flow of humour in Burns' *O for ane and twenty, Tam.* The idea of marriage, which makes these songs preserve the freshness of some nobler emotions in the Scottish heart, is found giving a tone to the feelings of actual life in a letter by one of the songstresses of Scotland, which is worth quoting in illustration of our subject. "I am just come," writes Mrs. Cockburn, "from a wedding that has neither tochers, jointures, nor wheeled carriages, yet made six people happy, viz., the couple themselves, their two fathers and their two mothers, not forgetting some sisters and brothers, who love *love* better than riches—a very uncommon case."[1]

It is not surprising, however, that this trustfulness of love should make itself conspicuous as long as it has never been tested by the trials of wedded life and by the long monotony of every-day existence; but that it should retain its freshness after all these manifold trials and through that long monotony, is one of the most beautiful features in the life of the people whom it blesses. Yet this is a very prominent characteristic of those Scotch songs which give utterance to the love of man and wife; and nothing in the study of these has brought me a more pleasing surprise than the number of songs by humble authors, expressing all the passionate fervour of a young love in union with the more thought-

---

"The Songstresses of Scotland," by Sarah Tytler and J. L. Watson, vol. i. p. 113.

ful tenderness derived from the teachings of wedded intimacy. A few of these songs may be briefly noticed, expressing different manifestations of conjugal love.

Well may Burns have spoken of *Nae Luck about the House* as "one of the most beautiful songs in the Scots or any other language"; for what language can ever express, in words that burn with truer passion, the exultant gladness of a wife over her husband's return from a long voyage?

"And are ye sure the news is true?
　　And are ye sure he's weel?
Is this a time to think o' wark?
　　Ye jauds, fling by your wheel!

"Is this a time to think o' wark,
　　When Colin's at the door?
Rax'down my cloak; I'll to the quay,
　　And see him come ashore.

"Rise up and mak a clean fireside,
　　Put on the mickle pat;
Gie little Kate her cotton gown,
　　And Jock his Sunday coat.

"And mak their shoon as black as slaes,
　　Their stockins white as snaw;
It's a' to pleasure our gudeman,
　　He likes to see them braw.

　　　*　　*　　*　　*　　*

"Sae sweet his voice, sae smooth his tongue;
　　His breath's like caller air;
His very foot has music in't,
　　As he comes up the stair.

> "And will I see his face again?
> And will I hear him speak?
> I'm downricht dizzy wi' the thocht:
> In troth I'm like to greet.
>
> "For there's nae luck about the house,
> There's nae luck at a';
> There's little pleasure in the house,
> When our gudeman's awa'."[1]

In Burns' *John Anderson* there is a tenderness of retrospect which is positively sacred, and probably unequalled in lyrical poetry. What a pleasant homeliness, again is there in the wifely care of *Johnnie's Grey Breeks*, with its gladdening memories of the times when the breeks "were neither auld nor duddy," and there "werena mony" like the goodman! Who does not feel a certain warmth of sympathy kindling in his heart, while he listens to the wife of *The Boatie rows*, prattling about her anxiety for the safe return of the boat "that wins the bairnies' bread," with "a heavy creel," the weight of which will "grow muckle lighter" by the help of Jamie's love? Examples would require, however, to be multiplied to tediousness to give an adequate conception of the amount of joyous confidence, which these songs display, in the sufficiency of conjugal love to support the burdens of life; but I cannot forbear to

---

[1] It is well known that the authorship of this song has been the subject of much dispute. The claims of Jean Adams, the Greenock schoolmistress, have found a new and very elaborate defence in "The Songstresses of Scotland," vol. i. pp. 41-8. It is a curious fact, if the most fervent expression of wifely affection in the Scottish language has been written by an elderly maiden; but I question whether the authorship is yet satisfactorily settled.

cite one additional specimen in the old lyric, *Bide ye yet*, which Herd fortunately rescued from the precarious tenure of the people's memories.

> "Gin I had a wee house and a cantie wee fire,
> A bonny wee wifie to praise and admire,
> A bonny wee yairdie aside a wee burn;
> Fareweel to the bodies that yammer and mourn.
>
> "When I gang afield and come hame at e'en,
> I'll get my wee wifie fou neat and fou clean,
> And a bonnie wee bairnie upon her knee,
> That will cry papa or daddie to me.
>
> "And if there should happen ever to be
> A difference atween my wee wifie and me,
> In hearty good humour although she be teased,
> I'll kiss her and clap her until she be pleased.
> Sae bide ye yet, and bide ye yet,
> Ye little ken what may betide ye yet;
> Some bonny wee body may be my lot,
> And I'll aye be cantie wi' thinking o't."

The concluding verse of this song recalls a pleasing feature which is met with in the Scots songs of conjugal love: many of them are animated with that generous forbearance towards human weaknesses which forms the soul of all true courtesy and the condition of happiness in all social intercourse. It must not be supposed, indeed, that the social life of Scotland has uniformly presented marriages such as are pictured in these happy songs; the lyrical poetry of the Scotch contains too many life-like portraitures of the unhappiness resulting from all sorts of misalliances, to allow the supposition that these were not common in the experience of the people. An old poet, possibly of the fifteenth century, of whom almost nothing but his name Clapperton is known, commences the dirge over the death of bridal hopes in a song, *Wa worth Mary-age*, which is the lament of a wife longing to be a maiden once more. Another old song, *God gif I wer Wedo now*,[1] which is perhaps by the same author, is a still stronger lamentation on the part of an unfortunate husband, who consoles himself, not by the vain wish that what is done might be undone, but by the prospect of a deliverance which, in the course of nature, must come to him sooner or later—the sooner the better. The hope of such a deliverance forms a solitary source of cheer in Burns' song of a husband who has learnt only too late to know his wife's temper.

> " How we live, my Meg and me,
> How we love, and how we gree,
> I carena by how few may see;
>   Sae, whistle ower the lave o't.
> Wha I wish were maggots' meat,
> Dished up in her winding sheet,
> I could write,—but Meg maun see't ;
>   Sae, whistle ower the lave o't."

On the other hand, the unhappy wretch whose wife will neither drink, feast, spend, dress, strike, sleep, nor speak, "hooly and fairly," would, in the perplexity of his despair, hail any possible escape.

---

[1] Both of these songs will be found in Sibbald's "Chronicles of Scottish Poetry," vol. iii. pp. 195-8.

I wish I were single, I wish I were freed,
I wish I were doited, I wish I were dead,
Or she in the mools, to dement me nae mair, lay;
What does't avail to cry hooly and fairly?
   Hooly and fairly, hooly and fairly,
   Wasting my breath to cry hooly and fairly!"[1]

Scottish lyrical poetry, therefore, contains not only many general satires on marriage, but also many satirical representations of particular incidents in unhappy marriages. Among the general satires, it is somewhat unpleasant to notice a parody on the cheerful little song, *Bide ye yet*, quoted above—a parody perpetrated by Miss Jenny Graham, a maiden lady of Dumfries, whose views are thus thrown into striking contrast with the generous sentiment ascribed to the reputed authoress of *Nae Luck about the House*. Fortunately the parody is never likely, on the ground of its poetical merits, to supplant the original, even if its theme had been more popular. The opening verse, with the chorus, will form a sufficient quotation:—

"Alas, my son, you little know
The sorrows that from wedlock flow;
Farewell to every day of ease,
When you have gotten a wife to please.
   Sae bide ye yet, and bide ye yet,
   Ye little ken what's to betide ye yet;
   The half of that will gane you yet,
   If a wayward wife obtain you yet."

---

[1] This is from a version, by Joanna Baillie, of an older song, in which the husband's complaint is merely that his wife will not "*drink* hooly and fairly."

The representation of conjugal differences has formed a favourite subject of humorous sketches in all literatures; and particular stories of this class seem to be the common property of various races. One of the most distinctively Scotch is the well-known ballad, *Get up and bar the Door*, which is excelled by none in liveliness of narrative and sharp portraiture of character. The quotation of it in its integrity will not be tedious, even to those who are familiar, not only with its general plot, but also with its detailed incidents :—

"It fell about the Martinmas time,
 And a gay time it was than,
That our gudewife got puddings to mak,
 And she boiled them in the pan.

"The wind blew cauld frae east and north,
 And blew into the floor;
Quoth our gudeman to our gudewife,
 'Get up and bar the door.'

"'My hand is in the hussy-skep,
 Gudeman, as ye may see;
An it shouldna be barred this hunder year,
 It's ne'er be barred by me.'

"They made a paction 'tween them twa,
 They made it firm and sure,
That the first word whaever spak,
 Should rise and bar the door.

"Then by there cam twa gentlemen
 At twelve o'clock at night,
When they can see nae ither house
 And at the door they light.

"'Now, whether is this a rich man's house,
    Or whether is it a poor?'
But ne'er a word wad ane o' them speak
    For barring o' the door.

"And first they ate the white puddings,
    And syne they ate the black:
Muckle thought the gudewife to hersel'
    Yet ne'er a word she spak.

"Then ane unto the other said,
    'Here, man, tak ye my knife;
Do ye tak aff the auld man's beard,
    And I'll kiss the gudewife.'

"'But there's nae water in the house,
    And what shall we do than?'
'What ails ye at the pudding bree
    That boils into the pan?'

"O up then started our gudeman,
    An angry man was he;
'Will ye kiss my wife before my een,
    And scald me wi' pudding bree?'

"O up then started our gudewife,
    Gied three skips on the floor;
'Gudeman, ye've spoken the foremost word;
    Get up and bar the door.'"

Another ballad of a similar strain, in which also the wife comes out victorious, is that commonly entitled *Tak your auld Cloak about ye*. Here the dispute arises from the wife requesting the husband one day when the wintry winds were threatening the safety of the cattle, to put on his cloak and go out to look after the cow. This ballad, however, is greatly inferior to the other in the peculiar excellences which have won for the latter its popularity.

Besides these more distinctively Scottish lyrics, there are others whose theme is met with in other literatures. Chief among these must be ranked *The Wyf of Auchtermuchty*, preserved in the Bannatyne MS., where it is attributed to "Moffat"—Sir John Moffat, a poet belonging to the beginning of the sixteenth century. The ballad pictures a man of Auchtermuchty, who was not unmindful of comfort,

> " Quha weill could tippill owt a can,
> And naithir luvit hungir nor cauld,"

coming home tired with his work at the plough on a day which had been "foull for wind and rane," and finding his wife seated comfortably at a tidy hearth. He cannot repress a grumble over the difference in the toil which falls to the lot of men and the comfortable ease which women seem to him to enjoy; whereupon the wife consents to his request to take the plough in hand next day, if he will attend to the affairs of the house. I shall not attempt to reproduce the inimitable humour with which the results are detailed in the old ballad, the wife returning home after a good day's ploughing to find her husband distracted with the multiplicity of his labours, none of which, in his perplexity, he had succeeded in finishing.

This story is attempted again in a more modern snog, *John Grumlie*, which Allan Cunningham found a favourite among the peasantry of Nithsdale.¹ A similar tale was pointed out by Ritson in the "*Silva Sermonum Jocundissimorum*" (Basel, 1568)²; and there has been preserved the first *fit* of an English ballad, as well as an English nursery rhyme on the same subject.³ It may be added that the story is also familiar among our Scandinavian kinsmen, whose version of it will be found in the tale of "The Husband who was to mind the House."⁴

It is remarkable that, in all these tales of domestic quarrels, the wife vindicates her claim to be "the better half:" in Scots lyrical poetry the instances are extremely few in which the "dour" self-will of the wife is successfully resisted by the goodman. The idea, therefore, of taming a shrew, which is so familiar in English literature, and appears among the Norse Tales,⁵ is scarcely to be met in Scottish song. One of our later poets, indeed, Alexander Wilson, has, in his *Watty and Meg*, produced a ballad on the subject, which has attained not only general popularity, but the distinction of special praise from Burns; for the greater poet, hearing from his window the ballad offered for a plack as a new production of his own, called out to the hawker, "That's a lee; but I would make your plack a bawbee if it *were* mine."⁶ But most of the songs which represent

---

¹ See his "Songs of Scotland," vol. ii. p. 124.
² Quoted in the Appendix to Mr. Laing's "Select Remains of the Ancient Popular Poetry of Scotland."
³ Child's "English and Scottish Ballads," vol. viii. pp. 116-7.
⁴ Dasent's "Tales from the Norse," No. 37.
⁵ Ibid. No. 16.
⁶ This incident is related in Chambers' "Cyclopædia of English Literature" (vol. ii. p. 106), on the authority of Mrs. Burns.

a shrewish temper as successfully tamed, ascribe the success to a process which the wiser tales of the taming of a shrew discard as inefficient, even if allowable. The hero of the song, for example, who complains that his " wife's a wanton wee thing,"

> "Took a rung and clawed her,
> And a braw good bairn was she!"

A similar expedient is adopted by *The Cooper of Fife*.

More frequently, however, the conviction of the goodman, who is doomed to the domestic unhappiness pictured in these lyrics, expresses itself in the sentiment of the song, *My Wife shall hae her will;* and there are not wanting instances, therefore, in which the distracted victim of such infelicity is described as settling into the despair which has been already brought before the reader in the above-mentioned songs *God gif I wer Wedo now*, and *Whistle o'er the Lave o't*. There is one ballad on this theme with which this whole series of lyrics may be closed. It is founded on the idea of a wife being carried off by the devil with the hearty consent of her spouse, and being brought back as an intolerable nuisance even in the place to which she had been carried. The ballad may possibly have suggested to Burns the climax of his *My spouse Nancy* :—

> "'Well, sir, from the silent dead
> Still I'll try to daunt you;
> Ever round your midnight bed
> Horrid sprites shall haunt you.'

"'I'll wed another like my dear,
   Nancy, Nancy;
Then all hell will fly from fear,
   My spouse, Nancy.'"

The ballad in question is *The Carle of Kellyburn Braes*. The original version of it has disappeared, though an English ballad on the subject, *The Farmer's Old Wife*,[1] has been preserved. The original, however, is evidently old; and one might almost be justified in surmising that a faint trace of the pre-Christian origin of the story is retained in the conception of the devil, which bears a similarity to the conception with which we are familiar in the Norse Tales. "Whenever the devil appears in these tales, it is not at all as the arch-enemy, as the subtle spirit of the Christian's faith, but rather as one of the old Giants, supernatural, and hostile indeed to man, but simple and easily deceived by a cunning reprobate, whose superior intelligence he learns to dread, for whom he feels himself no match, and whom finally he will receive in hell at no price."[2] But whatever may be the antiquity from which the story dates, it was taken up by Burns and put into shape for Johnson's Museum. Subsequently it was retouched by Allan Cunningham, with the help of some versions which still existed in his time.[3] I give his revision, as, without destroying the spirit of the tale, it removes a

---

[1] Child's "English and Scottish Ballads," vol. viii. p. 257.
[2] Dasent's "Tales from the Norse," Introduction, p. xlv. Compare Cox's interesting section on "the Semitic and Aryan Devil," in his "Mythology of the Aryan Nations," vol. ii. pp. 358-366.
[3] See his "Songs of Scotland," vol. ii. pp 199-201.

few expressions somewhat unpalatable to the tastes of the present day.

"There dwalt a carle on Kellyburn braes,
And he had a wife was the plague o' his days ;
Ae day as the carle was hauding the plow,
Up came the devil, says, ' How d'ye do ? '
' I've got a bad wife, sir ; that's a' my complaint.
For, saving your presence, to her you're a saint.'

" ' It's neither your colt nor your cow that I crave,
But gie me your wife, man, and her I shall have.'
' O welcome ! most kindly,' the glad carle said ;
' Ye'll no keep her lang, and that I'm afraid.
I'll lay baith my plow and my pettle to wad,
That, if ye can match her, ye're waur than ye're ca'd.'

"Auld Clootie took kimmer fu' kind on his back,
And away like a pedler he trudged wi' his pack ;
He cam to the pit and he shook her aboon,
Till the brass buckles melted like snaw in her shoon.
The wee fiends looked up wi' loud laughter and din,
And Cloots gae a shout and whomeled her in.

"She dropt on her foot, and in Satan's arm-chair
She clapt hersel down wi' so regal an air,
That the fiend-imps came round wi' a stare and a shout,
And she gae them a kick, and she lent them a clout.
On Belzebub's dog, at the door of his den,
She frowned—the tyke howled, and the carlin gaed ben.

"A reekit wee devil glowered over the wa',
'O help ! master, help ! else she'll ruin us a'.'
The deil caught the carlin wi' mickle ado,
And sought out the auld man hauding the plow :
And loudly the gray carle ranted and sang,
'In troth, my friend Spunkie, ye'll no keep her lang.'

"In sorrow he looked up, and saw her and said,
'Ye're bringing me back my auld wife, I'm afraid:
But bide ye a blink, for the day is but young,
Hae ye mended her manners, or silenced her tongue?
Her nails are grown langer, her look has grown dourer:
Alas! wha can mend her, if ye canna cure her?'

"Says Satan, 'I vow by the edge of my knife,
I pity the man who is tied to a wife.
I swear by the kirk, and rejoice by the bell,
That I live not in wedlock, thank heaven! but hell:
There hae I been dwelling the maist o' my life,
But I never could thole it if I had a wife.'"

We were led into this digression about one of the less agreeable classes of lyrics, by having remarked that many of the songs of conjugal love express that generous forbearance towards human weaknesses which forms the soul of all true courtesy. Even the satirical poems, which have just been described, must be regarded as having a tendency to soften the aspects of character which they satirise; but the songs of conjugal love themselves often recognise, with homely truthfulness and homely tenderness, the presence of less amiable qualities in the object of affection, who is described as

"A creature not too bright or good
For human nature's daily food;
For transient sorrows, simple wiles,
Praise, blame, love, kisses, tears, and smiles."

The spirit of these songs may be illustrated by another quotation from those letters of Mrs. Cockburn, which are so full of Scotch good sense. Referring to the popularity of Richardson's great novel, she says: "I'm clear for burning *Sir Charles Grandison* by the hands of the common hangman. The girls are all set agog seeking an ideal man, and will have none of God's corrupted creatures. I wonder why they wish for perfection: for my share I would none on't; it would ruin all my virtue and all my love. Where would be the pleasure of mutual forbearance, of mutual forgiveness?"[1] The distinctively Christian virtues, therefore, mould the sentiment of such songs as Lady Nairne's *Oh, Weel's me on my ain Man*, and give a happy point to a humorous little lyric like that preserved by Herd, *My Wife has taen the Gee*, in which the surly indignation of the wife dissolves, with amusing rapidity, before the penitence of the goodman.

"When that she heard, she ran, she flang
  Her arms about his neck;
And twenty kisses in a crack;
  And, poor wee thing! she grat.

"'If you'll ne'er do the like again,
  But bide at hame wi' me,
I'll lay my life, I'll be the wife
  That never taks the gee.'"

Even with the laugh, which cannot be repressed at the poor wife who has to complain that *Our Gudeman's an unco Body*, there mingles an emotion which is not wholly free from respect.

[1] "The Songstresses of Scotland," by Sarah Tytler and J. L. Watson, vol. i. p. 135.

"When he comes hame fou at e'en,
   He's sic a takin gate aye wi' him,
I sigh and think on what he's been,
   I flyte awee, and just forgie him.

"Twa score and ten has cooled his bluid,
   And whiles he needs a drop to warm him;
But when he taks 't to do him guid,
   He whiles forgets, and taks 't to harm him.

"When twa hae wrought, and twa hae fought
   For thretty year sae leal thegither,
A faut or flaw is nought ava',
   They may weel gree wi' ane anither."[1]

The nature of these songs of conjugal love would scarcely be exhibited in full, if we did not briefly refer to those in which that love appears after its office in life may be said to have been fulfilled. From the lady to whom we owe several of our most touching lyrics of domestic life, we have received that song which sounds more like the voice of a spirit already in "the land o' the leal," than of one who is merely "wearin awa'" to its sorrowless bliss. In a less familiar song, *The Widow's Lament*, by one of our more recent song-writers, Thomas Smibert, there is a wail over the loss of husband and children, which places the reader at once in sympathy with the bereaved heart.

"Afore the Lammas tide
   Had dun'd the birken tree,
In a' our water side
   Nae wife was blessed like me.

---

[1] First printed in the "Book of Scottish Song" (Blackie and Son, Glasgow, 1843).

A kind gudeman, and twa
   Sweet bairns were round me here,
But they're a' taen awa'
   Sin' the fa' o' the year.

" Sair trouble cam our gate,
   And made me, when it cam,
A bird without a mate,
   A ewe without a lamb.
Our hay was yet to maw,
   And our corn was to shear,
When they a' dwined awa'
   In the fa' o' the year.

downa look afield,
   For aye I trow I see
The form that was a bield
   To my wee bairns and me;
But wind, and weet, and snaw,
   They never mair can fear,
Sin' they a' got the ca'
   In the fa' o' the year.

" Aft on the hills at e'ens
   I see him 'mang the ferns—
The lover o' my teens,
   The faither o' my bairns;
For there his plaid I saw,
   As gloamin aye drew near,
But my a's now awa'
   Sin' the fa' o' the year.

" Our bonnie rigs theirsel
   Reca' my woes to mind,
Our puir dumb beasties tell
   O' a' that I hae tyned;

For whae our wheat will saw,
  And whae our sheep will shear,
Sin' my a' gaed awa'
  In the fa' o' the year?

" My hearth is growing cauld,
  And will be caulder still,
And sair, sair in the fauld
  Will be the winter's chill;
For peats were yet to ca',
  Our sheep they were to smear,
When my a' passed awa'
  In the fa' o' the year.

" I ettle whiles to spin,
  But wee, wee patterin feet
Come rinnin out and in,
  And then I just maun greet;
I ken it's fancy a'
  And faster rows the tear,
That my a' dwined awa'
  In the fa' o' the year.

" Be kind, O Heaven abune,
  To ane sae wae and lane,
And tak her hamewards sune
  In pity o' her maen.
Lang ere the March winds blaw,
  May she, far far frae here,
Meet them a' that's awa',
  Sin' the fa' o' the year."

Even the wild life of the Border rievers, with all its savage callousness to the sacredest human affections and rights, does not, as *The Lament of the Border Widow* shows, exclude the same wifely sorrow over a husband, though he has met with a well-merited fate from the laws of his country. In the spirit in which the old mythology represents Sigyu, wife of Loki, the mischief-maker of the gods, holding a cup over her husband to shelter him from the torture to which he was doomed— the incessant dripping of a serpent's venom on his face —in the same spirit this Border monody furnishes a deeply pathetic picture of a widow sitting in the loneliness of death, watching the corpse of her robber-husband gibbeted over the gate of his own tower, while she sewed his winding-sheet; and a natural regret follows her, as we think of her taking the corpse down and carrying it off on her back, while, staggering under the burden, she "sometimes gaed and sometimes sat," till she reached the grave she had made,

"And happed him wi' the sod sae green."

It cannot, therefore, be matter of surprise that scarcely one, if any, of the Scots songs or ballads pourtrays, except in a spirit of disapproval, that looseness of conjugal relationship which forms an unhappy feature of some communities, where marriage is not founded on the intimate personal acquaintance and fondness resulting from a previous courtship, and where consequently the husband does not necessarily expect affection from his wife, nor the wife fidelity in her husband. Conjugal virtue has, indeed, long formed a prominent trait in the race, of different branches of which the Scottish nation is mainly composed, appearing, as it does, in the domestic purity of the mythical Asgard, which, in its turn, must have reacted powerfully on the character of the people to whom it represented the most perfect condition of society.[1] This virtue characterises all the Scottish songs of family life, and the perpetuation of the virtue owes much undoubtedly to these songs. There are, indeed, some songs in which a relation between man and wife is exhibited, that makes no pretence of being founded on mutual affection. It is not every girl in the position of auld Robin Gray's wife, who recognises the duties of her situation with the same self-sacrificing resolution; and the wives introduced in *Wattie's the waur o' the Wear*, as well as in Burns' *What can a young Lassie do wi' an auld Man?*[2] are wholly destitute of Jenny's heroic virtue. Yet these songs are mainly satires on that "love of siller and land," which often seduces mother and father to sacrifice the natural affections of a daughter; and neither these nor any other songs of note represent the infidelity of man or wife in the light of a pleasure rather than in the light of a wrong. In one of the very few lyrics which refer to such a subject, the healthy sentiment of the Scottish heart comes out at the close. The story of *Lord Randal* issues in the following tragedy:—

> "Then out Lord Randal drew his brand,
> And straiked it o'er a strae;

---

[1] See the contrast which Motley draws between the social characteristics of the German and those of the Gaul ("Rise of the Dutch Republic," Introduc. ii.). Compare Burton's sketch of the Northern mythology in its moral aspects ("History of Scotland," vol. i. pp. 236-7).

[2] The Maitland MS. contains some verses by Sir Richard Maitland, *On the Folye of ane auld Man maryand ane young Woman*.

> And through and through that fause knight's waste
> He gar'd the cauld iron gae ;
> And I hope ilk ane sall sae be served,
> That treats an honest man sae."[1]

With this may be compared the vigorous moral feeling of the ballads, *The weary Coble o' Cargill* and *The Laird o' Warristoun*, contrasting, as it does, with the effeminate sentiment which is unhappily growing up, especially on the western side of the Atlantic, where it is difficult to empannel a jury with the courage to convict a woman of any capital crime.

Not a few of the songs expressing conjugal love open to us scenes which are rendered beautiful by the general affections of family life; and, in this region of our inquiry, the student of Scottish song is sure of a pleasing surprise at the number of lyrics, by authors of narrow fame, embodying the most elevating sentiments on the only true sources of domestic happiness. These remarks are made not so much in reference to *The auld House* or *The Rowan Tree*, by Lady Nairne, or *The Spinning Wheel*, by Robert Nicoll, since their authors are well known ; but it is pleasant to notice that the theme of the domestic affections is a favourite among the recent song-writers of Scotland. It is almost invidious to make a selection ; but a reader glancing through any of the more modern collections, will probably be attracted by several of the following :

---

[1] In this ballad the name of Lord Randal was introduced by its first editor, Mr. Jamieson ("Popular Ballads and Songs," vol. i. p. 162). The ballad must, therefore, be distinguished from another of the same title in the "Border Minstrelsy" (vol. iii. p. 43). The story, as Jamieson points out, is very like that of the ballad, *Little Musgrave and Lord Barnard*.

Robert Gilfillan's *Janet and Me*, J. G. Cumming's *Wife and Me*, W. Millar's *My bonny Wife*, Alexander Laing's *The Happy Mother*, Andrew Mercer's *The Cottar's Sang*, and a song by a Mrs. J. S., of Rutherglen, beginning *If on Earth there is Enjoyment*, which is of a similar tenor, and not unworthy of comparison, with Elizabeth Hamilton's *My ain Fireside*. With these may be mentioned not inappropriately the charming nursery songs of William Miller. This group of lyrics contains happy pictures of home-life in "wee bit bields," of the bonny goodwife stepping out with the "toddlin weans" to welcome the weary goodman as he comes home in the gloaming, of the family gathered around the "cosy ingle," perhaps with a "crony" or two who can sing a "canty sang," while the bass hum of the spinning-wheel or the treble click of the stocking-wires mingles with the talk that is flowing around, and these louder noises drown the low whispers of Peggie and Jamie, who in a corner are speaking what they do not wish other ears than their own to hear. Every verse in these songs delights us with their cheerful trust in the mutual love of husband and wife, of parent and child, of brother and sister—their outspoken conviction, that in a home blessed with such reciprocal affection, man is secured in a fortress which is impregnable by any of the real evils of human life, and wants none of its real blessings.

> "O happy's the father that's happy at hame,
> And blythe is the mither that's blythe o' the name;
> The cares o' the warld they fear na to dree
> The warld is naething to Johnnie and me." [1]

[1] From Alex. Laing's *The Happy Mother*.

> "We're no without our toil
>   At our ain fireside,
> Care mixes wi' the smile
>   At our ain fireside ;
> But wi' hearts sae leal and true,
> We hope to wuddle through
> Life's linked and ravelled clew
>   At our ain fireside.
>
> " Though we hae na muckle wealth
>   At our ain fireside,
> Yet wi' sweet content and health
>   At our ain fireside,
> We envy not a king,
> For riches canna bring
> The blessings we can sing
>   At our ain fireside." [1]

When I think of the profound ethical wisdom of this conviction, when I think of this wise conviction being embodied, with felicitous homeliness of language, in numerous lyrics, some of which are familiarly known and sung in almost every Scottish home, my heart bows in gratitude to the Giver of every good and perfect gift, for giving to the Scottish people these songs of domestic love.

§ 3.—*Lyrics of General Social Relations.*

By this group of lyrics I mean the songs and ballads which describe the affections and the events of social life beyond the limited range of the family circle. As this chapter began with the songs which celebrate the

---

[1] From the verses, *If on Earth there is Enjoyment*, by Mrs. J. S.

intensest of social affections, so the present section opens appropriately with the songs of friendship, in the most restricted application of the term. Though Caligula would have liked mankind to be endowed with but one neck, that he might set his foot on it, and though Byron more amiably wished womankind to have "but one rosy mouth, that he might kiss them all at once," the heart of man is not big enough to embrace the world either in love or in hatred; and general benevolence must display itself in a special intensity of affection for a narrow circle of acquaintances, or even for "one friend that sticketh closer than a brother." Are there any Scots songs which celebrate a friendship of this sort—anything like the close of the song in which David laments over Saul and Jonathan: "I am distressed for thee, my brother Jonathan; very pleasant hast thou been unto me; thy love to me was wonderful, passing the love of women"?[1]

As a lay of friendship may be cited the intensely interesting ballad of *Graeme and Bewick*, which Scott considered remarkable as "containing, probably, the very latest allusion to the institution of brotherhood in arms,"[2] and which is undoubtedly remarkable as containing all the elements of a splendid mediæval tragedy. The ballad introduces us in the opening verses to two chiefs at Carlisle, good Lord Graeme and Sir Robert Bewick, going "arm in arm to the wine," and drinking together "till they were baith merrie." But like most of the merriment due to the same inspiration, that of

[1] 2 Samuel, i. 26.
[2] "Minstrelsy of the Scottish Border," vol. iii. p. 66.

Bewick and Graeme soon resolved itself into feelings of a less agreeable nature. A cup, pledged to their two sons, whose romantic friendship sheds its splendour over the story, excites a rivalry between the fathers as to the respective merits of the young men; and Graeme, stung by the taunts of Bewick, declares in drunken anger that his own son must establish his superiority in mortal combat with the son of Bewick. Returning home he announces his resolution to his son.

> "'I hae been at Carlisle town,
> Where Sir Robert Bewick he met me;
> He says ye're a lad, and ye are but bad,
> And billie to his son ye canna be.
>
> "'I sent ye to the schools, and ye wadna learn;
> I bought ye books, and ye wadna read:
> Therefore my blessing ye shall never earn,
> Till I see with Bewick thou save thy head.'"

The only answer to his remonstrance which the son obtains is, that if he will not fight with young Bewick he must fight with his own father.

> "'If thou do not end this quarrel soon,
> There's my right hand thou shalt fight with me.'"

The struggle which ensues in young Graeme's mind between the duties of chivalrous friendship and the duty of filial reverence, represents a conflict of motives which have died away with the old world which gave birth to them, and reminds one of the deeply affecting "Adventure"[1] in the *Nibelungenlied*, in which Rüdiger is

---

[1] The thirty-sixth.

distracted between the conflicting duties of hospitality to the Burgundians and of loyalty to his king.

> "Then Christie Graeme's to his chamber gane,
>   To consider weel what then should be;
> Whether he should fight with his auld father,
>   Or with his billie Bewick, he.
>
> "'If I should kill my billie dear,
>   God's blessing I shall never win;
> But if I strike at my auld father,
>   I think 'twald be a mortal sin.
>
> "'But if I kill my billie dear,
>   It is God's will, so let it be;
> But I make a vow, ere I gang frae hame,
>   That I shall be the next man's die.'"

The result is, therefore, that young Graeme seeks a rencounter with young Bewick, and, after two hours' fighting, the latter receives a mortal wound; upon which the former carries out his resolution by throwing himself on the point of his sword. Sir Robert Bewick, coming up and finding his son still alive, while the other combatant is dead, hastens to congratulate the survivor on having gotten the victory. But the reply is in the spirit of a morality in advance of the times in which such a tragedy was possible.

> "'O hald your tongue, my father dear!
>   Of your prideful talking let me be!
> Ye might hae drunken your wine in peace,
>   And let me and my billie be.

> "'Gae dig a grave baith wide and deep,
>   And a grave to hald baith him and me;
> But lay Christie Graeme on the sunny side,
>   For I'm sure he wan the victorie.'"

This lyric is probably the finest tribute which Scottish ballad poetry offers to the spirit of friendship. Lyrics of friendship, however, cannot be expected to be numerous in any literature. For a lyric—a poem intended to be sung—requires a certain intensity of emotion. Now, the love of mere friends seldom, if it ever, rises to lyrical fervour, except under certain stimulating circumstances, such as will be noticed presently; and undoubtedly David's appreciation of Jonathan's friendship gained in emotional intensity under the stimulus of sorrow at his death; while, but for its tragic close, the brotherhood in arms of Bewick and Graeme would never have become the theme of a ballad. This is, indeed, one of the most common circumstances to call forth poetical expressions of friendship; and in the English language alone, several poets have made friends immortal by celebrated poems on their death. The *Astrophel* of Spenser, the *Lycidas* of Milton, the *Adonais* of Shelley, the *In Memoriam* of Tennyson, will readily occur to every student of English literature. But these are not lyrics, in the strictest sense of the term. There are, however, several epistles of Burns, such as those to Davie and Lapraik, which, in the passionate fervour of friendly emotion, come nearer to the spirit of a song than any expression of friendship I remember.

" It's no in titles nor in rank ;
   It's no in wealth like Lon'on bank,
     To purchase peace and rest ;
   It's no in making muckle mair ;
   It's no in books ; it's no in lear,
     To mak us truly blest.
If happiness hae not her seat
     And centre in the breast,
We may be wise, or rich, or great,
     But never can be blest:
     Nae treasures nor pleasures
       Could mak us happy lang ;
     The heart aye's the part aye
       That maks us right or wrang.

* * * * * *

" But tent me, Davie, ace o' hearts !
   (To say aught less wad wrang the cartes,
     And flattery I detest):
This life has joys for you and I,
And joys that riches ne'er could buy,
     And joys the very best.
There's a' the pleasures o' the heart,
     The lover and the frien' ;
Ye hae your Meg, your dearest part,
     And I, my darling Jean !
     It warms me, it charms me,
       To mention but her name ;
     It heats me, it beets me,
       And sets me a' on flame.

* * * * *

" All hail, ye tender feelings dear !
   The smile of love, the friendly tear,
     The sympathetic glow !

> Long since, this world's thorny ways
> Had numbered out my weary days,
>   Had it not been for you.
> Fate still has blest me with a friend,
>   In every care and ill;
> And oft a more endearing band,
>   A tie more tender still.
>   It lightens, it brightens
>   The tenebrific scene,
>   To meet with, and greet with
>   My Davie or my Jean."

But while our lyrics do not sing of individual friends as they do of individual lovers, friendship, under the excitement of conditions in which it is enjoyed, and with which it becomes associated, forms the theme of many a song. It may be noticed, for example, that songs of friendship, like love-songs, take us back very frequently to the scenes in which the affection has sprung up, and with which it becomes ever afterwards linked in memory; and many of the songs that sing of the spots in which earlier days have been spent, may be appropriately described as referring to the companionships of those days. Such companionships are more likely to be thought of on leaving or on returning to the scenes with which they are associated. The *Farewell to Ayrshire*, which was attributed in Johnson's "Museum" to Burns, but which seems to have been the work of Richard Gall, as well as Burns' own song, *The gloomy Nicht is gathering fast*, may be taken as reminiscences of friendships on leaving the scenes where they have been formed; Miss Blamire's touching song, *The Nabob*, as a reminiscence of friendships on returning to such scenes.

There is no circumstance, however, in which all the emotions of friendship swell so readily to their full tide as under the stimulus of social gatherings, in which the song and the bowl pass round. Several of these songs, even of the best among them, express nothing more reprehensible than the talk, and jest, and song, and general merriment of a gathering among intimate friends; and at the head of this class will probably be placed, by all who know it well, the Rev. John Skinner's *Tullochgorum*, which Burns may well have called "the first of songs;"[1] for the torrent of unrestrained jollity which dances along the lilt of the strathspey to which it is sung—eddying around the iterations in the middle of each verse, only to gush on again in boisterous stream—is sufficient to bear down the barriers of decorum in the stiffest supporter of personal dignity.

> "O, Tullochgorum's my delight:
> It gars us a' in ane unite;
> And ony sumph that keeps up spite,—
>   In conscience I abhor him.
> Blithe and merry we's be a',
> Blithe and merry, blithe and merry,
> Blithe and merry we's be a',
>   And make a cheerfu' quorum.
> Blithe and merry we's be a',
> As lang as we hae breath to draw,

---

[1] See Chambers' "Life and Works of Burns," vol. iv. p. 290. In letter to Skinner, Burns even goes the length of calling *Tullochgorum* "the best Scotch song ever Scotland saw." (Ibid. vol. ii. p. 141.)

And dance, till we be like to fa',
The reel of Tullochgorum.

"There needna be sae great a phraise
Wi' dringing dull Italian lays;
I wadna gie our ain strathspeys
   For half a hundred score o' 'em.
They're douff and dowie at the best,
Douff and dowie, douff and dowie,
They're douff and dowie at the best
   Wi' a' their variorums.
They're douff and dowie at the best,
Their allegros, and a' the rest,
They canna please a Highland taste,
   Compared wi' Tullochgorum.

*   *   *   *   *   *

"May choicest blessings still attend
Each honest-hearted open friend;
And calm and quiet be his end,
   And a' that's good watch o'er him!
May peace and plenty be his lot,
Peace and plenty, peace and plenty,
May peace and plenty be his lot,
   And dainties a great store o' 'em!
May peace and plenty be his lot,
Unstained by any vicious blot;
And may he never want a groat,
   That's fond of Tullochgorum."

There are several songs suggested by this, whose specific object is the description of social gatherings; and a conspicuous place among these must be assigned to *The Blithesome Bridal*, which is commonly attributed to Francis Semple of Beltrees, though it has been claimed less probably for others. Few songs contain a livelier portraiture of varied characters, or a more humorous sketch of ancient manners; but, unfortunately, the coarseness in the life of old times makes the fun of the song a little too boisterous for the present generation; though it cannot be too strongly coloured for an earlier period, if Dunbar's poem, *On a Dance in the Queen's Chamber*, is not a piece of outrageous extravagance. It is a fortunate circumstance, however, that Joanna Baillie has put *The Blithesome Bridal* through the same process of refinement which she has carried out so successfully in the case of some other lyrics. Though long, this paraphrase sustains the humour of the description so capitally that it will be relished by all.

" Fy, let us a' to the wedding,
    For they will be lilting there;
For Jock's to be married to Maggie,
    The lass wi' the gowden hair.

" And there will be gibing and jeering,
    And glancing o' bonny dark een;
Loud laughing and smooth-gabbit speering
    O' questions baith pawky and keen.

" And there will be Bessy the beauty,
    Wha raises her cockup sae hie,
And giggles at preaching and duty;
    Gude grant that she gang not agee!

" And there will be auld Geordie Tanner,
    Wha coft a young wife wi' his gowd;
She'll flaunt wi' a new gown upon her,
    But now she looks dowie and cowed!

"And brown Tibby Fowler,[1] the heiress,
    Will poke at the tap o' the ha',
Encircled wi' suitors, wha's care is
    To catch up her gloves when they fa'.

"Repeat a' her jokes as they're cleekit,
    And haver and glower in her face,
When tocherless mays are negleckit—
    A' crying, a scandalous case!

"And Mysie, wha's clavering aunty
    Wad match her wi' Laurie the Laird,
And learn the young fule to be vaunty,
    But neither to spin nor to card.

"And Andrew, wha's granny is yearning
    To see him a clerical blade,
Was sent to the college for learning,
    And came back a coof as he gaed.

"And there will be auld Widow Martin,
    That ca's hersel thritty and twa!
And thrawn-gabbit Madge, wha for certain
    Has jilted Hal o' the Shaw.

"And Elspy, the swoster sae genty,
    A pattern of havins and sense,
Will straik on her mittens sae dainty,
    And crack wi' Mass John in the spence.

"And Angus, the seer o' ferlies,
    That sits on the stane at his door,
And tells about bogles, and mair lees
    Than tongue ever uttered before.

"And there will be Bauldy the boaster,
    Sae ready wi' hands and wi' tongue;

---

[1] See above, p. 73.

Proud Patty and silly Sam Foster,
    Wha quarrel wi' auld and wi' young.

"And Hugh, the town-writer, I'm thinking,
    That trades in his lawyerly skill,
Will egg on the fighting and drinking,
    To bring after-grist to his mill.

"And Maggie—na, na, we'll be civil,
    And let the wee bridie abee;
A vilipend is the devil,
    And ne'er was encouraged by me.

"Then, fy, let us a' to the wedding,
    For there will be lilting there,
From mony a far-distant haudin',
    The fun and the feasting to share.

"For they will get sheep's head and haggis,
    And browst o' the barley-mow;
E'en he that comes latest and lag is,
    May feast upon dainties enow.

"Veal florentins in the o'en bakin',
    Weel plenished wi' raisins and fat;
Beef, mutton, and chuckies all taken
    Het reekin' frae spit and frae pat.

"And glasses (I trow 'tis na said ill),
    To drink the young couple good luck,
Weel filled wi' a braw bucken ladle,
    Frae punch-bowl as big as Dumbuck.

"And then will come dancing and daffing,
    And reeling and crossing o' hauns,
Till e'en auld Luckie is laughing,
    As back by the aumry she stauns.

> "Sic bobbing, and flinging, and whirling,
>   While fiddlers are making their din ;
> And pipers are droning and skirling
>   As loud as the roar o' the lin.
>
> "Then fy, let us a' to the wedding,
>   For there will be lilting there ;
> "For Jock's to be married to Maggie,
>   The lass wi' the gowden hair."

Another of our female song-writers, the Baroness Nairne, has made an original attempt at a similar theme in her lyrical description of a *County Meeting*. These and many other social songs of the Scotch, draw a rich flavour from the lively relish which they express for the enjoyment of life,—a relish which compels us to give a brighter hue than is commonly given in the portraiture of the national character, and which probably tended to brighten the more sombre shade thrown upon the spirit of the people by their civil and religious history. Even the Whig, Sir Patrick Home, writing from Utrecht —a solitary exile—before his family joined him, instructs his wife, that "Care be taken to keep the children hearty and merry, laughing, dancing, and singing. . . . . Lost estates can be recovered again, but health once lost by a habit of melancholy can never be recovered."[1] Perhaps in these instructions, and in the healthy mirth which they encouraged, may be seen the source of the fine old song, *Were na my Heart licht, I wad dee*, which we owe to the exile's daughter, Lady Grizzel Baillie. At all events, the

---

[1] "The Songstresses of Scotland," by Sarah Tytler and J. L. Watson, vol. i. pp. 5. 6.

songs of Scotland prove that beneath the harder and sadder surface of the national character there was a perennial spring of genial mirth, which was probably kept flowing over the social life of the people mainly by the singing of these songs.

But unhappily songs of this class do not limit themselves to the description of harmless, wholesome fun; there are, indeed, few good social songs which do not praise the zest imparted to friendly gatherings by means of a more material stimulant. This introduces us to the large collection of Scottish lyrics, which may be described in general as *Drinking Songs*. The most cursory acquaintance with Scottish poetry will convince anyone that these songs represent a very extensive literature, and a literature of a very remarkable character. I will not say that they surpass, in lyrical force, anything of the kind to be met with in any other literature: for sweeping assertions of that sort generally betray merely ignorance of any literature but one; while, without going beyond the modern languages, there are several German students' songs which would make such an assertion extremely questionable. But there is something distinctive in the drinking songs of the Scotch. They do not express the refined, but more artificial enjoyment of one who is politely sipping a beverage like wine, the delicate flavour of which can be appreciated only by the educated connoisseur, nor the exulting gratification of one who is quaffing a beverage like beer, which is drunk in quantities as much to quench thirst as for the sake of its mildly stimulating effect: the Scots drinking song is purely and avowedly in praise of the general elevation in mental and bodily power excited by

"Inspiring bold John Barleycorn!"

The happy play of fancy and language in which this theme is variously wrought out is excelled by nothing in the whole compass of Scottish song; but the literary skill of these productions cannot, in the present inquiry, hide from us their effect on the habits of the people. Though some of these songs express simply the impulse which is given by a stimulant to the more rapid flow of social enjoyment, yet against others I do not hesitate —and no one who studies them dispassionately can hesitate—to bring the charge of seriously contributing to perpetuate what used to be a prevalent vice among all classes, what continues to be a prominent vice and the most hopeless obstacle to social reform among the working classes of Scotland. There is none of our best songs which deliberately represents any other gross vice in an attractive aspect; but in many of the drinking songs, all the charm of lyrical thought and expression is thrown around that sacrifice of intelligence to the demon of Unreason, which is truthfully represented only in language of pity or of scorn. It is true that the lyrical poet must catch an emotion while it is flowing at white heat, and run it then into the mould of song; and this may explain the extravagance with which many of the drinking songs are characterized. But the license which this principle of lyrical poetry allows is certainly exceeded in the drunken merriment to which some, though few, of these songs give utterance, over the personal degradation resulting from the vice they encourage:—

> "O gude ale comes, and gude ale goes;
> Gude ale gars me sell my hose,
> Sell my hose, and pawn my shoon;
> Gude ale keeps my heart aboon.
>
> "I had sax owsen in a pleuch,
> And they drew teuch and weel eneuch:
> I drank em a' just ane by ane;
> Gude ale keeps my heart aboon."

The remainder of this old song, which took some touches from the hand of Burns, describes a lower stage of degradation, which does not admit of being cited. An equal transgression of the limits of all legitimate license may be charged against the old song, *Cauld Kail in Aberdeen*, in callously making light of those who suffer most directly by the excess which it praises:—

> "Johnnie Smith has got a wife,
>   Wha scrimps him o' his cogie;
> But were she mine, upon my life,
>   I'd douk her in a bogie.
>
> "Twa three toddlin weans they hae,
>   The pride o' a' Stra'bogie:
> Whene'er the totums cry for meat,
>   She curses aye his cogie.
>
> * * * * *
>
> "Yet here's to ilka honest soul
>   Wha'll drink wi' me a cogie;
> And for ilk silly whinging fool,—
>   We'll douk him in a bogie.

> "For I maun hae my cogie, Sirs,
> I canna want my cogie;
> I wadna gie my three-gir'd cog
> For a' the wives in Bogie."[1]

With the unhappy exception of these drinking songs, the lyrics of Scotland, which are expressive of general social affection, may well evoke a gratitude similar to that which is due to the songs of domestic love. Many of them are written by authors of limited fame, and most of them give us glimpses of homes brightened by none of the elegances or luxuries, and even by few of the comforts, of earthly existence; but nearly all express, in cheery rhythm, the same deep consciousness of the absolute worth of human love, the same hearty, jeering contempt of riches without that love, the same generous regard for true worth of character even when concealed behind a lowly external appearance, the same manful self-respect in the midst of "honest poverty,"—in a word, the same clear insight into "the real guid and ill" of human life, which bursts into unrestrained utterance in every verse of the domestic songs. The Scotch have been blamed—and not altogether without justice—for an absence of genial warmth in the outward expression of their affections; yet it is probably in the Scotch *Auld lang syne*, as revised by Burns, that we must seek the most universally recognised hymn of friendship, and of the splendour with which friendship lights up all our memories of "the days that are no more." And well is

---

[1] This is one of the older versions of *Cauld Kail in Aberdeen*. Several song-writers have tried their hand at the theme.

it for the people who possess, in language of which all can feel the pith, and adapted to a simple melody which all can appreciate, an expression of courageous reliance on moral worth, whose fervour carries away the soul, like *A Man's a Man for a' that.*

> "Is there, for honest poverty,
>   That hangs his head, and a' that?
> The coward slave—we pass him by,
>   We dare be poor for a' that!
> For a' that, and a' that,
>   Our toils obscure, and a' that;
> The rank is but the guinea's stamp,
>   The man's the gowd for a' that.
>
> "What though on hamely fare we dine,
>   Wear hoddin gray, and a' that:
> Gie fools their silks, and knaves their wine,
>   A man's a man for a' that!
> For a' that and a' that,
>   Their tinsel show, and a' that;
> The honest man, though e'er sae poor,
>   Is king o' men for a' that.
>
> "Ye see yon birkie, ca'd a lord,
>   Wha struts, and stares, and a' that;
> Though hundreds worship at his word,
>   He's but a coof for a' that.
> For a' that, and a' that,
>   His ribbon, star, and a' that;
> The man of independent mind,
>   He looks and laughs at a' that.
>
> "A prince can mak a belted knight,
>   A marquis, duke, and a' that;

But an honest man's aboon his might,
    Guid faith, he maunna fa' that!
For a' that, and a' that,
    Their dignities and a' that;
The pith o' sense, and pride o' worth,
    Are higher rank than a' that.

"Then let us pray that come it may,
    As come it will for a' that;
That sense and worth, o'er a' the earth,
    May bear the gree, and a' that.
For a' that, and a' that,
    It's coming yet for a' that,
That man to man, the warld o'er,
    Shall brothers be for a' that."

CHAPTER III.

ROMANTIC BALLADS AND SONGS.

> " What resounds,
> In fable or romance, of Uther's son
> Begirt with British and Armoric Knights;
> And all who since, baptized or infidel,
> Jousted in Aspramont, or Montalban,
> Damasco, or Marocco, or Trebisond,
> Or whom Biserta sent from Afric shore,
> When Charlemain with all his peerage fell
> By Fontarabbia."
>
> *Paradise Lost*, Book I.

THE poems included under this title are based on events which, if not wholly ideal, are at least incapable of being certainly identified with any known historical transactions. This limitation of the term *Romantic* does not claim to be an adequate definition of it for all purposes; but it expresses a prominent characteristic of Romance, and it would be difficult to find an equally suitable term.

This definition, it will be observed, does not exclude some of the poems on which remarks have been made in the previous chapters. All the legendary ballads, for example, must, as a rule, be considered romantic in this sense of the term; and many of the social ballads and songs are evidently founded on unreal or uncertain relationships. But in explanation of this it has been already observed, in the Introduction, that a perfectly logical classification of literary works is impossible; and the reason is evident. The characteristic, on the ground of which a number of works are included in one class, will often be found to be possessed by a number of other works which, on the ground of a different characteristic, are relegated to a separate group. Moreover, although the classification of romantic ballads and songs as a distinct group crosses the other divisions of legendary and social lyrics; yet, as our object is to discover the influence of the ballads and songs on the Scottish character, it is in the light of their most prominent characteristics that that influence is to be traced. We may, therefore, consider the same poems as legendary, as social, as romantic; and the effect upon character which is traced to them will be different in all these different points of view. Accordingly, in the present chapter, the ballads and songs are considered simply as romances.

There are, however, many poems which appropriately go by the name of romantic, inasmuch as their romantic nature is more prominent than any other characteristic; and different groups of these, clustering around different ideal heroes or events, are referred to so many cycles of romance. In English ballad literature two of such cycles claim a considerable number of poems—the cycle of Arthurian romance, and that which centres on Robin Hood; but neither of these is represented by a corresponding group in the ballad poetry of Scotland.

With regard to the former, if it be possible to discover

its original birthland, the south of Scotland, with the six counties of northern England which are more Scotch than English in the outline of their scenery, may present perhaps a stronger claim than any other place. At least this theory, started originally by Sir Walter Scott,[1] and subsequently supported by Allan Cunningham,[2] finds an elaborate defence in the most recent contribution to the subject of Arthurian localities.[3] But even if this claim be well founded, the heroic story has wandered far into other literatures, and scarcely a fragmentary segment of the whole cycle has been deposited in the ballad minstrelsy of Scotland.

Robin Hood, again, is emphatically "the English ballad-singer's joy," even though, under critical analysis, he should evaporate into the atmosphere of Teutonic mythology, leaving only the slight solid residuum of Odin or Woden.[4] For, whatever may be the origin of his name, the hero of this romance is clothed in a distinctively English costume by the ballad-singers of England; and the absence of any corresponding group of ballads in Scotland is one of the strongest collateral proofs of the true historical origin of the romance. The hero, indeed, is not unknown in Scottish literature. He is referred to by Gavin Douglas, in *The Pal..*

---

[1] Introduction to *Sir Tristrem*. See especially pp. xxxiv. lxv.—lxvi.

[2] "Songs of Scotland," vol. i. pp. 61 63.

[3] Mr. Glennie's "Essay on Arthurian Localities," prefixed to the Prose Romance of Merlin, published by the Early English Text Society in 1869.

[4] See Simrock's "Deutsche Mythologie," pp. 249 et seq.; Child's "English and Scottish Ballads," vol. v., Introd.

Honour,[1] along with Fin MacCowl and other legendary heroes; an isolated exploit or two of his has strayed into the Scottish ballads;[2] while "Robert Hude and Lytill Johne" took a place, alongside of the Abbot of Unreason, in the interludes and other satirical representations by which at first the Reformation was advanced, and afterwards the Puritanism of Scottish piety was scandalised.[3] But the true Scottish counterpart of the southern hero is not the Robin Hood of Scottish literature, but the legendary Wallace. Both became, in popular imagination and in the literature which popular imagination creates, ideal representatives of the popular struggle against Norman oppression; and the difference in the portraiture of the two heroes must be ascribed to the difference of the forms in which that oppression came to be most keenly felt north and south of the Tweed respectively. The cruel forest laws of Norman England were unknown in the north;[4] and the Normans first made themselves felt for evil in Scotland when Edward I. began the long-sustained attempt to bring it into feudal subjection to the English crown.

If the ballads of Scotland had kept up in the Scottish mind an enthusiasm for different great cycles of

---

[1] Stanza CVI.
[2] Child's "English and Scottish Ballads," vol. v. p. 187.
[3] Irving's "History of Scottish Poetry," pp. 445-450.
[4] See Burton's "History of Scotland," vol. ii. pp. 156, 157. It is not impossible, therefore, to combine the theory of the mythological origin of the Robin Hood legend with all that is essential to Thierry's theory of its historical origin ("History of the Norman Conquest," vol. ii. pp. 223-232, Hazlitt's translation). The reader of *Ivanhoe* need scarcely be reminded that Scott takes the same view as Thierry.

romance, we might have been able to trace a different influence to the ballads which form each of the different cycles; but, as it is, we have simply to contemplate the effect on the Scottish character of that romance which infuses a peculiar spirit into many of our ballads. What is it, then, that essentially constitutes an incident, a life, a character, which is described as romantic, because partaking of this spirit?

Any phenomenon in human nature is said to be romantic, when it is not a spiritless obedience to external rule, but the outflowing of a spirit from within. A romantic life, therefore, does not present the uniformity of one that is destitute of romance, for the spirit of a man is more varied in its impulses than an external law in its operations. It is on this account that a man who moves unswervingly in a rut which has long been worn by the wheels of custom, and whose life is but the monotonous repetition of similar tasks from day to day, is spoken of as unromantic; whereas we attribute more or less romance to a character in proportion to the eccentricity of the movements in which it reveals the changeful centre of its action—the variable moods of the human soul. This is the sense which must be attached to romance, when it is traced to its source in human nature; and it is in this sense that the critics have distinguished the Romanticists of literature from the French or classical school. It is evidently, therefore, in this sense also that we must seek to discover the romance of the Scottish character, of which the romantic ballads are at once an outgrowth and a support.

Where, then, are we to look for romance of this sort in the character of the Scottish people? The national peculiarities of the Scots may be, in a large measure, explained by the fact that Norman feudalism never became thoroughly organized among them, as many idioms of their dialect are due to its having been comparatively so little affected by the Norman-French. To this they owe the strong love of personal freedom which has distinguished them from a very early period, appearing in the peculiar mildness of their laws in reference to thralls,[1] and in the recognition of rights possessed by the meanest peasant, at a time when the recognition of such rights was incomprehensible to the feudalism of other nations.[2] It need not be observed, that the love of personal freedom is of the very essence of the romantic spirit.

The spirit of romance may also be traced in every great epoch of Scottish history. The love of national freedom, which characterised the long struggle against feudal subjection to a powerful neighbour, was but a manifestation of that romantic tendency which rejects the tyranny of any force foreign to the spirit of the nation. The next great movement—the Reformation of the sixteenth century—was, in many of the peculiar features which that movement assumed in Scotland, an exhibition of the noblest spirit of romance. Perhaps more unequivocally than any other Reformed national Church, that of Scotland proclaimed the great principles of Protestantism. It ignored any real dis-

---

[1] Burton's "History of Scotland," vol. ii. pp. 151-154.
[2] Ibid. vol. iii. pp. 54 and 110.

tinction between clergy and laity, asserting the direct responsibility of each human being to God, who, in the memorable language of its symbols, is declared to be "the alone Lord of the conscience." It therefore recognized the independent worth of each individual in God's universe; and while this is implied in several remarkable facts connected with the organization and service of the Church, it also found the most beneficent practical embodiment in the first national system which attempted to educate each individual into fitness for the responsibilities and the rights accorded to him by the Reformation. In the great struggle of the following century appeared another of the nobler outgoings of romance: the struggle was simply a passionate but indomitable protest against the imposition of Church forms which were not the outgrowth of the national spirit, and by which the national spirit could not be fettered. The great events of Scottish history subsequent to the Union have been mainly ecclesiastical; but in these may be traced the same spirit of romance. This spirit throws light perhaps on the almost fanatical horror of read prayers or even of read sermons in the service of the Church; but certainly it is displayed in the persistent opposition to any system of appointing pastors without the choice of the congregation being consulted; and everyone acquainted with the history of Scotland during the last hundred years, knows what an important part that opposition has played.

Perhaps, in conclusion, some will see the most unequivocal proof of a romantic spirit among the Scottish people in the love of adventure which has characterised "the Scot abroad." I believe that I have sketched some profounder and more general manifestations of that spirit; but there cannot be a doubt that the narrow boundaries of their fatherland, and the extremely limited nature of its material resources in former times, have been felt by many Scotsmen to afford but a small range for the play of a romantic spirit, and have consequently driven many, in whom that spirit was strong, into foreign lands. It is also unquestionable that the inheritance of the national spirit, which they have carried with them, has given them a force to clear a way for themselves through the obstacles of nature and the entanglements of society, wherever they have gone, from the time when nearly every European university boasted of its Scotch professor[1] till the present day, when Scotsmen or their descendants are found occupying prominent situations in the United States and in all the colonies of Great Britain.

[1] See Sir William Hamilton's "Discussions," pp. 119-121.

CHAPTER IV.

HISTORICAL BALLADS AND SONGS.

> " There are in ancient story
>   Wonders many told,
> Of heroes in great glory,
>   Of courage strong and bold,
> Of joyances and hightides,
>   Of weeping and of woe,
> Of noble warriors striving,
>   Mote ye now wonders know."
>
> *Niebelungenlied*, translated by CARLYLE.

THE ballads and songs which refer to known historical transactions do not present the same difficulty, which was met in the case of the romantic ballads, of being referred to different groups. The history of Scotland, like that of all progressive countries, may be divided into certain more or less definitely marked periods, each of which has become an epos—a theme for song. We may therefore briefly notice the lyrical poetry of each epos, pointing out the effect which it may be shown to have produced on the national life of Scotland.

For this purpose we may distinguish four epochs in the history of Scotland, to one or other of which its historical ballads and songs may be referred, viz. the War of Independence; the Border Feuds; the Reformation; and the Jacobite Struggle.

§ 1.—*The War of Independence.*

The history of the Scots, as one distinct people, begins properly with this war; and in the enthusiasm which the common resistance to Anglo-Norman oppression created, may be recognized the force which welded together the different tribes that peopled Scotland.[1] In such an enthusiasm will also be found a fruitful source of national song; and, consequently, the period of this struggle is, perhaps more than all others, worthy of being dignified with the title of an epos, while it has given birth to two poems—Blind Harry's *Wallace* and Barbour's *Bruce*—which have some claim to be called epic. But the period does not seem to have created a minor poetry of sufficient value to be traditionally preserved; or the two greater poems have absorbed the popular favour so entirely, that the contemporary ballads and songs have been allowed to sink into oblivion. The latter supposition is indeed the more probable, as there are not a few indications of a lyrical poetry, belonging to the period, which has been lost. This is not the place to sketch the history of Scottish song, but it may be worth while to collect here the references which have been discovered to those early national lyrics.

A proof that, even before this time, songs on national themes were not unknown in Scotland, is furnished by the well-known song on the death of Alexander III., preserved by Wyntoun :

---

[1] Before this time the royal notifications to all classes of the people addressed them as Franks and Angles, Scots and Galwegians. See Burton's "History of Scotland," vol. ii. p. 127.

> "When Alysandyr our Kyng was dede,
>   That Scotlande led in luve and le,
> Away was sons of ale and brede,
>   Of wyne and wax, of gamyn and gle.
> Our gold was changyd into lede,
>   Cryst born into virgynyte,
> Succour Scotland and remede,
>   That stad is in perplexyte."

This, which is probably the earliest extant specimen of Scottish verse, is of peculiar interest as revealing the bitterness with which the people remembered the good old times of plenty preceding the War of Independence, and enabling us to understand the intensity of national feeling which the war called forth, and which found utterance in the popular songs of the period. A fragment which, in various forms, has been preserved from one of the oldest of these songs, refers to the siege of Berwick by Edward I., and hits at the prominent feature of his person, which gave him the nickname of *Longshanks*.

> "What wende the Kyng Edward
>   For his langge shanks,
> For to wynne Berewyke
>   Al our unthankes?
>   Go pike it him,
>   And when he it have wonne
>   Go dike it him."[1]

In connection with the battle of Bannockburn another fragment has been preserved in Fabyan's *Cronycle*, with

---

[1] Burton's "History of Scotland," vol. ii. p. 266, n. Irving's "History of Scottish Poetry," p. 79.

the interesting information that it continued long afterwards to be sung by the maidens and minstrels of Scotland:

"Maydens of Englande, sore may ye mourne
 For your lemmans he have loste at Bannockysborne,
  With a heue a lowe.
 What! weneth the Kinge of Englande
 So soone to have wonne Scotlande?
  With rumbylowe."

In relating a victory which a small body of Scots gained over a larger body of English in Eskdale, Barbour dispenses with a detailed narrative on the ground that
 "Young wemen, quhen thai will play,
 · Sing it amang thaim ilk day."

Another satirical song, hitting at "the deformyte of clothyng that at those days was used by Englyshmenne," is said by Fabyan to have been composed on the occasion of the marriage of the infant David Bruce to the Princess Jane of England—*Jane Makepiece*, as she was popularly nicknamed:

"Long beardes heartles,
 Paynted hoodes witles,
 Gay cotes graceles,
 Maketh Englande thriftles."

Besides these songs on particular events, Wintoun gives us the general information about poems having been written on Sir William Wallace:—

"Of his gud Dedis and Manhad
 Gret Gestis, I hard say, are made."

On the exploits of Wallace in France, it is said by Fordun,[1] that songs were written in France itself, as well as in Scotland.

With all this evidence it is impossible to avoid the conclusion that there must have been at one time a considerable amount of popular lyrical poetry, created by the national enthusiasm which gathered around the events and the heroes of the great War of Independence in Scotland. But, in addition to the unimportant fragments cited above, we have a couple of ballads which deserve notice at least. The ballad of *Auld Maitland*, though maintained by Aytoun and Child to be a modern production, is regarded by Leyden, Scott, and Hogg as being of very ancient date; while we have the testimony of the last to its popularity in the district of the Ettrick forest.[2] Whatever may be the decision of criticism on this question, we cannot be far wrong, with the opinion of Scott and Leyden, in taking *Auld Maitland* as a fair representative of the ballads of the time.

The ballad *Gude Wallace*, a defective version of which first appeared in Johnson's "Museum," and the ballad of *Sir William Wallace*, first published in *The Thistle of Scotland*,[3] refer to one of the well-known adventures in the legendary life of the popular hero. Though their original date is wholly uncertain, and they are evidently to a great extent modernised, they appear to me to retain unmistakable traces of old origin. At least they,

---

[1] Fordun's "Scotichronicon," II. 176 (edit. Goodall).
[2] Scott's "Border Minstrelsy," vol. i. pp. 314, 315.
[3] Both of these ballads will be found in Child's "English and Scottish Ballads," vol. vi. pp. 232-242.

as well as the ballad of *Auld Maitland*, preserve, in its freshness, the thoroughly military spirit of the time—the exhilaration at the prospect of battle,

> —"That stern joy which warriors feel
> At foemen worthy of their steel."

These can be but meagre representatives, so far as number is concerned, of the lyrical poetry in which the struggle to maintain national independence was celebrated; but, when examined with care, they reveal the influence which must have been exerted by the literature they represent. There is in these ballads, as there was undoubtedly in all of the same group, an admiring love of the heroes who assumed the championship of the popular cause; while there is also the fierce hatred of the foe which characterises a warlike age.

> "It's ne'er be said in France, nor e'er
> In Scotland, when I'm hame,
> That Englishman lay under me,
> And e'er gat up again!"[1]

In the ballads and songs of this period, therefore, we may see one of the influences which served to perpetuate the dread of any interference with Scottish independence, and the jealous dislike of England lest she might seize some opportunity to crush that independence. This dread and jealousy are visible, not only throughout the particular struggle in which they

---

[1] From *Auld Maitland*. Another reading of the third line in this verse gives—
> "That *Edward* once lay under me;"

but either reading illustrates the point of the quotation.

originated: they weakened the hands of Knox and Murray, who were among the first Scotchmen to see clearly the identity of Scottish interests with those of England, while they strengthened the conservative French party at the court of Holyrood; they gave an additional bitterness to the long contest of the seventeenth century; they formed a principal obstacle to the Union of the century following; they put a fresh vigour into the dying struggle of the Stuart cause; they are still discernible in the strongly marked character which makes the Scotchman retain so many distinctive peculiarities of his country, even in the midst of powerful foreign influences; and they are now only beginning to give way before that wiser legislation and more frequent intercourse which are at last welding the two nations into one.

§ 2.—*The Border Feuds.*

The influence pointed out at the close of the previous section may be attributed to another group of ballads but these possess some characteristics so distinctive that they are more appropriately gathered into a class by themselves. The general hostility between England and Scotland was, of course, hottest in the Border counties of each kingdom; and the special feuds between the clans on opposite sides of the Border paid little or no regard to the general relations of the two countries—were, in fact, as likely to break out in as in war. This was owing mainly to two circumstan —the general system of warfare in feudal tim, and t special kind of warfare adopted by the Scots. Under the feudal system the defence of the Border was necessarily entrusted to the great families on either side; while the Scots, unable generally to cope in the open field with the armies of a comparatively populous and wealthy kingdom, carried on the war by retiring before the superior invading forces of the enemy, and retaliating in predatory raids. A state of society was thus created which aroused in intensity various human passions, such as form fit materials for the fierce minstrelsy of warlike tribes, and the habits of the people encouraged the minstrel to celebrate in song the exploits of favourite heroes.

The earliest Scottish ballad of this group is *The Battle of Otterbourne*, which is, without doubt, the finest of the historical ballads that have been preserved. The ballad refers to a chivalrous combat which took place in connection with one of the most formidable invasions of England ever made by the Scots. Their forces amounted to about 50,000, the main body entering by the west, while a small body of 2,000 or 3,000, under the Earl of Douglas, made a diversion in the east. The smaller division penetrated as far as Newcastle, where they were met by a force under Sir Henry Percy—the familiar Harry Hotspur, son of the Earl of Northumberland. In one of several passages at arms, Hotspur's pennon was carried off by Douglas. Incited by a chivalrous challenge from Douglas, Hotspur followed the little Scotch army with a force of above 8,000 men, and came upon it at Otterburn by moonlight on the 19th of August, 1388. The Scots were strongly encamped; and after a bloody contest, in which Douglas was slain and Percy taken prisoner, the English were obliged to retire. This is one of the actions which fascinated most strongly the imagination of Froissart, and makes his narrative glow with his finest enthusiasm.[1] But the features of the battle which attracted the chronicler of chivalry made the minstrels, on both sides of the Border, seize upon it as a splendid theme for their ballads. In the course of tradition the story assumed various forms; and the celebrated ballads of the *Chevy Chase*,[2] though an attempt has been made to connect them with a different event, are undoubtedly to be ascribed to the treatment which the great tournament at Otterburn received among the popular poets: at least it would be gratifying if the license of the ballad-mongers always allowed us to trace their narratives so easily to the events in which these originated. It is now uncertain what form of these old songs about Percy and Douglas moved Sir Philip Sidney "more than with a trumpet;" but few who retain any taste for our popular poetry can read the ballad of *The Battle of Otterbourne* without catching some of the enthusiasm which it must have kindled among the ruder audiences of the old times.

This ballad might, with sufficient propriety, be em

---

[1] The reader will find some of the best episodes of Froissart selected by Scott in his notes to the ballad.

[2] "In the changes to which traditional poetry is subjected, Chevy Chase connects itself with the Cheviot Hills; but the term is evidently a variant or corruption of *chevauchée*, which in the Norman-French of the day meant the sort of plundering expedition now better known by the name of *raid*." — BURTON's *History of Scotland*, vol. iii. p. 275.

braced among the ballads described in the previous section, and it forms a fit transition to the Border ballads proper. For our purposes it is unnecessary to enter into a detailed narrative of the events celebrated in these ballads; but I shall endeavour to sketch some of the main characteristics by which the ballads are distinguished, that we may appreciate the influence which they have exerted on those by whom they have been sung.

It is exceedingly difficult, if precision is desired, to find one's way through a state of society so disorganized as that which appears in the Border ballads, so as to arrive at very definite conclusions as to the principles by which it was governed. The following statements must therefore be taken as true only in general, while admitting of occasional exceptions. The moral code, for example, of the Border ballads is, as a rule, plain even to *naïveté*. It is merely

"the good old rule,
 · · the simple plan,
That they should take who have the power,
And they should keep who can."

For the most part, therefore, in these ballads there is implied, while in many there bursts out in exceedingly natural, straightforward language, an admiration, a worship of physical force—of sheer power to take, to hold what is taken, to retake what is lost, and, if retaking is impossible, to revenge at least. Let us see how this rude morality shows in some of the Border ballads.

The raiders who march to rescue Kinmont Willie

from Carlisle, in the ballad which takes its title from him, are described as meeting "the fause Sakelde," who, in reply to their questions as to his object, is deluded at first by various evasions; but evidently the minstrel's sympathies go, and those of his audience would follow, with Dickie of Dryhope who "had nevir a word o' lear."

"The nevir a word had Dickie to say,
  Sae he thrust the lance through his fause bodie."

Might becomes, therefore, with this class of men, the main standard of right; power to hold, the real justification of property. King James V., annoyed at the exploits of Murray of Philiphaugh, determined that the outlaw should be compelled to recognize his feudal lord. Accordingly he despatched James Boyd, who appear in front of Murray's castle, and summons him to his allegiance:—

"The King of Scotlande sent me here,
  And, gude Outlaw, I am sent to thee:
I wad wot of whom ye hald your landis,
  Or, man, wha may thy master be."

The spirited reply throws a peculiar light on the idea of the time and country:—

"'Thir landis are MINE!' the Outlaw said;
  'I ken nae King in Christentie;
Frae Soudron I this foreste wan,
  When the King nor his Knightis were not to see.

The fact is, that some of the estates within the limit the Debatable Land had been won from their so th foes by the Border chiefs, without assistance from the crown of Scotland; and, with the weak central government which was the perennial source of the country's misfortunes, the captors had to trust to their own swords for continued possession of their property. Their own power, therefore, to take and hold their lands constituted, in their eyes, a more indefeasible title than the most accurately drawn charter from the lawyers of Edinburgh.[1]

With these ideas it is not surprising that the Borderers should have looked to their swords for their right, not only to their lands, but to all the necessaries of life; and it is perfectly in accordance with this principle that they should have cherished a popular prayer, which quaintly combines their savage morality with the limited Christian conceptions that had made way into their minds.

> "He that ordained us to be born,
> Send us mair meat for the morn:
> Come by right, or come by wrang,
> Christ, let us never fast owre lang,
> But blithely spend what's gaily got—
> Ride, Rowland, hough's in the pot."[2]

In the spirit of this prayer, closing with the hint that the *hough* (the poorest and therefore the last piece of meat) was in the pot, was a practice related of the wife

---

[1] An excellent sketch of the Border chiefs will be found in Burton's "History of Scotland," vol. iii. pp. 323–329. Many interesting facts are also given by Scott in his General Introduction to the "Border Minstrelsy," as well as in his special introductions and notes to the different ballads.

[2] Allan Cunningham's "Songs of Scotland," vol. i. p. 139.

of Walter Scott of Harden—Auld Wat of Harden, as he was familiarly called. This Border chief, who flourished about the middle of the sixteenth century, married Mary Scott—the Flower of Yarrow, as she is named in poetical style; and by her he had six stalwart sons. When meat became scarce at Harden, it is said the hungry lads, on sitting down to dinner and uncovering the dishes, used to find a clean pair of spurs for each, placed there by their mother's hand, and

"Come by right, or come by wrang,"

the meat was sure to be on the table next day.[1]

Among such a people, all laws which distinguish *meum* and *tuum* on any other principle than that of power to take and hold, are ridiculed as on the face of them absurd; and the interference of a force from Edinburgh, swooping down on the robbers' keeps and gibbeting the refractory chiefs on the most convenient tree, if not on their own gateways, was an action the necessity of which did not come within the range of their ethical or political conceptions. Like that of a ballad[2] which represents a similar state of society the sentiment of the Border ballads runs against the laws of civilized states with a simplicity which, though amusing, is thoroughly sincere:—

"Wae worth the loun that made the laws
 To hang a man for gear;
 To reave of life for ox or ass,
  For sheep or horse or mare!"

---

[1] "Border Minstrelsy," vol. i. p. 211, note, and vol. ii. p. 10, note 3.
[2] The ballad of *Gilderoy*.

And therefore it is that the sympathies of the people, as expressed in the fine ballad of *Johnie Armstrang*, side not with the government which had rid the country of a dangerous predatory chief, but with the sufferer :—

>"John *murdered* was at Carlinrigg,
>   And all his gallant companie ;
>But Scotland's heart was ne'er sae wae,
>   To see sae mony brave men die,—
>
>"Because they saved their country deir
>   Frae Englishmen ! Nane were sae bauld,
>Whyle Johnie lived on the Border syde,
>   Nane of them durst cum neir his hauld."

This admiration of sheer strength is also seen in the grim humour in which the Borderers could sport with danger or pain to themselves or others. Hughie Graham, who gives his name to a ballad, had stolen a mare belonging to the Bishop of Carlisle in revenge for a worse offence which the Bishop had done to him. The dignitary of the Church, however, was of influence sufficient to get Hughie sent to the gallows for the theft ; but the spirit of the condemned man was not to be broken, and his last message to his father, as he looked down upon him from the gallows-knowe, is one of the most remarkable utterances ever delivered in such a situation :—

>"And ye may tell my kith and kin,
>   I never did disgrace their blood,
>And when they meet the Bishop's cloak,
>   *To mak it shorter by the hood.*"

When Kinmont Willie is being rescued from the castle at Carlisle,—so runs the ballad named after him,—the task of carrying him down the ladder, with his chains still about him, is given to "Red Rowan,"

"The starkest man in Teviotdale."

The rescued prisoner, who was to have been led out to execution in the morning, can still keep spirit enough for a jest:—

"'O mony a time,' quo' Kinmont Willie,
 'I have ridden a horse baith wild and wood;
But a rougher beast than Red Rowan,
 I ween my legs have ne'er bestrode.'

"'And mony a time,' quo' Kinmont Willie,
 'I've pricked a horse out owre the furs;
But since the day I backed a steed,
 I never wore sic cumbrous spurs.'"

But this worship of force did not, as Alexander Smith supposes,[1] exclude the use of lying and deceit, when these suited the purpose of the Borderers. Remarkable instances of their fidelity may undoubtedly be adduced; but fidelity was with them a passion, not a principle, and could not be relied upon where passion was involved.[2] The truth is, that all tribes and individuals of strong muscle, but moderately developed brain, will, as a rule, go straight to their object with sheer physical strength. Only one instance is recorded in which the

[1] See his fine, suggestive essay on the Scottish Ballads in the "Edinburgh Essays," p. 229.
[2] Compare Scott's remarks in the "Border Minstrelsy," vol. i. pp. 173, 174.

god Thor departed from this rule, and the instance is one in which the rule was suspended by a higher. " Salus populi suprema lex :" the safety of the universe was involved in Thor's recovery of Miölnir, his red-hot hammer, which had been stolen by the giant Thrym, and therefore it had to be recovered, even if it could be so only by the trickery of Loki. The Borderer had retained the spirit of his forefathers' religion, and an emergency justified him in a trick or a lie, though he was readier in the use of his muscle than in the exertion of brain which cunning requires. The desperate police expedients which the government at Edinburgh itself adopted in dealing with the Border chiefs, the equally desperate stratagems by which the contemporary English government attempted to secure the refractory chiefs of Ireland, the international diplomacy of Europe, at the time, exhibit the practical standard of truthfulness in circles which claimed to represent the highest civilization of their age ; and it would certainly have been surprising if we had found a virtue, which was practically discarded in such circles, shining with untarnished splendour in the semi-savage society of the Scottish Border.

But the genial writer of the Edinburgh Essay has not looked quite deep enough. In the ballad of *Kinmont Willie*, as we have seen, Dickie of Dryhope is the only one of his party who does not try to deceive Salkelde; and the reason why he did not follow the example of his comrades was the very satisfactory one that "he had nevir a word o' lear,"—he had not sufficient learning to concoct a lie! In the English

Border ballad, *Northumberland betrayed by Douglas*,[1] an atrocious breach of faith is imputed to Hector of Harlaw. In the previously noticed ballad of *Auld Maitland*, which obviously exhibits a social condition not unlike that of the Borders at the time we speak of, the son of Maitland is represented as saying, in the English camp before "Billop-Grace" (Ville de Grace?) in France, that he was born in the North of England; and the falsehood is justified precisely as a murder in the same circumstances would have been:—

"It needed him to lie!"

In fact, the Borderer felt like Thomas the Rhymer—*true* Thomas though he is called, in simple sincerity, by the minstrel—in the ballad, of which an account was given in the first chapter. "The tongue that can never lie" is a gift, the offer of which the freebooter would have rejected with as much scorn as the mythical lover of the Fairy Queen; for his tongue was to him a weapon, like his arm or his sword, any use of which was allowable in order to attain his ends.

But though mistaken in attributing to the Borderers in any eminent degree the virtue of truthfulness, Mr. Smith is right in believing that the fierce fire of their nature did not dry its tenderness.[2] A kindlier feeling often flashes its softer light up through the furious glare of their hotter passions, and a gentle voice of pity can be caught at times amid the din of their usual strife. We have seen already, in the ballad of *Je..*

---

[1] Child's "English and Scottish Ballads," vol. vii. p. 92.
[2] "Edinburgh Essays," p. 229.

Armstrang, how their hard nature melts into sorrow at the fate of an admired leader; and in the fragment known as *Armstrong's Goodnight*, which professes to be the farewell of a Borderer belonging to that powerful clan, who was executed for the murder of Sir John Carmichael, there is a subdued sentiment which is not without its pathos :—

> "This night is my departing night,
> For here nae langer must I stay;
> There's neither friend nor foe o' mine,
> But wishes me away.
>
> "What I hae done through lack o' wit
> I never can recall,
> I hope ye're a' my friends as yet,
> Goodnight, and joy be with you all."[1]

Few can read, without feeling that the rude old singer must have been deeply affected as he chanted, the death of Douglas in *The Battle of Otterbourne*. In the ballad an old prophecy, that a dead man should gain a field, which was encouragingly quoted by Douglas as he was dying,[2] is poetically transmuted into a dream which he

---

[1] Buchan, in his "Songs of the North of Scotland," gives a version, thrice as long as this, which he looks upon as the original in its completeness; but it is worthy of the neglect with which it has generally been treated.

See *Hume of Godscroft*, quoted by Scott in the "Border Minstrelsy," vol. i. pp. 346, 347. The ballad runs :—

> "But I have dreamed a dreary dream,
> Beyond the Isle of Sky;
> I saw a dead man win a fight,
> And I think that man was I."

had dreamt the night before the battle. When he felt that his wound was mortal, he sent his page to fetch his "ain dear sister's son, Sir Hugh Montgomery." Think of this interview between men who had just been fighting with the fury of the combatants at Otterburn!

> "'My nephew good,' the Douglas said,
>   'What recks the death of ane?
> Last night I dreamed a dreary dream,
>   And I ken the day's thy ain.
>
> "'My wound is deep; I fain would sleep;
>   Take thou the vanguard of the three,
> And hide me by the braken bush,
>   That grows on yonder lilye lee.
>
> "'O bury me by the braken bush,
>   Beneath the blooming brier,
> Let never living mortal ken
>   That ere a kindly Scot lies here.'
>
> "He lifted up that noble lord,
>   Wi' the saut tear in his ee;
> He hid him in the braken bush,
>   That his merrie-men might not see."

It will not be altogether out of place to introduce in this connection one of the most pathetic pictures which the ballad-singers of Scotland have drawn, though it is found in a ballad about an event which took place, not on the Border, but in a more northern part of the country; for the event originated from one of those feuds between the great families of the north, which resembled, in their savage displays, the feuds of the

Border tribes. The ballad bears the title, *Edom o' Gordon*, which is but a corrupted form of the name of Adam Gordon of Auchendoun, brother to the Marquis of Huntly, and his deputy as a lieutenant of Queen Mary. The Gordons had long been at feud with their neighbours, the Forbeses, and took many opportunities of abusing their official position under the Queen for the purpose of private revenge. On one occasion Auchendoun commissioned a Captain Ker, or Car, with a party of soldiers to demand the surrender of the castle of Torvie, one of the chief seats belonging to the Forbeses. The lady, whose husband was absent at the time, not only refused to surrender the castle, but replied to Ker's demand in taunting language; upon which the irritated captain ordered the castle to be burnt with all its inmates, amounting to twenty-seven persons. As Ker was acting under the commission of Adam Gordon, and received no punishment for what he had done, the guilt of his crime was naturally charged upon the latter, who figures in the ballad as the perpetrator himself. The scene, in which the mother and her children appear as they see the flames climbing up the battlements and the smoke closing round them, is perhaps unsurpassed in popular poetry; while the picture of the beautiful dead face smiting even the ruffian soldier with a feeling which he cannot bear, is sketched as if by the hand of Nature herself:—

> "O then bespake her youngest son,
>   Sat on the nurse's knee;
> 'O mother dear, gie ower your house,
>   For the reek it smothers me.'

"'I wad gie a' my gowd, my bairn,
    Sae wad I gie my fee,
For ae blast o' the westlan wind
    To blaw the reek frae thee.

"'But I winna gie up my bonny house
    To nae sic traitor as he;
Come weel, come wae, my jewels fair,
    Ye maun tak share wi' me.'

"O then bespake her dochter dear—
    She was baith jimp and sma'—
'O row me in a pair o' sheets,
    And tow me ower the wa'.'

"They rowed her in a pair o' sheets,
    And towed her ower the wa';
But on the point of Edom's spear
    She got a deadly fa'.

"O bonny, bonny was her mouth,
    And cherry were her cheeks,
And clear, clear was her yellow hair,
    Whereon the red bluid dreeps.

"Then wi' his spear he turned her ower,
    O gin her face was wan!
He said, 'Ye are the first that e'er
    I wished alive again.'

"He turned her ower and ower again,
    O gin her skin was white!
'I might hae spared that bonny face,
    To been some man's delight.'

"'Busk and boun my merry men all,
   For ill dooms I do guess;
I cannae look in that bonny face,
   As it lies on the grass.'"

The Borderers of these ballads were, in truth, children in their moral habits and in their social customs. But they were not the children of that effeminacy which is born of a relaxing climate or of enervating manners. They bore the spirit of the North—the fierce power which grew from their unremitting struggle for existence with nature and with one another. Their character is, therefore, that which is formed by passion, fiery or tender, rather than by principle; and even their adherence to a principle becomes a passion.

This is the character which these ballads have contributed to transmit in the people by whom they have been sung. The sturdy strength and the stern daring of the old Border clans have not passed away. Nothing dies altogether; and the force of those strong natures gushes out in other channels now. The arm, which in those wild times would have poised a spear or carried off the load of booty from a plundered grange, is now swinging a hammer, or toiling with an engine that moves a hundred looms or bears a thousand tons over the sea. The head, which would then have led a party of freebooters to drive home the cattle of a hostile tribe, is now directing the beneficent industry of our factories and railways and ships. But the old Border ballads are interesting still, as preserving, in the freshness of nature, the material out of which these valuable forces of modern Scottish life have been formed. "The stream which of yore rushed wastefully from fount to sea, is banked and bridged; it turns the wheels of innumerable mills, carries on its bosom barge and stately ship, sweeps through mighty towns where thousands live and die beneath an ever-brooding canopy of smoke, and melts at last into peaceful ocean-rest a labourer grimed and worn; but its cradle is still, as of old, on the mountain top among the sacred splendours of the dawn, its companions the flying sunbeams and the troops of stars, its nurses the dews of heaven and the weeping clouds."[1]

Long after civilization had leavened the Border tribes, their spirit was kept alive in the North; and, till the Highland clans were broken up for ever by the irretrievable ruin of Culloden and the policy which followed, they maintained a state of society founded on ideas of right and property similar to those met with in the ballads which have just been described. The remarks, therefore, which have been made on the influence of these ballads, may be applied with equal truth to those which celebrate the deeds of Rob Roy and Gilderoy and Macpherson and other Highland freebooters who subsisted by plundering or black-mailing their Lowland neighbours.

§ 3.—*The Reformation Period.*

The lyrics of this period, in so far as they reflect the condition of the people, will not occupy us so long as their number might seem to justify. The lyrical and

[1] Alexander Smith in "Edinburgh Essays," p. 238.

other poetry of Reformation times was unquestionably extensive and varied—more extensive and varied than that of any previous epoch in the history of Scotland. There is, in fact, every evidence to show that Scotland was even taking the start of England in that reviving culture which was spreading throughout Europe, and which mingled itself, partly as cause, partly as effect, with the ecclesiastical revolution of the sixteenth century. A very slight inquiry into the literature of the time soon reveals to the inquirer an extraordinary number of names which had risen to no mean distinction in poetry. The songs and ballads which reflect the condition of the period have mostly for their aim to advance the cause of the Reformers, and, as will presently appear, contributed powerful aid to that cause. In so far, therefore, as the Reformation assisted in the development of a national character among the Scotch, the same influence may be indirectly ascribed to the ballads and songs by which the Reformation was promoted.

It is unnecessary to go into a detailed examination of these lyrics, but it may be worth while to notice some of the more prominent kinds. As is the case with most of the lyrics called forth in any contest, the songs of the Reformation period are, many of them, of a satirical cast—parodies of the Catholic hymnology, burlesques of Catholic dogma, and jeering exposures of clerical and monastic vices. But the most curious and apparently the most popular parodies of the time are those which, in all seriousness, give a religious turn to purely secular songs, sometimes even to songs of a coarsely licentious character. This has been a favourite kind of parody with a certain class of minds at various periods: the Puritans of England are ridiculed in the *Winter's Tale*[1] for "singing psalms to hornpipes," and similar practices are still being perpetually revived at times of religious excitement. Though the most of these parodies, which formed part of the religious instruction of our ancestors, are characterised by a silliness and incongruity astonishing to us, yet some possess a good deal of that rough vigour which makes their popularity and their polemical usefulness not altogether unintelligible. Here is one, for example, which parodies what is known to have been a favourite old song :—

"With huntis up, with huntis up,
  It is now perfite day :
Jesus our King is gane in hunting ;
  Quha lykes to speid, they may.

"Ane cursit fox lay hid in rocks
  This lang and mony ane day,
Devouring scheip ; quhyle he micht creip,
  Nane micht him 'schape away.

"It did him gude to laip the blude
  Of yung and tender lammis ;
Nane could him nis, for all was his,—
  The yung anis with thair dammis.

"The hunter is Christ, that huntis in haist,
  The hundis are Peter and Paul :
The Paip is the fox, Rome is the rocks,
  That rubbis us on the gall.

[1] Act iv. scene 2.

> "That cruel beist, he never ceist
>   Be his usurpit powr,
> Under dispence to get our pence,
>   Our saullis to devour.
>
> "Quha could devyse sic merchandyse
>   As he had there to sell,
> Unless it were proud Lucifer,
>   The grit master of hell?"

And so the poet goes on to describe more minutely the misdeeds of the Papal power.

Others of these parodies, which have no polemical aim, are scarcely characterised by bolder language than that which an excessive mysticism employs in the utterance of pious emotions. The following seems to be based on one of the old love-songs referred to in the *Complaint of Scotland*:—

> "My lufe murnis for me, for me,
>   My lufe that murnis for me;
> I am not kinde, he's not in minde,
>   My lufe that murnis for me.
>
> "Quha is my lufe but God abuve,
>   Quhilk all the warld hes wrocht;
> The King of blisse, my lufe he is,
>   Full deir he hes me bocht.
>
> "His precious blude he sched on rude,
>   That was to make us fre;
> This sall I prove by Goddis love,
>   That my lufe murnis for me.
>
> "This my lufe came from abuve," &c.

The most of these parodies, however, exhibit their authors floundering helplessly in the management of an intractable allegory, the incongruity of which produces on modern tastes the effect of an intentional jest. One illustration will be sufficient :—

"Johne, cum kiss me now,
    Johne, cum kiss me now,
Johne, cum kiss me by and by,
    And mak no more adow.

"The Lord thy God I am,
    That Johne dois thee call,
Johne representis man
    By grace celestiall.

*   *   *   *   *

"My prophites call, my preachers cry,
    Johne, cum kiss me now,
Johne, cum kiss me by and by,
    And mak no more adow.

"Ane spreit I am incorporat,
    No mortallis eye can see,
Yet my word does intimat,
    Johne, how thou must kiss me.

"Repent thy sinne unfeinyeitlie,
    Beleve my promise in Christis death ;
This kiss of faith will justifie thee,
    As my Scripture plainlie saith."

These parodies and other sacred lyrics of the Reformation were collected into "A Compendious Book of Psalms and Spiritual Songs," which was published at Edinburgh after the middle of the sixteenth century, and, besides being frequently republished, has recently appeared under the care of the most competent of editors.[1] The chief authors of these lyrics appear to have been John and Robert Wedderburn. The influence which they exerted is undoubted. It is probably to collections of some of these lyrics that reference is made in a canon of the Provincial Council held in 1549, denouncing all those who should keep in their possession books of vulgar rhymes or songs, attacking the clergy or containing any heresy. It is remarkable, moreover, that of the various editions of the *Gude and Godlie Ballads* which were issued, very few copies are to be found at the present day. "Old copies of the book," Mr. Burton observes, "are extremely rare, and the cause of the rarity evidently is, not because few copies were printed, but because the book was so popular and so extensively used that the copies of it were worn out."[2]

It was not in the nature of compositions violating so outrageously all the principles of taste, to obtain a permanent place in the sacred poetry of Scotland. But it is a fact worthy of notice, that no original lyrics on sacred themes have ever reached an equal popularity. The Scotch have no hymnology which can for a moment be put in comparison with that of England and Germany. This seems astonishing when it is remembered that the service of the Church in Scotland, requiring from the laity no responses nor any audible participa-

---

[1] "A Compendious Book of Psalms and Spiritual Songs, commonly known as the Gude and Godlie Ballads," edited by David Laing, 1868.
[2] "History of Scotland," vol. v. p. 88.

tion beyond the singing, has given extraordinary prominence to this act. The want of a Scottish hymnology it is not difficult to explain. The demand for sacred lyrics has been abundantly satisfied by metrical translations of the Psalms. The reason of this may not be readily discovered, but the fact is certain, and the Psalms have thus come to be intricately interwoven with the religious sentiments of the Scottish people. The strength of this attachment it is impossible for an alien to realize. It is observable, not so much in the fanatical horror with which many congregations shrink from using in their service hymns "of merely human composition," as in the warmth of affection with which the old Psalter is spoken of even by those whose culture might be supposed to be offended by its rude versification.[1] This attachment to the Psalms will probably be traced to peculiarities in the religious character of the Scotch, as developed by the scenery of their country, by their history, and by the Reformation. But whatever may have been the cause of this attachment, few will fail to ascribe to it the effect of imparting to Scottish piety the prominently Old Testament type by which it has been generally marked.

§ 4.—*The Jacobite Struggle*

The omission of any reference to the lyrical literature of this struggle would be liable to misapprehension, and the slight notice which it receives here may be a dis-

---

[1] See A. Cunningham's "Scottish Songs," vol. i. pp. 164, &c. expresses only what anyone who has mixed in the educated of Scotland may have heard.

appointment to some; but the object of this essay must form the justification of such treatment. The extent of this literature is indeed extraordinary—perhaps unequalled by the polemical songs of any other contest in the history of the world. Hogg, speaking of the first volume of his "Jacobite Relics," after observing that he confines himself in that volume to the songs previous to the battle of Sheriffmuir (13th November, 1715), adds: " Indeed there is no scarcity of them during that era. In the reign of Queen Anne the hopes of the Jacobites were at the full, and they seem to have adopted the sentiment lately expressed by a modern lawyer, 'Suffer us to make the songs of our country, and do you make its laws.' Every Muse that could string a rhyme must certainly have then been put in requisition; for of the songs which I have received, that have apparently been written about that time, I have not thought proper to admit above *one-fifth*, and yet I am sure the peruser will think there is enough of them in all conscience."[1]

It is not, however, in number alone that these lyrics are surprising. After throwing aside a considerable amount of dreary rubbish, unreadable as controversial pamphlets after the passions of a controversy have died away, there are a large number of Jacobite songs whose literary excellence is likely to give them a place, for a long time to come, in the lyrical poetry of Scotland. And this excellence is of a very varied character, fitted to gratify the lover of song in the various moods in which poetical gratification is desired. I know of no contest which has produced such a number of songs, equal

---

[1] "Jacobite Relics," vol. i. Introd. pp. xi., xii.

to those of the Jacobites in defiant resolution, in reckless satire, in subduing pathos, and in exuberant mirth.

With all this literature of song on their side, the wonder naturally arises that the Stuarts should have been so perpetually unsuccessful, that men began to talk mysteriously of their evil star, and the devout to see in their fate an answer from heaven to the cry of the people whom they had oppressed. It is for the historian to investigate the causes of this defeat; but it is not wholly beyond the province of this essay to observe, that the Whigs were the men of work, the Jacobites the men of sentiment, in their times. If the sterner nature and more practical activity of the former gave them little opportunity for indulging the enthusiasm which finds its natural outlet in song, the sentimentalism of the latter took from them that practical force which is absolutely essential to success. It is not surprising, therefore, that there should have been few songs, and these few of small poetical merit, on the side of the Whigs, while the force of their enemies, which ought to have been directed to political and military tactics, overflowed wastefully in lyrical effusions.

The poetical excellence of the Jacobite songs claim for them a place in this inquiry, as contributing, along with other popular Scottish poems, to the cultivation of that poetical taste which is so widely diffused among the people of Scotland; but beyond this effect, which is merely common to them with all other good Scots songs, their influence on the national character is quite inappreciable. In fact, even with reference to their power in preserving the traditional history of the struggle out of which they took their origin, it must be admitted that louder in the ear of the Scottish people than *Wae's me for Prince Charlie* is the wail over the martyrs of the Covenant; and tales of the heroism these displayed amid their sufferings are cherished in the memory and told with enthusiasm, when the name of the Chevalier is never mentioned, except in singing the Jacobite songs for the enjoyment of their poetry and music.

CHAPTER V.

GENERAL INFLUENCE OF THE BALLADS AND SONGS.

> "O Caledonia, stern and wild,
> Meet nurse for a poetic child!"
> *The Lay of the Last Minstrel.*

"Take up Burns. How is he great, except through the circumstance that the whole songs of his predecessors lived in the mouth of the people — that they were, so to speak, sung at his cradle; that, as a boy, he grew up amongst them, and the high excellence of these models so pervaded him, that he had therein a living basis on which he could proceed further?" GOETHE, *in* ECKERMANN'S *Conversations.*

THE previous chapters have endeavoured to trace the influence on the Scottish character which has been exerted by different classes of ballads and songs; but it is still necessary to point out the influence which the ballads and songs in general have exerted, without reference to the particular classes into which they may be divided. It is on this subject, therefore, that I propose to make some observations in the present chapter.

There need be no hesitation in saying that the general influence of the Scottish songs and ballads has been to diffuse among the people of Scotland a poetical taste and even a considerable poetical faculty. Of course, the existence of such an amount of excellent popular poetry as these songs and ballads compose, is itself, in the first instance, proof of a widely diffused poetical taste and power among the people; but it must, in the second instance, have contributed very greatly to keep alive, to strengthen, and to extend the taste and the power from which it derived its existence at first. It seems scarcely necessary to say anything on the poetical character of these ballads and songs, or to prove their extensive distribution among the people; but the nature of their general influence will be made clear by some remarks on both of these points.

§ 1.—*Poetical Character of the Ballads and Songs.*

What, then, in the first place, are the peculiar characteristics of the poetry which has been reviewed in the previous chapters? These chapters make no claim to be considered as an adequate critical treatment of the ballads and songs, but they can scarcely have failed to impress on the reader one prominent peculiarity of these lyrics. This peculiarity may be expressed by different terms: it may be described negatively, from the poetry never being violently strained into accordance with rules, as *artlessness;* positively, from the whole style being that which the subject spontaneously creates, as *naturalness*. Occasionally in more minute and excessive forms, this peculiarity is designated by a term of the same origin and the same grammatical meaning as naturalness, *naïveté*, which is merely the French form of our *nativity*. This characteristic of an artless or natural (naïve or native) style is the distinctive excellence of popular poetry. There was a period of British literature—indeed, of European literature—so dazzled by the glitter of artistic finish as to be blind to the charm of natural expression; and it is only in recent times that the appreciation of this charm has revived. We are apt, therefore, to take credit to the superior discernment of these times for the recognition of this excellence, and consequently to overlook the merits of those who, in the midst of prevalent artificial tastes and in opposition to all the critical authorities by whom they were surrounded, had yet the insight to discover and the courage to proclaim the superior literary power of natural sentiment and natural action artlessly expressed to the most perfect work of art without these. Now, I do not know that this critical principle, though much has since been written in its illustration, has ever been more clearly stated than by Addison in his delightful critique of the popular English ballad, *The Children in the Wood.* "This story," he says—and it is still refreshing to read his words—"is a plain simple copy of nature, destitute of the helps and ornaments of art. The tale of it is a pretty tragical story, and pleases for no other reason but because it is a copy of nature. There is even a despicable simplicity in the verse; and yet because the sentiments appear genuine and unaffected, they are able to move the mind of the most polite reader with inward meltings of humanity and compassion. The incidents grow out of the subject, and are such as are most proper to excite pity; for which reason the whole narrative has something in it very moving, notwithstanding the author has delivered it in such an abject phrase and poorness of expression, that quoting any part of it would look like a design of turning it into ridicule. But though the language is mean, the thoughts, as I have said, from the one end to the other, are natural, and therefore cannot fail to please those who are not judges of language, or those who, notwithstanding they are judges of language, have a true and unprejudiced taste of nature."[1]

These words, with reference to one of the old English ballads, might be taken as a general description of the peculiar charm which is felt in reading the Scottish ballads and songs; but it is necessary to be more specific, and even to modify somewhat the language of Addison, in order to avoid misapprehension. The artlessness or naturalness which is predicated of the ballads and songs may suggest two very different qualities. It may be applied either to the absence of all ornaments whatever —even of those by which art seeks to imitate nature; or to that perfect imitation of nature, in which, if it be the result of artistic effort, the art is wholly concealed.

I. Now, in relation to the first of these meanings, it must be admitted that there is, especially in the ballads, a baldness which renders almost every one of them insipid in some passages. This arises of course from that absence of effort, which certainly frees the ballads from all strained sentiment and language; but the same cause results too often in a slovenliness which a very slight artistic ambition would have avoided. This want of labour in the composition of the ballads is seen at once in the tameness of incident, by which the interest of the plot often flags, and in the use of phrases which have become so tarnished by long service that they take

[1] *Spectator*, No. 85.

from the dignity of any work in which they are introduced. The fault is peculiarly noticed, however, in the recurrence of incidents and expressions which became a sort of common property among the ballad-makers, and with which the reader of ballads very soon becomes familiar, at times even nauseated. For an example of such incidents I need only refer to the uniform intertwining of the rose and the briar which grow out of the graves of unfortunate lovers. It is unnecessary to burden these pages with examples of the insipid repetition of commonplace phrases, which seem to fall into their position as a matter of course, because they have done service on similar occasions before. The reader who does not recall a number of these, will find enough by glancing through any collection of ballads.

The same deficiency, even in respect to the essential requisites of poetic art, is observable in the excessive similarity of the rhymes employed in the ballads, the minstrels evidently having been content to draw from a very slender common stock, neither afraid of the unpardonable fault of monotony, nor ambitious of producing the pleasure of variety. The whole structure of the ballad versification, in fact, shows but a rough attempt at observing the principles of metre and of rhyme. Few even of our modern poets are perfectly faultless in regard to the rhymes they employ, and our older poets are not to be criticised in the light of the definition of rhyme which guides us at the present day. In the ballads, however, the idea of rhyme adhered to is of the vaguest character, requiring at times nothing but a similarity of vowel sounds, without reference to the identity or difference either of the consonantal sounds which precede or of those which follow. The metrical structure, also, of the ballads knows none of the regularity which English versification has attained since the Earl of Surrey's time. It binds itself by no condition but the equality in the number of accented syllables which each verse contains, assuming a license, limited only by necessity, as to the number of unaccented syllables that may intervene. It is still possible, however, for the reader who enters into the spirit of the ballads, by laying a vigorous stress on the accented syllables, to reproduce the rude rhythm at which the ballad-singers aimed, and in which their audiences found delight.

This excessive artlessness of the ballads is much more prominent in the form in which they were preserved in the memories of the people, than in that which they assume in modern ballad-books. For the collectors, to whose labours we owe the permanent preservation of the ballads in literature, generally make up the versions which they print from a number of versions which they have obtained from various sources. and each of which may present not only important discrepancies with the others, but also a mere fragment of the whole. In their natural state, therefore, as they were known to the people among whom they have been traditionally preserved, the ballads showed a ruder destitution of all artistic labour than might be supposed by the reader who knows them only from ballad-books.[1] It is true

---

[1] The importance of remembering this fact in the study of the ballads is well illustrated in Motherwell's "Minstrelsy, Ancient and Modern," vol. i. pp. 7, 8 (Amer. ed.).

that the imperfections of the ballads are not to be ascribed wholly, or even mainly, to their original authors; for the most superficial acquaintance with them discovers proofs of various corruptions which they have undergone in the course of transmission from one district and from one generation to another.[1] But for the more immediate purpose of this essay it is necessary to bear in mind that the ballads have exerted an influence on the people in the ruder forms in which they were traditionally sung; while it may be questioned whether any ballad was ever more polished than a well-collated version by an industrious modern collector.

II. But while the simplicity of our popular lyrics degenerates at times into all the defects of careless composition, it oftener attains instinctively that perfect imitation of nature, at which the conscious artist frequently strives in vain. This excellence may be noticed in various forms.

There is, first of all, a naturalness in the choice of language, which is more than a compensation for all the staleness and monotony of phrase by which the ballads become occasionally insipid. The ballad-maker expresses himself in the words which most readily suggest themselves to his mind, even though the readiness of the suggestion may be due to the fact that the words have grown familiar from having been frequently used for a similar purpose in previous ballads. Without any fear of being charged with plagiarism, he relates an event in any well-known verse; and he never hesitates

---

[1] This is interestingly illustrated by Scott in the "Border Minstrelsy," vol. i. pp. 18-27.

to describe an object by an epithet, or to illustrate it by a simile, because these have been applied to the same object before. He knows nothing of that morbid craving for originality which results in the substitution of quaint instead of luminous expressions, which starts the author on a hunt after far-fetched analogies that darken rather than illustrate his subject, which produces all sorts of spasmodic efforts to contrive novel literary artifices. The events, therefore, of the life pictured in these old poems, the objects of the world around, the feelings of the human heart, appear in all the natural colours which they have originally imprinted on the minstrel's mind. The sunshine is bright, the winter nights are long and *mirk*, the heroes are bold, the fair Teuton lass is blue-eyed, with cheeks like roses and hair as yellow as gold, the burns run clear as crystal, the snow is white, the leaves are green, just as they are in nature.

This naturalness in the style of the ballads is also seen in their thorough objectivity. The minstrel endeavours not to express his sentiments about the events he narrates; he seeks to relate them as they actually took place. His soul is in immediate contact with the facts of nature and of life; and his narrative is but a reproduction of these facts without the colouring of his own personal character. It is this that makes the style of the ballads so uniform, numerous and various though their authors must have been: probably no compositions contain fewer internal traces of the persons from whom they have emanated. It is this also that imparts to the ballads a vividness of narrative and a dramatic distinctness in the portraiture of character, equal at times to the finest efforts of a cultivated historical imagination.

A curious and interesting illustration of the thorough objectivity of the ballads is to be found in the child-like credulity with which they narrate legendary marvels—a credulity which continued to be manifested by ballad-singers as long as the ballads continued to be traditionally preserved. "It is well known," says Motherwell, "by all who have personally undergone the pleasant drudgery of gathering our traditionary song, that the old people who recite these legends attach to them the most unqualified and implicit belief. To this circumstance may be ascribed the feeling and pathos with which they are occasionally chanted,—the audible sorrow that comes of deep and honest sympathy with the fates and fortunes of our fellow kind. In the spirit, too, with which such communications are made, in the same spirit must they be received and listened to. The audacious sceptic, who, in the plenitude of his worldly wisdom, dared to question their being matter of incontrovertible fact, I may state for the information of those who may hereafter choose to amuse themselves in the quest of olden song, would eventually find the lips of every venerable sibyl in the land most effectually sealed to his future inquiries." And he adds in a foot-note: "From no discourteous motive, but from sheer ignorance of this important article of belief, I have, unfortunately for myself, once or twice notably affronted certain aged virgins, by impertinent dubitations touching the veracity of their songs, an offence which bitter experience will teach me to avoid repeating, as it has, long ere this, made me rue the day of its commission."[1]

The natural style of the popular lyrics is observable still further in a skilfulness of structure which is evidently the result of an instinct rather than of art. While there has been noticed an occasional tameness arising from the introduction of superfluous incident, the ballads also exhibit that power of arresting interest which is attained by dashing at once "in medias res" and hurrying on "ad eventum." This has been already pointed out in the commencement of *The Dowie Dens of Yarrow*, and it is also characteristic of the frequent opening—

"It fell about the Martinmas," &c.,

or—

"It fell about the Lammas tide," &c.

None of the ballads, in fact, ever falls into the blunder of carrying the narrative back to antecedent circumstances which have no essential connection with the main interest of the plot. It is a distinctive merit of them all that they advance straight to their story. In like manner, in the body of the ballads there is often the same vigorous brevity of narrative, a complete picture being at times brought out distinctly as if by a single stroke of a master. This power of the ballad-makers has struck me specially in their descriptions of battles: the confused mingling of arms seems to be more truthfully represented by a vague, but apposite phrase, than by a more elaborate narration. Take, for example, the

---

[1] "Minstrelsy, Ancient and Modern," vol. i. pp. 36, 37 (Amer. ed.)

account of the combat between Percy and Douglas in *The Battle of Otterbourne* :—

> "When Percy wi' the Douglas met,
>   I wat he was fu' fain!
> They swakked their swords, till sair they swat,
>   And the blood ran down like rain."[1]

The passionate ardour of the combatants, the din, the bloodshed of a mortal duel could not well be put into a more powerful picture. In like manner, the contest of the hero with his nine assassins in *The Dowie Dens of Yarrow* is disposed of briefly in a single verse :—

> "Four has he hurt, and five has slain,
>   On the bloody braes of Yarrow,
> Till that stubborn knight came him behind,
>   And ran his body thorough."

I question whether brief descriptions like the above are not truer to reality than the detailed narrative of the combat between Fitz-James and Roderick Dhu.

The preceding remarks, which have had the ballads chiefly in view, may be applied also in general to the songs of Scotland, except that the latter class of lyrics are marked by fewer of the defects which have been noticed as belonging to the former. The songs also owe their most prominent excellences to their freedom from

---

[1] Compare the later verse on the combat of Percy and Montgomery :

> "The Percy and Montgomery met,
>   That either of other were fain ;
> They swapped swords, and they twa swat,
>   And aye the blood ran down between."

the restraint of those artificial rules which too often check the spontaneous expression of natural feeling. The poet, who summed up in himself all that was most admirable in the previous song-writers of his country, understood this, when, in the preface to his first publication, he wrote of himself: " Unacquainted with the necessary requisites for commencing poet by rule, he sings the sentiments and manners, he felt and saw in himself and his rustic compeers around him, in his and their native language."[1] And one of those numerous song-writers, whose poetical nature was nurtured chiefly by Burns and old Scottish song and those national influences under which the lyrical muse of Scotland grew up, has but expressed the same feeling in the preface to his first volume of songs: " I composed them by no rules excepting those which my own observation and feelings formed: I knew no other. As I thought and felt, so have I written."[2]

§ 2.—*Extent of the Popularity of the Ballads and Songs.*

The previous section has sketched the character of the poetry whose general influence on the Scottish mind we are now considering. To determine this influence, we must inquire into the extent of its popularity.

Without entering into disputed questions, it is sufficient to say, with reference to the minstrels, that there

---

Preface to the Kilmarnock edition of Burns' Poems.

[2] Alexander Hume, quoted in "The Scottish Minstrel," by Dr. C. Rogers (Edin. 1870), p. 287.

is abundant evidence of the part which they played in the old times, and of the power which they wielded, by the charm of music and song, at festivals and social gatherings. The ballads themselves occasionally give us glimpses of this. The old tragic ballad of *Glenkindie*,[1] for example, turns on the skill of a minstrel and the influence which he won by its means:—

> " Glenkindie was ance a harper gude,
>   He harped to the king;
> And Glenkindie was ance the best harper
>   That ever harped on a string.
>
> " He'd harpit a fish out o' saut water,
>   Or water out o' a stane;
> Or milk out o' a maiden's breast,
>   That bairn had never nane."

Instances have already been given in the preceding pages of the more stately romances being broken down into ballads for the common people. It now remains to go more minutely into the evidences of the extensive popularity enjoyed by these ballads.

References have already been collected in a previous chapter to show that there existed at one time a number of historical lyrics called forth by events connected with the War of Independence. The ballads which relate to the feuds of the Border tribes have also been seen to be numerous; and the testimony of Lesley the historian,[2] in

---

[1] This ballad, which seems to be of the same origin with the English ballad of *Glasgerion*, first appeared in Jamieson's "Popular Ballads and Songs," vol. i. p. 91. Compare the ballads *Young Hastings the Groom* and *The Water o' Wearie's Well*.

[2] Quoted by Sir W. Scott in the "Border Minstrelsy," vol. i. p. 213.

a chapter on the manners of the Borderers, may be cited as evidence of the pleasure which they took in the chanting of such ballads. It has been observed further that the mass of lyrical poetry which arose from the influence of the Reformation is probably greater than that of any former period in the history of Scotland; while the Jacobite struggle has been made illustrious by the innumerable ballads and songs in which its memory is preserved. The account of the legendary ballads has proved, moreover, that Scottish poetry possesses a large number of lyrics illustrating popular superstitions, and that some of these lyrics must have been traditionally preserved for several hundred years. The popularity of these ballads cannot have been more extensive at a recent date, when printed literature was already beginning to be widely circulated, than it was in times when the greater part of the information, now got from book and newspaper and magazine, was conveyed through the pulpit, the fireside tale, and the ballad or song. It is, therefore, interesting to collect some of the latest testimonies we possess to the extent of the popularity which the ballads enjoyed down to the period when they were first extensively committed to the press by our modern collectors.

No man was in a better position to bear such testimony than Sir Walter Scott, and a passage from the introduction to the "Border Minstrelsy" is peculiarly suitable to our purpose:—"The causes of the preservation of these songs have either entirely ceased, or are gradually decaying. Whether they were originally the composition of minstrels professing the joint arts of poetry and music, or whether they were the occasional effusions of some self-taught bard, is a question into which I do not mean here to inquire. But it is certain that, till a very late period, the pipers, of whom there was one attached to each Border town of note, and whose office was often hereditary, were the great depositaries of oral, and particularly of poetical, tradition. About spring time, and after harvest, it was the custom of these musicians to make a progress through a particular district of the country. The music and the tale repaid their lodging, and they were usually gratified with a donation of seed-corn. This order of minstrels is alluded to in the comic song of *Maggie Lauder*, who thus addresses a piper:

'Live ye upo' the Border?'

"By means of these men, much traditional poetry was preserved, which would otherwise have perished. Other itinerants, not professed musicians, found their welcome to their night's quarters readily ensured by their knowledge in legendary lore . . . . The shepherds also, and aged persons, in the recesses of the Border mountains, frequently remember and repeat the warlike songs of their fathers. This is more especially the case in what are called the South Highlands, where, in many instances, the same families have occupied the same possessions for centuries.

"It is chiefly from this latter source that the editor has drawn his materials, most of which were collected many years ago, during his early youth." [1]

With reference to the class of persons to whom Scott

---

[1] "Border Minstrelsy," vol. i. pp. 224-226.

alludes as the principal source of his materials, no one was in a better position to speak than the Ettrick Shepherd. Speaking of his native district, he says:— "Many are not aware of the manners of this country; till this present age, the poor illiterate people in these glens knew of no other entertainment in the long winter nights than repeating and listening to the feats of their ancestors, recorded in songs which I believe to be handed down from father to son for many generations, although, no doubt, had a copy been taken at the end of every fifty years, there must have been some difference occasioned by the gradual change of language."[1] Interesting allusions to the fondness of the Scottish people for ballads and songs will be found scattered throughout the introduction to Allan Cunningham's "Songs of Scotland," deepening our regret that one who possessed such splendid opportunities for collecting the popular lyrical poetry of his country, should rather have bewildered other inquirers by substituting for the genuine remains of ancient song modern revisions by himself.

The observations just quoted from Scott and from Hogg imply that even in their time, and in the most poetical districts of Scotland, the knowledge of the ballads had already begun to fade from the memory of the people, in consequence of the spread of book literature. Even yet, indeed, few Scotchmen who have had their tastes for popular poetry awakened can have failed to catch, from mother, or nurse, or peasant friend, some snatches at least of ballad verse which were evidently preserved by mere tradition; but

[1] "Border Minstrelsy," vol. i. p. 315.

most of the living generation find it difficult to realize how the ballads have been preserved at all without writing. Still, the recitation and chanting of these ballads have done their work in former times; while it would be wrong to suppose that their withdrawal from the perilous safe-keeping of mere recollection and their preservation in books have destroyed their influence. We shall presently see that their influence has thus been only extended and intensified.

The preceding remarks have been confined to the ballads: it is necessary to add a few remarks of a similar purport in reference to the songs. Passing over those lyrics, which may be called songs rather than ballads, connected with the War of Independence, we come, in the earlier half of the fifteenth century, on the first of the Jameses,—the first of the royal poets of Scotland. Besides abundant evidence of his celebrity as a musician having extended even to the continent of Europe, there is the testimony of Joannes Major, the historian, who was nearly contemporaneous with James, to the fact that songs of his composition in the vernacular language were held in high esteem by his people. In the humorous poem of *Peblis to the Play*, attributed to James by Major, there are two songs referred to as if they were popular at the time: *There fure ane Man to the Holt*, and *There sall be Mirth at our Meeting yet*.

From this period till more than a century afterwards there have been preserved several detailed allusions to Scottish songs by their titles. These allusions are of very great value in studying the history of Scottish lyrical poetry: to us they are of interest mainly as showing that the songs of Scotland were numerous and popular even in those early times. The first of these allusions occurs in an amusing poem, called *Cockleby's Sow*, which must have been written about the period of James I. Gavin Douglas's Prologues to his translation of the Æneid, which belongs to the beginning of the sixteenth century, contain also the title of some songs popular in his time. But the most valuable list of the kind is to be found in *The Complaint of Scotland*—a work published in 1549, which is remarkable as the first original composition printed in Scottish prose. These allusions it is useless to quote at length, because they are little more than mere catalogues of the titles of songs, and in themselves are not more interesting than other catalogues, while they are unintelligible to the general reader without an antiquarian commentary. It is only necessary to add that the *Gude and Godlie Ballads*, referred to in a previous chapter, throw further light on the number, nature, and popularity of the secular songs which they parody. As illustrating the same period ought to be mentioned the two great collections made by Sir Richard Maitland and George Bannatyne, which have been frequently referred to in previous chapters as the Maitland MS. and the Bannatyne MS. respectively; but these are of more value for the general history of Scottish poetry than in the special connection of Scottish songs.

During the seventeenth century the life of the Scottish people was absorbed in a struggle which withdrew intellectual activity from everything else, and blighted the brilliant literary promise of the century preceding. Comparatively few traces now remain to tell us the state of Scottish song throughout this period; but the indications are, that, while the lyrical Muse of Scotland undoubtedly seems to have diminished her productiveness, the people retained their hereditary fondness for their old songs. There are not wanting even, in this period whose barrenness is deplored by all the historians of Scottish literature, evidences that the lyrical Muse was worshipped by votaries who were not unworthy of her service. Without going into detail, it may be stated that to this century belong the Semples of Beltrees—father, son, and grandson—all honoured in the history of Scottish poetry, and the two last as the authors of Scottish songs whose popularity is still as fresh as in their own day. It is to the son, Robert Semple, that we owe the *Elegy on the Death of Habbie Simson*, which not only possesses the flavour of the finest Scottish lyrics, but seems to have been the originator of the stanza which afterwards became the favourite of Ramsay, Fergusson, Burns, and subsequent versifiers in the Scottish dialect:—

> "Now, who shall play *The Day it daws?*
> Or *Hunt up, when the Cock he craws?*
> Or who can for our Kirktown cause
>   Stand us in stead?
> On bagpipes now nobody blaws,
>   Sen Habbie's dead."

But the grandson, Francis Semple, is indeed a name worthy of being treasured in the history of Scottish song, associated as it is with such songs as *Hallow Fair*, *Maggie Lauder*, *The Blythesome Bridal*, *She rose and loot me in*,[1] as well as with the earliest known lyric on the theme of *Auld lang syne*, which grew, through subsequent revisions, into the imperishable song of Burns. The quotation given above from the *Elegy on Habbie Simson* indicates that the old songs of an earlier generation were still popular; and the general strain of that poem, as well as of Francis Semple's songs, implies a state of society which must have given abundant encouragement to the lyrics of social life.

As soon as the great struggle of the seventeenth century was over, the literary productiveness of the Scotch revived; and for the first time the popular lyrics of the country became fashionable enough to obtain a place in printed collections. Even before this, snatches of Scottish lyrical poetry had found their way south of the Tweed; but about the close of the century the songs and airs of Scotland seem to have attained sufficient favour among the better classes of English society to encourage such imitations of them as may be found in Tom D'Urfey's *Pills to purge Melancholy*—a collection published at London in 1719. Previous to this, in 1706, Watson's *Comic and Serious Scots Poems* appeared at Edinburgh. But the collection which eclipsed all its predecessors, both in popularity and in value to the student of Scottish song, was Ramsay's *Tea-Table Miscellany*, which first appeared in 1724. From this period Scottish song is no longer traditional; it takes

---

[1] I follow here the common tradition, though it has been questioned with reference to some of these songs.

a distinct place as a department of book literature. It is remarkable, however, that this circumstance has diminished neither the general taste of the Scottish people for their songs, nor even the activity of that poetical power by which their songs have been created. While the ballads have been dying out of the memory of the people, and will hereafter influence the literary world more than the men and women of ordinary life, the songs continue to be cherished still. The day has long gone by when a genuine ballad could be produced ; but within recent years new songs have been written, which may take their place in the song-literature of the country. Nor is it difficult to see the cause of this difference between the fate of the ballads and that of the songs. The ballads owe their origin to interests which are limited in locality, and still more limited in time ; so that as the appearance of localities changes with the progress of civilization, and as the events celebrated in popular poetry recede further into the past, the ballads become forgotten amid the new interests which are continually obtruding their claims. It is not so with songs: they express those universal passions of human life which are unvarying from age to age ; and, consequently, the singer who gives a favourite utterance to the joys and griefs, the loves and hates, the hopes and fears, which the human heart experienced in his own time, will find his words suited to men of any subsequent generation who have undergone the same emotions.

In order to estimate the amount of the influence which the songs of Scotland have been exerting on the life of her people, it is not necessary to hazard any comparison between these songs and those of any other country, even though such a comparison need not be dreaded by the most patriotic Scotsman. But no one, who makes any inquiry upon the subject, can fail to be struck with the prominent place which the songs of Scotland occupy in the life of the Scottish people. There is no occupation of Scottish life whose toil is not made at least more tolerable, if not positively pleasant ; there is no sorrow whose shadow is not brightened ; there is no aspiration of the human heart which is not quickened into a more ardent glow ; there is no joy which does not receive an additional zest, from the songs which the Scots—men and women, lads and lasses —sing, or try to sing, or, if they cannot even try, hum at least with inward satisfaction.

Anecdotes, pathetic and amusing too, are not wanting to illustrate the fondness of the Scotch for their music and songs, and the cheer which the gratification of their fondness afforded, under circumstances extremely unfavourable to cheer of any kind. Dr. Cameron, a brother of Lochiel, the friend of Prince Charlie, was overheard, in his prison after the disaster at Culloden, indulging his feelings in singing *We'll may be return to Lochaber no more*.[1] A still more remarkable indulgence in song and music is related of a town-piper of Falkirk who was sentenced to be hanged for horse-stealing. In the spirit in which Hughie Graham of Border ballad notoriety addressed a witty message to his father from the gallows-knowe—in the spirit in

[1] Hogg's "Jacobite Relics," Second Series, p. 434.

which the northern freebooter, Macpherson, played his violin under the gallows-tree, the condemned piper invited, by permission, a number of his professional brethren to spend with him the night before his execution. "As the liquor was abundant, and the instruments were in tune, the noise and fun grew fast and furious. The execution was to be at eight o'clock, and the poor piper was recalled to a sense of his situation by morning light dawning on the window. He suddenly silenced his pipe, and exclaimed, 'O but this wearyfu' hanging rings in my lug like a new tune!'"[1]

But the beneficent influences of Scottish song are more touchingly evidenced in the ordinary life of the people; and I do not know that these influences could be better illustrated than by a glimpse of the office which the cherished popular songs are performing still in the less favoured spheres of Scottish society. We draw from the experience of William Thom of Inverury, one of the best of those numerous humble poets who, in the midst of unremitting toil for the bare necessaries of life, have been led to cherish nobler thoughts mainly by the influence of Burns and the popular poetry of Scotland. "Moore," he says, in his *Rhymes and Recollections of a Handloom Weaver*, "was doing all he could for love-sick boys and girls, yet they never had enough! Nearer and dearer to hearts like ours was the Ettrick Shepherd, then in his full tide of song and story; but nearer and dearer still than he, or any living songster, was our ill-fated fellow-craftsman, Tannahill. Poor weaver chiel! what we owe to you! Your *Braes of Balquidder*,

---

[1] Allan Cunningham's "Songs of Scotland," vol. iv. pp 23, 24.

and *Yon Burnside*, and *Gloomy Winter*, and the *Minstrel's* wailing ditty, and the noble *Gleniffer*. Oh how they did ring above the rattle of a thousand shuttles! Let me again proclaim the debt we owe to these song spirits, as they walked in melody from loom to loom, ministering to the low-hearted; and when the breast was filled with everything but hope and happiness, let only break out the healthy and vigorous chorus, 'A man's a man for a' that,' and the fagged weaver brightens up. . . . Who dare measure the restraining influences of these very songs? To us they were all instead of sermons. Had one of us been bold enough to enter a church, he must have been ejected for the sake of decency. His forlorn and curiously patched habiliments would have contested the point of attraction with the ordinary eloquence of that period. Church bells rang not for us. Poets were indeed our priests: but for those, the last relics of moral existence would have passed away. Song was the dewdrop which gathered during the long night of despondency, and was sure to glitter in the very first blink of the sun. You might have seen *Auld Robin Gray* wet the eyes that could be tearless amid cold and hunger and weariness and pain."

Those who have mixed much with Scottish society, especially among the middle and working classes, know that Thom's is not an isolated experience,—that, in fact, the higher sentiments by which, among these classes, life is ennobled into something more than a mere gratification of animal cravings, or a monotonous round of insipid tasks, are drawn from the inspirations of popular song. The people of Scotland have indeed lived in an atmosphere of song; their minds are saturated with its spirit; their talk is moulded by its language. The national mind has thus become a richly cultivated soil, in which popular poetry strikes its roots deep, and, finding congenial nourishment, produces fresh fruits with ever renewed fertility. The astonishing fertility of the Scottish mind in the production of popular poetry is witnessed, not only by the innumerable names which make up the long roll of Scottish song-writers, but perhaps far more by the royal munificence with which gems of song have been scattered abroad, unclaimed by individuals, to become the common property of the people, like modest wild-flowers which bloom alike for all,—for all at least who are sufficiently natural to appreciate their bloom. It is to this poetical fertility of the Scottish mind that we owe also the constant revision through which many of our finest lyrics have passed into the more finished forms in which they are familiar to us at the present day; for numberless conscious and unconscious efforts of unknown lovers of song have been carrying on the process, by which Ramsay and Burns, and Lady Nairne and Joanna Baillie, have entered, like spirits of light, into the genius of old songs which had been blighted by the touch of grosser spirits, and have breathed into them a purer life.

It is scarcely possible to suppose that any nation can exhibit a more extensive lyrical taste and lyrical productiveness: of few nations can it be said that song influences their life even to the same extent. The marvellous character of the Scottish mind in this respect has not failed to attract the attention of one of the wisest students of literature. "We admire the tragedies of the ancient Greeks," said Goethe to Eckermann one day; "but, to take a correct view of the case, we ought rather to admire the period and the nation in which their production was possible, than the individual authors; for though these pieces differ a little from each other, and though one of these poets appears somewhat greater and more finished than the other, still, taking all things together, only one decided character runs through the whole. . . . .

"Now, take up Burns. How is he great, except through the circumstance that the whole songs of his predecessors lived in the mouth of the people,—that they were, so to speak, sung at his cradle; that as a boy, he grew up amongst them, and the high excellence of these models so pervaded him, that he had therein a living basis on which he could proceed further? Again, why is he great, but from this, that his own songs at once found susceptible ears amongst his compatriots; that, sung by reapers and sheaf-binders, they at once greeted him in the field; and that his boon companions sung them to welcome him at the ale-house? Something was certainly to be done in this way.

"On the other hand, what a pitiful figure is made by us Germans! Of our old songs—no less important than those of Scotland—how many lived among the people in the days of my youth? Herder and his successors first began to collect them and rescue them from oblivion; then they were at least printed in the libraries. Then, more lately, what songs have not

Bürger and Voss composed! Who can say that they are more insignificant or less popular than those of the excellent Burns? But which of them so lives among us that it greets us from the mouth of the people? They are written and printed, and they remain in the libraries, quite in accordance with the general fate of German poets. Of my own songs, how many live? Perhaps one or another of them may be sung by a pretty girl to the piano; but among the people, properly so called, they have no sound. With what sensations must I remember the time when passages from Tasso were sung to me by Italian fishermen!"[1]

It is not to be forgotten in estimating the value of these words, so far as they refer to Germany, that, while they come to us through the medium of a German Boswell, they are but the conversational expressions of a cultured poet, who drew his knowledge from comparatively limited intercourse with the mass of his countrymen. But whether his account of the popular taste for song in Germany be absolutely correct or not, his language indicates the impression produced upon a foreign student by contemplating the extensive diffusion among the Scottish people of the taste for popular poetry and of the faculty for producing it, as the causes to which mainly the astonishing genius of Burns was due. What may be the future of the popular poetry of Scotland, it is difficult and would be unwise to prophesy. There is much, as already hinted, to indicate that the national peculiarities of the Scotch are fading away in the assimilating process carried on by the increasing international

[1] Eckermann's "Conversations of Goethe," vol. i. pp. 4, 41.

intercourse of modern times; and the result of this may be, that the difference of dialect will wholly disappear in the literary productions which emanate from different sides of the Tweed. Still, even if this is to be the result of the new influences under which we live, the popular poetry of Scotland need not, and probably will not, cease to be a power in the life of her people.

It has been already remarked that the ballads are fast dying out of the memories of the people, and that the day has long gone by when a genuine ballad could be produced. But the ballads are now more extensively known, and more thoroughly studied, than they were in those old times when they were preserved entirely by traditional memory. They have passed into literature, and become one of the powers from which the literary culture of our time receives its tone. Such may be the fate of all the popular poetry written in a distinctly Scottish language. Even if such should be its fate, however, that is no mean function which it is yet called to perform; and its future influence upon literature may well be cherished, if we may judge from the beneficence of its power in the past.

The place taken by the early songs and ballads of the Teutonic nations in the revival of a more natural literature during the past hundred years has become a commonplace of literary history. It is not yet quite a century, since among these nations the memory revived of that early popular literature which is now being studied with enthusiasm by numerous critical historians. Undoubtedly this revival of memory was due to the deeper and more loving look with which these nations began to turn to the past in general, and to that past especially to which they as separate nations were linked as the grown-up man to what he was when a child. But whatever may have been the source of this restored taste for the inartificial literature of earlier times, the taste spread rapidly over Europe, mingling itself, partly as cause, partly as effect, with the endeavour to attain the freer forms which distinguish the literature of our century from that of the eighteenth. For if the study of the old songs and ballads, in which our less cultured forefathers found pleasure, is in one sense to be viewed as having been brought about by the general effort to produce a simpler and more natural literature, scarcely anything could contribute to the success of this effort so largely as the simplicity and naturalness of style with which men became acquainted in those old ballads and songs. What could teach men that genius must create a form for itself, but cannot be created by mere forms —what could emancipate them from the thraldom of misunderstood literary prescriptions, more completely than the discovery of a poetry distinguished only by an inner beauty which sought its readiest utterance with little regard to regularity of outward structure? It is not surprising, therefore, that as the literary culture of Europe grew to its nineteenth century type, the study of early Teutonic literature in every dialect advanced with increasing ardour; and while the old libraries of Germany, Scandinavia, and Britain were ransacked, the memories of the people were plied, in order to recover, as far as possible, the tales and the songs of former times. The ordinary histories of literature sketch the progress of these researches, and their influence on the literary development of recent years; but there is one fact, which has probably never received the prominence it deserves in this section of literary history.

There is properly no period in which a natural literature was so completely extinct in Scotland, as it seems to have been in the other countries of Europe. The period which critics of the nineteenth century unite in deploring as inundated by the watery insipidities which Frenchified tastes dignified with the title of "classic," was the era of richest efflorescence in the history of Scottish song. It is true, the Scottish authors of the period, who abandoned their native dialect, partook in a considerable degree of the tastes prevalent throughout Europe, though their contributions to philosophy and science represent an entirely original school; but it is always worthy of memory, that when we turn from the general literature of Europe produced under the reign of French criticism, to the lyrical poetry of Scotland, we find ourselves amid the productions of Ramsay and Fergusson and Burns, as well as of those obscurer contemporaries of theirs, authors of many capital songs which still live in the hearts and in the voices of the Scottish people.

Is it a wholly groundless hope which looks to the future of Scottish literature with some confidence that it may continue to draw a fuller health and life from the popular lyrics of Scotland, even if a distinctive dialect should be disused? Already several of those poets who have started from the most crowded ranks of the people, and in an earlier age would have sung in the popular language, have adopted a dialect indistinguishable from that of the contemporary poets of England; but few of them fail to show, in their happiest characteristics, the influence of the popular poetry which they have learnt with their native tongue. These poets have not made the impression which they might have left on the mass of their countrymen, if they had used the language which is still alone familiar, and is spoken still with much of its living power, in the every-day life of the people. But they probably represent the direction which even the popular poetry of Scotland is to take; and they encourage the hope that, even if it take such a direction, it may continue to draw much of its inspiration from the old Scottish ballads and songs. It will be some time yet, indeed, before these lyrics can cease to be familiar and endeared to the people of Scotland at large; but it will be pleasant to know that, even if they are forgotten by the people, they continue to attract the poets of Scotland away from the hot-house processes of art to the wildings which grow up under the tending of nature alone, deep in the undisturbed glens and along the open mountain-sides of song. And to the historian of literature these lyrics carry an imperishable interest; for to her ballads, more than to any other literary influence, Scotland owes Sir Walter Scott; while without her songs, as Goethe correctly saw, she could never have produced her Burns.

INDEX.

ABBOT of Unreason, 130.
Adams, Jean, 88.
Addison, 169, 170.
Adonais, Shelley's, 112.
Ae fond Kiss, and then we sever, 62.
Alcmena, 7.
Alison Gross, 8—12.
A Man's a Man for a' that, 125.
Animism, 24.
Apuleius' *Golden Ass*, 6.
Archestratus, 18.
Ariadne, 34.
Armstrong's Goodnight, 152.
Arthurian Romance, 128.
Asgard, 11, 104.
Astrophel, Spenser's, 112.
Auld lang syne, 124, 186.
Auld Maitland, 139, 140, 151.
Auld Robin Gray, 64—8, 105.

Ballad, defined, *Introd. xi.*
Bannatyne MS., 184.
Barbara Allan, *Introd. xii.*, 55.
Barnard, Lady Ann, 65.
Battle of Otterbourne, 142, 152, 177.
Bessie Bell and Mary Gray, 71, 72.
Bide ye yet, 89, 91.
Billy Blind, 7, 12.
Bluebeard, 14.
Bride of Abydos, Byron's, 62.
Broomfield Hill, 41.
Brown, Mrs., of Falkland, 8.
Brownie, 7, 11.
Bruce, Barbour's, 136.

Cauld Kail in Aberdeen, 123, 124.
Chevy Chase, 143.
Clapperton, 90.
Clarinda, Burns', 61.

Clerk Colvill, or the Mermaid, 29.
Clerk Saunders, 25, 27, 28.
Cockleby's Sow, 184.
Come under my Plaidie, 70, 71.
Complaint of Scotland, 184.

Däumling, 18, 36.
Douglas, Gavin, 129, 184.
Druidism, 4.
Duncan Gray, 77.

Elves, 11—13.
Edom o' Gordon, 154.
Edda, 12.
Eery, meaning of, 17.
Egeria, 31.
Elegy on the death of Habbie Simpson, 185, 186.
Ewain, 22.

Fair Annie of Lochroyan, 55.
Fair Helen of Kirconnell, *Introd. xii.*, 60, 61.
Fairies, 11—13.
Farewell to Ayrshire, 114.
Fetichism, 4.
Fin Mac Cowl, 130.

Galanthis, 7.
Gentle Tibby and Sonsy Nelly, 72.
Get up and bar the Door, 92, 93.
Gie me a Lass wi' a Lump o' Land, 82.
Gilderoy, 147, 157.
Glasgerion, 179.
Glenkindie, 179.
God gif I wer Wedo now, 90, 96.
Goethe, *Introd. vii.*, 67, 102.
Graeme and Bewick, 109—112.

Green grow the Rashes, O, 54.
Gude and Godlie Ballads, 162, 184.
Gude Wallace, 139.

Hallow Fair, 186.
Hey! for a Lass wi' a Tocher, 82.
Hooly and fairly, 90, 91.
Hughie Graham, 148, 188.
Huntly Bank, 31.
Hunt up, when the Cock he craws, 185.

If on earth there is enjoyment, 107, 108.
I hae laid a Herrin in Saut, 71.
I'll wager, I'll wager, I'll wager with thee, 41.
In Memoriam, Tennyson's, 112.

Jack the Giant-killer, 36.
James Herries, 16, 24.
Jamie o' the Glen, 83.
Janet and Me, 107.
Jenny's Bawbee, 78.
Jock o' Hazeldean, 83.
John Anderson, 88.
John Grumlie, 94.
Johnie Armstrong, 148, 151.
Johnnie's Grey Breeks, 88.

Kelpies, 11, 15.
Kempion, or *Kemp Owyne*, 21—24.
King Lear, 16.
Kinmont Willie, 144, 149, 150.
Koempeviser, 22.

Lady Isabel and the Elf-knight, 15, 19.
Lament of the Border Widow, Introd. xii., 103.
Last May a braw Wooer, 77.
Little Musgrave and Lord Barnard, 106.
Locksley Hall, Tennyson's, 70.
Logie o' Buchan, 86.
Loki, 104, 150.
Lord Gregory, 55.
Lord Randal, 105, 106.
Lord Salton and Auchanachie, 83.
Lycidas, Milton's, 112.

Macbeth, 42.
Maclehose, Mrs., 61.

Maggie Lauder, 181, 186.
Maggie's Tocher, 77.
Magic, 5.
Maitland MS., 184.
May Colvin, 33.
Mermaids, 11.
Minotaur, 35.
Miölnir, 39, 150.
Moses, Song of, Introd. xii.
Muirland Willie, 77.
My ain Fireside, 107.
My bonny Wife, 107.
My Heart's my ain, 69, 74—76.
My Luve murnis for me, 160.
My Nannie's awa, 61, 62.
My Spouse Nancy, 96.
My Wife has taen the Gee, 100.
My Wife's a wanton wee thing, 96.
My Wife shall hae her Will, 96.

Nae Luck about the House, 87, 88, 91.
Niebelungenlied, 110.
Northumberland betrayed by Douglas, 151.
Numa Pompilius, 31.

O, Gude Ale comes, and Gude Ale goes, 123.
O for ane and twenty, Tam, 86.
On a Dance in the Queen's Chambers, 117.
On the Folye of an Auld Man maryand ane Young Woman, 105.
O Tibbie, I hae seen the day, 72.
Our Gudeman's an Unco Body, 100, 101.
Owain ap Urien, 22.
O, weel's me on my ain Man, 100.

Palace of Honour, Gavin Douglas', 129.
Peblis to the Play, 27.
Philytas, 18.
Pills to purge Melancholy, Tom D'Urfey's, 186.

Robene and Makyne, 76, 77.
Robin Hood, 128.
Romances, 24.

INDEX.

Rowland, Child, 16.
Roy's Wife of Aldivalloch, 69, 70.

Schiller, 13.
Scott, Alexander, 52.
Seely Court, the, 10.
Seely Wichts, the, 10.
Semples of Beltrees, the, 185, 186.
She rose and loot me in, 186.
Sigyu, 104.
Silva Sermonum Jocundissimorum, 95.
Sir Oluf and the Elf-king's Daughter, 31.
Sir Roland, 16, 24.
Sir Tristrem, 129.
Sir William Wallace, 139.
Skrymir, the Giant, 36.
Song, defined, *Introd. xii.*
Song on Absence, 52, 53.
Still under the Levis Green, 63.
Superstitions, 1—4.

Tak your auld cloak about ye, 93.
Tamlane, see *The Young Tamlane.*
Tam o' Shanter, 42.
Tam o' the Linn, see *The Young Tamlane.*
Tea-table Miscellany, Ramsay's, 186.
The Auld House, 106.
The Blythesome Bridal, 116—120, 186.
The Boatie rows, 88.
The Braes of Gleniffer, 78.
The Braes of Yarrow, 59.
The Bridegroom grat when the Sun gaed down, 65.
The Carle of Killyburn Braes, 96—99.
The Children in the Wood, 169.
The Clerk's twa Sons o' Owsenford, 25—28.
The Cooper o' Fife, 96.
The Cottar's Sang, 107.
The Country Lass, 76.
The County Meeting, 120.
The Day it daws, 185.
The Demon Lover, 16.
The Dowie Dens of Yarrow, 55—59, 177.
The Drowned Lovers, 55.
The Earl of Mar's Daughter, 20, 21.

The Elfin Knight, 19, 20.
The Farmer's Old Wife, 97.
The Gloomy Nicht is gathering fast, 114.
The Gowans sae gay, 15.
The Happy Mother, 107.
The Husband who was to mind the House, 95.
The Laidley Worm of Spindleston-heugh, 21.
The Laird of Cockpen, 77.
The Laird o' Warristoun, 106.
The Lass of Lochroyan, 55.
The Mermaid, 29, 30.
The Merman and Marstig's Daughter, 15.
The Murning Maiden, 63.
The Nabob, 114.
The Outlaw Murray, 145.
The Rowan Tree, 106.
The Spinning Wheel, 106.
The Water o' Wearie's We'l, 14, 15, 179.
The Weary Coble o' Cargill, 106.
The Wee Wee Man, 18, 19.
The Widow, 82.
The Widow's Lament, 101 103.
The Wife of Usher's Well, 25—28.
The Wooing of Jock the Weaver and Jenny the Spinner, 77.
The Wowing of Jok and Jynny, 76, 77.
The Wyf of Auchtirmuchty, 94.
The Young Tamlane, 9, 18, 19, 35—45.
There fure ane Man to the Holt, 183.
There sall be Mirth at our Meeting yet, 183.
Theseus, 34.
Thomas the Rhymer, 31 35, 151.
Thomlin, see *The Young Tamlane.*
Thom, William, of Inverury, 189.
Thor, 11, 36, 37, 150.
Thrym, 150.
Tibbie Fowler o' the Glen, 73, 74.
To Mary in Heaven, 60.
Tom Linn, see *The Young Tamlane.*
Tom Thumb, 18, 19, 35—37.
Tullochgorum, 115, 116.

Utgard, 36, 39.

Valkyrs, 8.

Wae's me for Prince Charlie, 166.
Wallace, Blind Harry's, 136.
Wallace, the legendary, 130.
Waly, waly, but Love be bonny, 63, 64.
Wap at the Widow, my Laddie, 82.
Wattie's the Waur o' the Wear, 105.
Watson's *Comic and Serious Scots Poems*, 186.
Watty and Meg, 95.
Wa warth Maryage, 90.
Wedderburns, The, 162.
We'll may be return to Lochaber no more, 188.

Werena my heart licht, I wad dee, 120.
What can a Young Lassie do wi' an Auld Man? 105.
When the Kye comes Hame, 79, 80.
Whistle o'er the Lave o't, 90, 96.
Wifie and Me, 107.
Willie and May Margaret, 55.
Willie's Ladye, 6, 7.
Winter's Tale, 159.
Witchcraft, 4—11.
With Huntis up, 159.
Wooed and Married and a', 84, 85.

Yarrow, the river, 55, 56.
Young Hastings the Groom, 179.

GLOSSARY.

Aboon, above.
Ae or *ane*, one.
Agee, aside.
Aik, oak.
Ain, own.
Airn, iron.
Arblast-bow, cross-bow.
Aumrie, cupboard.

Bairn, child.
Bawbee, halfpenny (English).
Beet, add fuel, excite.
Ben, in the inner room.
Bent, (1) coarse grass, (2) open field.
Bield, shelter.
Billie, comrade.
Birkie, young fellow.
Bogle, hobgoblin.
Bot, see *But*.
Boun, make ready.
Brae, hill.
Braken, female fern.
Braw, pretty, finely dressed.
Bree, broth, juice.
Breeks, breeches.
Browst, a brewing.
Bucken, beechen.
Busk, deck.
But, in the outer room, without.
But and, and also.
Byre, cowhouse.

Caller, fresh.
Cant or *canty*, merry.
Care na by, to be indifferent.
Carle, an old man.
Carlin, an old woman.
Channerin, fretting.
Chiel or *chield*, fellow.
Chuckie, hen or chicken.

Claver, talk idly.
Cleck, hatch.
Clink, cash.
Coble, boat.
Cocknp, a kind of hat.
Coft, bought.
Cog or *cogie*, a bowl.
Coof, simpleton.
Cosy, comfortable.
Couthie, pleasant.
Cowt, colt.
Crack, chat.
Cramasie, crimson.
Crap, crept.
Crony, companion.
Curisey, kersey.

Daff, make sport.
Daft, made sport of, mad.
Daw, to dawn.
Daunton, daunt.
Daur, dare.
Deid, death.
Deil, devil.
Den or *dean*, a hollow.
Doited, in dotage.
Doo, dove.
Douce, sedate, sober.
Douff, dull.
Dought, could.
Douk, dive.
Dour or *dourie*, stern.
Dowie, drearie.
Dring, sing in a melancholy ton
Dree, endure.
Duddy, ragged.
Duke, see *Douk*.
Dule, sorrow.
Dunt, thump.
Dwine, fade.

Eee or *eie*, eye. Plural, *een*.
Eery. See p. 17.
Elritch or *erlish*, elvish, preternatural, awful.
Ernand, running.
Ettil or *ettle*, to aim, endeavour.

Ferlie, a wonder.
Fient, fiend.
Fleech, flatter, wheedle.
Flyte, scold.
Fou, full, tipsy.
Free or *freely*, noble.
Fure, fared, went.
Fyle, to soil.

Gab, mouth, talk.
Gad, a rod, a bar.
Gae, *gaed*, *gane*, go, went, gone.
Gait or *gate*, way.
Gang, go.
Gar, cause.
Gear, goods, wealth.
Geck, make sport.
Gee, *tak the*, take offence.
Genty, neat.
Gie, give.
Glaikit, giddy, foolish.
Glist, glistened.
Gloamin, twilight.
Glowr, gaze.
Gowd, gold.
Gree, pre-eminence.
Greet, *grat*, weep, wept.
Gryce or *grice*, a young pig.

Hap. See p. 27, note 2.
Haud, hold.
Haver, talk foolishly.
Havins, good manners.
Hende, handsome.
Hoddin-gray, applied to cloth which has the natural grey of the wool.
Holt, wood.
Hooly, gently.
Houm, holm.
Howlet, owl.
Hussyskep, housewifery.

Ilk or *ilka*, each, every.
Ingle, fireside.
Ither, other.

Jaud, a jade.
Jimp, neat, slender.

Kain or *kane*. See p. 34, note 2.
Kame, comb.
Kelpie, water spirit.
Kemb, comb.
Ken, know.
Kimmer, a gossip.
Kist, chest.
Kye, cows.

Lain or *lane*, alone.
Laird, landlord.
Lave, remainder.
Laverock, lark.
Lawing, reckoning.
Le, lee, tranquillity.
Lear, lore, learning.
Leman or *lemman*, sweetheart.
Leuch, laughed.
Lightly or *lichtly*, to slight.
Links, locks.
Loot, let.
Loup, leap.
Lout, bow down.
Luckie, a title applied to an old woman.
Lug, ear.
Luppen, leapt.
Lykewake, watch over a dead body.
Lythe, joint, limb.

Maik, a mate.
Marrow, a match.
Maukin, a hare.
Maun, must.
May, a maid.
Meikle, much.
Minnie, mother.
Mools, mould.
Mou, mouth.
Muckle, much.

Nae, no.
Nocht, not.
Neist, next.

Oure or *owre*, over, too.
Owreturn, refrain.
Owsen, oxen.

Pawky, sly.
Pearling, a kind of lace.

GLOSSARY.

Pettle, a stick for clearing away the earth that adheres to a plough.
Phraise, flattery.
Plack, about one-third of a penny (English).
Plenishing, house-furnishing.
Pleuch, plough.
Plum, a deep pool in a stream.
Poortith, poverty.

Rashes, rushes.
Rax, reach.
Rede, advise.
Reek, smoke.

Scant, scanty, scarcely.
Scrimp, to be niggardly.
Seely. See p. 10, note.
Shathmont, a measure of six inches.
Sheuch, trench, furrow.
Shoon, shoes.
Siller, silver, money.
Sinsyne, since.
Skelp, to scud.
Slae, sloe.
Snell, keen.
Speer, inquire.
Spence, pantry, inner room.
Stern, star.
Stour, dust.
Strae, straw.
Straik, stroke.
Stythe, stead, place.
Sumph, a soft, stupid fellow.
Swak, strike violently.
Swap, strike violently.
Swither, hesitation, doubt.
Swoster, sister.
Syke, a marsh with a rill running through it.
Syne, since, afterwards.

Tarrie, hindrance, trouble.
Tent, attend.
Thoil or *thole*, endure.
Thowless, powerless.
Thraw, twist.
Tine (*tyne*), *tint*, lose, lost.
Tocher, dowry.
Tod, fox.
Toddle, totter.
Toom, empty.
Tosh, neat.
Totum, a term of endearment for a child.
Tryst (verb), engage to meet; (subst.) appointment.
Tyke, a large dog of common breed.

Unco, extraordinary.

Vaunty, boastful.

Wa or *wae*, woe.
Wad, would.
Wale, choose.
Waly, alas!
Wap, throw.
Warlock, wizard.
Wat, wot, knew.
Waur, worse.
Wean, child.
Wee, little.
Weird (verb or subst.), doom.
Whinging, whining.
Whomel, overturn.
Wicht (subst.), wight; (adj.) powerful.
Won, dwell.
Wuddle, waddle.

Yammer, whine, grumble.
Yaud, an old mare.

THE END.

MACMILLAN AND CO.'S PUBLICATIONS.

SCOTTISH SONG. A Selection of the Choicest Lyrics of Scotland, compiled and arranged, with brief Notes, by MARY CARLYLE AITKEN. 18mo. cloth extra. 4s. 6d. GOLDEN TREASURY SERIES.

THE POETICAL WORKS OF ROBERT BURNS. Edited, with Biographical Memoir, Notes, and Glossary, by ALEXANDER SMITH. Two Vols. 8vo. 9s. GOLDEN TREASURY SERIES.

WILLIAM DRUMMOND OF HAWTHORNDEN: The Story of his Life and Writings. By PROFESSOR MASSON. With Vignette and Portrait engraved by JEENS. Crown 8vo. 10s. 6d.

THE GOLDEN TREASURY OF THE BEST SONGS AND LYRICAL POEMS IN THE ENGLISH LANGUAGE. Selected and arranged, with Notes, by FRANCIS TURNER PALGRAVE. 18mo. cloth extra. 4s. 6d.

THE BALLAD BOOK. A Selection of the Choicest British Ballads. Edited by WILLIAM ALLINGHAM. 18mo. cloth extra. 4s. 6d. GOLDEN TREASURY SERIES.

THE SONG BOOK. Words and Tunes from the best Poets and Musicians. Selected and arranged by JOHN HULLAH. 18mo. cloth extra. 4s. 6d. GOLDEN TREASURY SERIES.

A HOUSEHOLD BOOK OF ENGLISH POETRY. Selected and arranged, with Notes, by R. C. TRENCH, D.D., Archbishop of Dublin. Second Edition. Extra fcap. 5s. 6d.

SHAKESPEARE'S SONNETS AND SONGS. Edited by FRANCIS TURNER PALGRAVE. Gem Edition. 18mo. 3s. 6d.

MACMILLAN & CO., LONDON.

MACMILLAN'S GLOBE LIBRARY.

Beautifully printed on toned paper, and bound in extra cloth, with gilt edges, price 4s. 6d. each ; and in plain cloth, price 3s. 6d. each.

Also kept in various morocco and calf bindings, at moderate prices.

The SATURDAY REVIEW says—"The Globe Editions are admirable for their scholarly editing, their typographical excellence, their compendious form, and their cheapness."

The DAILY TELEGRAPH calls it "a series yet unrivalled for its combination of excellence and cheapness."

The following are Now Ready:—

SHAKESPEARE'S COMPLETE WORKS. Edited by W. G. CLARK, M.A., and W. ALDIS WRIGHT, M.A. With Glossary.

"A marvel of beauty, cheapness, and compactness. . . . For the busy man, above all for the working student, this is the best of all existing Shakespeare's."—*Athenæum.*

MORTE D'ARTHUR. Sir Thomas Malory's Book of King Arthur, and of his Noble Knights of the Round Table. The Edition of Caxton, revised for Modern Use. With an Introduction, Notes, and Glossary, by Sir EDWARD STRACHEY.

"It is with perfect confidence that we recommend this edition of the old romance to every class of readers."—*Pall Mall Gazette.*

BURNS' COMPLETE WORKS. The Poems, Songs, and Letters. Edited, with Glossarial Index and Biographical Memoir, by ALEXANDER SMITH.

"The works of the bard have never been offered in such a complete form in a single volume."—*Glasgow Herald.*

"Admirable in all respects."—*Spectator.*

ROBINSON CRUSOE. Edited after the Original Editions, with Biographical Introduction, by HENRY KINGSLEY.

"A most excellent and, in every way, desirable edition."—*Court Circular.*

SCOTT'S POETICAL WORKS. With Biographical and Critical Essay, by FRANCIS TURNER PALGRAVE.

"We can almost sympathize with a middle-aged grumbler, who, after reading Mr. Palgrave's Memoir and Introduction, should exclaim, 'Why was there not such an edition of Scott when I was a schoolboy?'"—*Guardian.*

GOLDSMITH'S MISCELLANEOUS WORKS. With Biographical Introduction by PROFESSOR MASSON.

"Cheap, elegant, and complete."—*Nonconformist.*

SPENSER'S COMPLETE WORKS. Edited, with Glossary, by R. MORRIS ; and Memoir by J. W. HALES.

"Worthy—and higher praise it needs not—of the beautiful 'Globe Series.'"—*Daily News.*

POPE'S POETICAL WORKS. Edited, with Notes and Introductory Memoir, by PROFESSOR WARD.

"The book is handsome and handy."—*Athenæum.*

DRYDEN'S POETICAL WORKS. Edited, with a Revised Text and Notes, by W. D. CHRISTIE, M.A., Trinity College, Cambridge.

"It is hardly possible that a better or more handy edition of this poet could be produced."—*Athenæum.*

COWPER'S POETICAL WORKS. Edited, with Notes and Biographical Introduction, by W. BENHAM, M.A., Professor of Modern History in Queen's College, London.

"An edition of permanent value. Altogether a very excellent book."—*Saturday Review.*

VIRGIL'S WORKS. Rendered into English Prose. With Introductions, Analysis, and Index, by J. LONSDALE, M.A., and S. LEE, M.A.

"A more complete edition of Virgil in English it is scarcely possible to conceive than the scholarly work before us."—*Globe.*

HORACE. Rendered into English Prose. With Introductions, Analysis, Notes, &c., by J. LONSDALE, M.A., and S. LEE, M.A.

"This charming version is the closest and most faithful of all renderings of Horace into English."—*Record.*

MACMILLAN & CO., LONDON.

BEDFORD STREET, COVENT GARDEN, LONDON.
March 1874.

Macmillan & Co.'s Catalogue of Works in Belles Lettres, including Poetry, Fiction, etc.

Allingham.—LAURENCE BLOOMFIELD IN IRELAND; or, the New Landlord. By WILLIAM ALLINGHAM. New and Cheaper Issue, with a Preface. Fcap. 8vo. cloth. 4s. 6d.

The aim of this little book is to do something, however small, towards making Ireland, yet so little known to the general British public, better understood. Several of the most important problems of life, Irish life and human life, are dealt with in their principles, according to the author's best lights. In the new Preface, the state of Ireland, with special reference to the Church measure, is discussed. "It is vital with the national character. . . . . It has something of Pope's point and Goldsmith's simplicity, touched to a more modern issue."—ATHENÆUM.

An Ancient City, and other Poems.—By A NATIVE OF SURREY. Extra fcap. 8vo. 6s.

Archer.—CHRISTINA NORTH. By E. M. ARCHER. Two vols. Crown 8vo. 21s.

"The work of a clever, cultivated person, wielding a practised pen. The characters are drawn with force and precision, the dialogue is easy: the whole book displays powers of pathos and humour, and a shrewd knowledge of men and things."—SPECTATOR.

Arnold.—THE COMPLETE POETICAL WORKS. Vol. I. NARRATIVE AND ELEGIAC POEMS. Vol. II. DRAMATIC AND LYRIC POEMS. By MATTHEW ARNOLD. Extra fcap. 8vo. Price 6s. each.

> The two volumes comprehend the First and Second Series of the Poems, and the New Poems. "*Thyrsis is a poem of perfect delight, exquisite in grave tenderness of reminiscence, rich in breadth of western light, breathing full the spirit of gray and ancient Oxford.*"—SATURDAY REVIEW. "*The noblest in it is clothed in clearest words. There is no obscurity, no useless ornament: everything is simple, finished, and perfect.*"—SCOTSMAN.

Atkinson.—AN ART TOUR TO THE NORTHERN CAPITALS OF EUROPE. By J. BEAVINGTON ATKINSON. 8vo. 12s.

> "*We can highly recommend it; not only for the valuable information it gives on the special subjects to which it is dedicated, but also for the interesting episodes of travel which are interwoven with, and lighten, the weightier matters of judicious and varied criticism on art and artists in northern capitals.*"—ART JOURNAL.

Baker.—(For other Works by the same Author, see CATALOGUE OF TRAVELS.)

CAST UP BY THE SEA; OR, THE ADVENTURES OF NED GREY. By SIR SAMUEL BAKER, M.A., F.R.G.S. With Illustrations by HUARD. Fifth Edition. Crown 8vo. cloth gilt. 7s. 6d.

> "*An admirable tale of adventure, of marvellous incidents, wild exploits, and terrible dénouements.*"—DAILY NEWS. "*A story of adventure by sea and land in the good old style.*"—PALL MALL GAZETTE.

Baring-Gould.—Works by S. BARING-GOULD, M.A.:—

IN EXITU ISRAEL. An Historical Novel. Two Vols. 8vo. 21s.

> "*Some of its most powerful passages—and prodigiously powerful they are—are descriptions of familiar events in the earlier days of the Revolution.*"—LITERARY CHURCHMAN. "*Full of the most exciting incidents and ably portrayed characters, abounding in beautifully attractive legends, and relieved by descriptions fresh, vivid, and truth-like.*"—WESTMINSTER REVIEW.

Baring-Gould—*continued.*

LEGENDS OF OLD TESTAMENT CHARACTERS, from the Talmud and other sources. Two vols. Crown 8vo. 16s. Vol. I. Adam to Abraham. Vol. II. Melchizedek to Zachariah.

Mr. Baring-Gould has here collected from the Talmud and other sources, Jewish and Mohammedan, a large number of curious and interesting legends concerning the principal characters of the Old Testament, comparing these frequently with similar legends current among many of the nations, savage and civilized, all over the world. "These volumes contain much that is very strange, and, to the ordinary English reader, very novel."—DAILY NEWS.

Barker.—Works by LADY BARKER:—

"Lady Barker is an unrivalled story-teller."—GUARDIAN.

STATION LIFE IN NEW ZEALAND. New and Cheaper Edition. Crown 8vo. 3s. 6d.

These letters are the exact account of a lady's experience of the brighter and less practical side of colonization. They record the expeditions, adventures, and emergencies diversifying the daily life of the wife of a New Zealand sheep-farmer; and, as each was written while the novelty and excitement of the scenes it describes were fresh upon her, they may succeed in giving here in England an adequate impression of the delight and freedom of an existence so far removed from our own highly-wrought civilization. "We have never read a more truthful or a pleasanter little book."—ATHENÆUM.

SPRING COMEDIES. STORIES.

CONTENTS:—A Wedding Story—A Stupid Story—A Scotch Story—A Man's Story. Crown 8vo. 7s. 6d.

"Lady Barker is endowed with a rare and delicate gift for narrating stories,—she has the faculty of throwing even into her printed narrative a soft and pleasant tone, which goes far to make the reader think the subject or the matter immaterial, so long as the author will go on telling stories for his benefit."—ATHENÆUM.

STORIES ABOUT:—With Six Illustrations. Third Edition. Extra fcap. 8vo. 4s. 6d.

Barker—*continued.*

> This volume contains several entertaining stories about Monkeys, Jamaica, Camp Life, Dogs, Boys, &c. "There is not a tale in he book which can fail to please children as well as their elders."—PALL MALL GAZETTE.

A CHRISTMAS CAKE IN FOUR QUARTERS. With Illustrations by JELLICOE. Second Edition. Extra fcap. 8vo. cloth gilt. 4s. 6d.

> In this little volume, Lady Barker, whose reputation as a delightful story-teller is established, narrates four pleasant stories showing how the "Great Birth-day" is kept in the "Four Quarters" of the globe,—in England, Jamaica, India, and New Zealand. The volume is illustrated by a number of well-executed cuts. "Contains just the stories that children should be told. 'Christmas Cake' is a delightful Christmas book."—GLOBE.

RIBBON STORIES. With Illustrations by C. O. MURRAY. Second Edition. Extra fcap. 8vo. cloth gilt. 4s. 6d.

> "We cannot too highly commend. It is exceedingly happy and original in the plan, and the graceful fancies of its pages, merry and pathetic turns, will be found the best reading by girls of all ages, and by boys too."—TIMES.

SYBIL'S BOOK. Illustrated by S. E. WALLER. Second Edition. Globe 8vo. gilt. 4s. 6d.

> "Another of Lady Barker's delightful stories, and one of the most thoroughly original books for girls that has been written for many years. Grown-up readers will like it quite as much as young people, and will even better understand the rarity of such simple, natural, and unaffected writing . . . . That no one can read the story without interest is not its highest praise, for no one ought to be able to lay it down without being the better girl or boy, or man or woman, for the reading of it. Lady Barker has never turned her fertile and fascinating pen to better account, and for the sake of all readers we wish 'Sybil's Book' a wide success."—TIMES.

Bell.—ROMANCES AND MINOR POEMS. By HENRY GLASSFORD BELL. Fcap. 8vo. 6s.

> "Full of life and genius."—COURT CIRCULAR.

Besant.—STUDIES IN EARLY FRENCH POETRY. By WALTER BESANT, M.A. Crown 8vo. 8s. 6d.

The present work aims to afford information and direction touching the early efforts of France in poetical literature. "In a moderately sized volume he has contrived to introduce us to the very best, if not to all of the early French poets."—ATHENÆUM.

Betsy Lee: A FO'C'S'LE YARN. Extra fcap. 8vo. 3s. 6d.

"*There is great vigour and much pathos in this poem.*"—MORNING POST.

"*We can at least say that it is the work of a true poet.*"—ATHENÆUM.

Black (W.)—Works by W. BLACK, Author of "A Daughter of Heth."

THE STRANGE ADVENTURES OF A PHAETON. Illustrated by S. E. WALLER. Seventh and Cheaper Edition. 8vo. 10s. 6d.

"*The book is a really charming description of a thousand English landscapes and of the emergencies and the fun and the delight of a picnic journey through them by a party determined to enjoy themselves, and as well matched as the pair of horses which drew the phaeton they sat in. The real charm and purpose of the book is its open-air life among hills and dales.*"—TIMES. "*The great charm of Mr. Black's book is that there is nothing hackneyed about it, nothing overdrawn,—all is bright and lifelike. All is told naturally, pleasantly, and with so infectious a sense of enjoyment, that the reader longs to have been with him in real earnest, not merely accompanying him in fancy by the winter fireside. Should Castor and Pollux take him on any future journey, he will not lack eager inquiries for another of his delightful travel stories; none the less delightful that they tell of familiar scenes, familiar English faces, homely customs, and homely pleasures.*"—MORNING POST.

A PRINCESS OF THULE. Three vols. Fifth Edition. Crown 8vo. 31s. 6d.

"*A beautiful and nearly perfect story.*"—SPECTATOR.

Brooke.—THE FOOL OF QUALITY; OR, THE HISTORY OF HENRY, EARL OF MORELAND. By HENRY BROOKE. Newly revised, with a Biographical Preface by the Rev. CHARLES KINGSLEY, M.A., Rector of Eversley. Crown 8vo. 6s.

The Preface to the book tells all that is known of this remarkable man of last century, and of his varied works. Over "The Fool of Quality" he spent several years, and in it we have the whole man; the education of an ideal nobleman has given him room for all his speculations on theology, political economy, the relation of sex and family, and the training, moral and physical, of a country gentleman. The pathos is healthy and simple.

Broome.—THE STRANGER OF SERIPHOS. A Dramatic Poem. By FREDERICK NAPIER BROOME. Fcap. 8vo. 5s.

Founded on the Greek legend of Danaë and Perseus. "Grace and beauty of expression are Mr. Broome's characteristics; and these qualities are displayed in many passages."—ATHENÆUM. *"The story is rendered with consummate beauty."*—LITERARY CHURCHMAN.

Cabinet Pictures.—Oblong folio, price 42s.

This is a handsome portfolio containing faithfully executed and beautifully coloured reproductions of five well-known pictures:— "Childe Harold's Pilgrimage" and "The Fighting Téméraire," by J. M. W. Turner; "Crossing the Bridge," by Sir W. A. Callcott; "The Cornfield," by John Constable; and "A Landscape," by Birket Foster. The DAILY NEWS *says of them, "They are very beautifully executed, and might be framed and hung up on the wall, as creditable substitutes for the originals."*

CABINET PICTURES. A Second Series.

Containing:—"The Baths of Caligula" and "The Golden Bough," by J. W. M. Turner; "The Little Brigand," by T. Uwins; "The Lake of Lucerne," by Percival Skelton; "Evening Rest," by E. M. Wimperis. Oblong folio. 42s.

BELLES LETTRES.

Carroll.—Works by "LEWIS CARROLL:"—

ALICE'S ADVENTURES IN WONDERLAND. With Forty-two Illustrations by TENNIEL. 40th Thousand. Crown 8vo. cloth. 6s.

A GERMAN TRANSLATION OF THE SAME. With TENNIEL's Illustrations. Crown 8vo. gilt. 6s.

A FRENCH TRANSLATION OF THE SAME. With TENNIEL's Illustrations. Crown 8vo. gilt. 6s.

AN ITALIAN TRANSLATION OF THE SAME. By T. P. ROSSETTE. With TENNIEL's Illustrations. Crown 8vo. 6s.

"*Beyond question supreme among modern books for children.*"— SPECTATOR. "*One of the choicest and most charming books ever composed for a child's reading.*"—PALL MALL GAZETTE. "*A very pretty and highly original book, sure to delight the little world of wondering minds, and which may well please those who have unfortunately passed the years of wondering.*"—TIMES.

THROUGH THE LOOKING-GLASS, AND WHAT ALICE FOUND THERE. With Fifty Illustrations by TENNIEL. Crown 8vo. gilt. 6s. 32nd Thousand.

In the present volume is described, with inimitably clever and laughter-moving nonsense, the further Adventures of the favoured Alice, in the grotesque world which she found to exist on the other side of her mother's drawing-room looking-glass, into which she managed to make her way. The work is embellished with illustrations by Tenniel, exhibiting as amount of humour as those to which "Alice's Adventures in Wonderland" owed so much of its popularity.

Children's (The) Garland, FROM THE BEST POETS. Selected and arranged by COVENTRY PATMORE. New Edition. With Illustrations by J. LAWSON. Crown 8vo. Cloth.

Christmas Carol (A). Printed in Colours from Original Designs by Mr. and Mrs. TREVOR CRISPIN, with Illuminated Borders from MSS. of the 14th and 15th Centuries. Imp. 4to. cloth inlaid, gilt edges, £3 3s. Also a Cheaper Edition, 21s.

> "*A most exquisitely got up volume. Legend, carol, and text are preciously enshrined in its emblazoned pages, and the illuminated borders are far and away the best example of their art we have seen this Christmas. The pictures and borders are harmonious in their colouring, the dyes are brilliant without being raw, and the volume is a trophy of colour-printing. The binding by Burn is in the very best taste."*—TIMES.

Church (A. J.)—HORÆ TENNYSONIANÆ, Sive Eclogæ e Tennysono Latine redditæ. Cura A. J. CHURCH, A.M. Extra fcap. 8vo. 6s.

> *Latin versions of Selections from Tennyson. Among the authors are the Editor, the late Professor Conington, Professor Seeley, Dr. Hessey, Mr. Kebbel, and other gentlemen.* "*Of Mr. Church's ode we may speak in almost unqualified praise, and the same may be said of the contributions generally.*"—PALL MALL GAZETTE.

Clough (Arthur Hugh).—THE POEMS AND PROSE REMAINS OF ARTHUR HUGH CLOUGH. With a Selection from his Letters and a Memoir. Edited by his Wife. With Portrait. Two Vols. Crown 8vo. 21s.

> *The late Professor Clough is well known as a graceful, tender poet, and as the scholarly translator of Plutarch. The letters possess high interest, not biographical only, but literary—discussing, as they do, the most important questions of the time, always in a genial spirit. The "Remains" include papers on "Retrenchment at Oxford;" on Professor F. W. Newman's book, "The Soul;" on Wordsworth; on the Formation of Classical English; on some Modern Poems (Matthew Arnold and the late Alexander Smith), &c. &c.* "*Taken as a whole,*" *the* SPECTATOR *says,* "*these volumes cannot fail to be a lasting monument of one of the most original men of our age.*" "*Full of charming letters from Rome,*" *says the* MORNING STAR, "*from Greece, from America, from Oxford, and from Rugby.*"

Clough—*continued.*

THE POEMS OF ARTHUR HUGH CLOUGH, sometime Fellow of Oriel College, Oxford. Fourth Edition. Fcap. 8vo. 6s.

"*From the higher mind of cultivated, all-questioning, but still conservative England, in this our puzzled generation, we do not know of any utterance in literature so characteristic as the poems of Arthur Hugh Clough.*"—FRASER'S MAGAZINE.

Clunes.—THE STORY OF PAULINE: an Autobiography. By G. C. CLUNES. Crown 8vo. 6s.

"*Both for vivid delineation of character and fluent lucidity of style, 'The Story of Pauline' is in the first rank of modern fiction.*"—GLOBE. "*Told with delightful vivacity, thorough appreciation of life, and a complete knowledge of character.*"—MANCHESTER EXAMINER.

Collects of the Church of England. With a beautifully Coloured Floral Design to each Collect, and Illuminated Cover. Crown 8vo. 12s. Also kept in various styles of morocco.

"*This is beyond question,*" the ART JOURNAL *says,* "*the most beautiful book of the season.*" "*Carefully, indeed lovingly drawn and daintily coloured,*" *says the* PALL MALL GAZETTE. *The* GUARDIAN *thinks it* "*a successful attempt to associate in a natural and unforced manner the flowers of our fields and gardens with the course of the Christian year*"

Cox.—RECOLLECTIONS OF OXFORD. By G. V. COX, M.A., late Esquire Bedel and Coroner in the University of Oxford. Second and cheaper Edition. Crown 8vo. 6s.

Mr. Cox's Recollections date from the end of last century to quite recent times. They are full of old stories and traditions, epigrams and personal traits of the distinguished men who have been at Oxford during that period. The TIMES *says that it* "*will pleasantly recall in many a country parsonage the memory of youthful days*".

Culmshire Folk.—By IGNOTUS. Three vols. Crown 8vo. 31*s.* 6*d.*

"*Its sparkling pleasantness, its drollery, its shrewdness, the charming little bits of character which frequently come in, its easy liveliness, and a certain chattiness which, while it is never vulgar, brings the writer very near, and makes one feel as if the story were being told in lazy confidence in an hour of idleness by a man who, while thoroughly good-natured, is strongly humorous, and has an ever-present perception of the absurdities of people and things.*"—SPECTATOR.

Dante.—DANTE'S COMEDY, THE HELL. Translated by W. M. ROSSETTI. Fcap. 8vo. cloth. 5*s.*

"*The aim of this translation of Dante may be summed up in one word—Literality. To follow Dante sentence for sentence, line for line, word for word—neither more nor less, has been my strenuous endeavour.*"—AUTHOR'S PREFACE.

Days of Old; STORIES FROM OLD ENGLISH HISTORY. By the Author of "Ruth and her Friends." New Edition. 18mo. cloth, extra. 2*s.* 6*d.*

The Contents of this interesting and instructive volume are, "Caradoc and Deva," a story of British life in the first century; "Wolfgan and the Earl; or, Power," a story of Saxon England; and " Roland," a story of the Crusaders. "Full of truthful and charming historic pictures, is everywhere vital with moral and religious principles, and is written with a brightness of description, and with a dramatic force in the representation of character, that have made, and will always make, it one of the greatest favourites with reading boys."—NONCONFORMIST.

Deane.—MARJORY. By MILLY DEANE. Third Edition. With Frontispiece and Vignette. Crown 8vo. 4*s.* 6*d.*

The TIMES *of September* 11*th says it is "A very touching story, full of promise for the after career of the authoress. It is so tenderly* drawn, and so full of life and grace, that any attempt to analyse or describe it falls sadly short of the original. We will venture to say that few readers of any natural feeling or sensibility will take up 'Marjory' without reading it through at a sitting, and we hope we shall see more stories by the same hand." The MORNING POST *calls it "A deliciously fresh and charming little love story."*

De Vere.—THE INFANT BRIDAL, and other Poems. By AUBREY DE VERE. Fcap. 8vo. 7s. 6d.

"*Mr. De Vere has taken his place among the poets of the day. Pure and tender feeling, and that polished restraint of style which is called classical, are the charms of the volume.*"—SPECTATOR.

Doyle (Sir F. H.)—LECTURES ON POETRY, delivered before the University of Oxford in 1868. By Sir FRANCIS HASTINGS DOYLE, Professor of Poetry in the University of Oxford. Crown 8vo. 3s. 6d.

THREE LECTURES:—(1) *Inaugural, in which the nature of Poetry is discussed;* (2) *Provincial Poetry;* (3) *Dr. Newman's "Dream of Gerontius."* "*Full of thoughtful discrimination and fine insight: the lecture on 'Provincial Poetry' seems to us singularly true, eloquent, and instructive.*"—SPECTATOR. "*All these dissertations are marked by a scholarly spirit, delicate taste, and the discriminating powers of a trained judgment.*"— DAILY NEWS.

Estelle Russell.—By the Author of "The Private Life of Galileo." New Edition. Crown 8vo. 6s.

Full of bright pictures of French life. The English family, whose fortunes form the main drift of the story, reside mostly in France, but there are also many English characters and scenes of great interest. It is certainly the work of a fresh, vigorous, and most interesting writer, with a dash of sarcastic humour which is refreshing and not too bitter. "We can send our readers to it with confidence." —SPECTATOR.

Evans.—BROTHER FABIAN'S MANUSCRIPT, AND OTHER POEMS. By SEBASTIAN EVANS. Fcap. 8vo. cloth. 6s.

"*In this volume we have full assurance that he has 'the vision and the faculty divine.' . . . Clever and full of kindly humour.*"—GLOBE.

Evans.—THE CURSE OF IMMORTALITY. By A. EUBULE EVANS. Crown 8vo. 6s.

"*Never, probably, has the legend of the Wandering Jew been more ably and poetically handled. The author writes as a true poet, and with the skill of a true artist. The plot of this remarkable drama is not only well contrived, but worked out with a degree of simplicity and truthful vigour altogether unusual in modern poetry. In fact, since the date of Byron's 'Cain,' we can scarcely recall any verse at once so terse, so powerful, and so masterly.*"—STANDARD.

Fairy Book.—The Best Popular Fairy Stories. Selected and Rendered anew by the Author of "John Halifax, Gentleman." With Coloured Illustrations and Ornamental Borders by J. E. ROGERS, Author of "Ridicula Rediviva." Crown 8vo. cloth, extra gilt. 6s. (Golden Treasury Edition. 18mo. 4s. 6d.)

"*A delightful selection, in a delightful external form.*"—SPECTATOR. *Here are reproduced in a new and charming dress many old favourites, as "Hop-o'-my-Thumb," "Cinderella," "Beauty and the Beast," "Jack the Giant-killer," "Tom Thumb," "Rumpelstilzchen," "Jack and the Bean-stalk," "Red Riding-Hood," "The Six Swans," and a great many others.*—"*A book which will prove delightful to children all the year round.*"—PALL MALL GAZETTE.

Fletcher.—THOUGHTS FROM A GIRL'S LIFE. By LUCY FLETCHER. Second Edition. Fcap. 8vo. 4s. 6d.

"*Sweet and earnest verses, especially addressed to girls, by one who can sympathise with them, and who has endeavoured to give articulate utterance to the vague aspirations after a better life of pious endeavours which accompany the unfolding consciousness of the inner life in girlhood. The poems are all graceful; they are marked throughout by an accent of reality; the thoughts and emotions are genuine.*"—ATHENÆUM.

Garnett.—IDYLLS AND EPIGRAMS. Chiefly from the Greek Anthology. By RICHARD GARNETT. Fcap. 8vo. 2s. 6d.

"*A charming little book. For English readers, Mr. Garnett's translations will open a new world of thought.*"—WESTMINSTER REVIEW.

Gilmore.—STORM WARRIORS; OR, LIFE-BOAT WORK ON THE GOODWIN SANDS. By the Rev. JOHN GILMORE, M.A., Rector of Holy Trinity, Ramsgate, Author of "The Ramsgate Life-Boat," in *Macmillan's Magazine.* Crown 8vo. 6s.

"*The stories, which are said to be literally exact, are more thrilling than anything in fiction. Mr. Gilmore has done a good work as well as written a good book.*"—DAILY NEWS.

Gladstone.—JUVENTUS MUNDI. The Gods and Men of the Heroic Age. By the Right Hon. W. E. GLADSTONE, M.P. Crown 8vo. cloth extra. With Map. 10s. 6d. Second Edition.

This new work of Mr. Gladstone deals especially with the history element in Homer, expounding that element and furnishing by its aid a full account of the Homeric men and the Homeric religion. It starts, after the introductory chapter, with a discussion of the several races then existing in Hellas, including the influence of the Phœnicians and Egyptians. It contains chapters "On the Olympian System, with its several Deities;" "On the Ethics and the Polity of the Heroic Age;" "On the Geography of Homer;" "On the Characters of the Poems;" presenting, in fine, a view of primitive life and primitive society as found in the poems of Homer. To this New Edition various additions have been made. "*To read these brilliant details,*" *says the* ATHENÆUM, "*is like standing on the Olympian threshold and gazing at the ineffable brightness within.*" *According to the* WESTMINSTER REVIEW, "*it would be difficult to point out a book that contains so much fulness of knowledge along with so much freshness of perception and clearness of presentation.*"

Guesses at Truth.—By TWO BROTHERS. With Vignette Title and Frontispiece. New Edition, with Memoir. Fcap. 8vo. 6s. Also see Golden Treasury Series.

These "Guesses at Truth" are not intended to tell the reader what to think. *They are rather meant to serve the purpose of a quarry in which, if one is building up his opinions for himself, and only wants to be provided with materials, he may meet with many things to suit him.*

Hamerton.—A PAINTER'S CAMP. Second Edition, revised. Extra fcap. 8vo. 6s.

BOOK I. *In England;* BOOK II. *In Scotland;* BOOK III. *In France.*

"*These pages, written with infinite spirit and humour, bring into close rooms, back upon tired heads, the breezy airs of Lancashire moors and Highland lochs, with a freshness which no recent novelist has succeeded in preserving.*"—NONCONFORMIST. "*His pages sparkle with many turns of expression, not a few well-told anecdotes, and many observations which are the fruit of attentive study and wise reflection on the complicated phenomena of human life, as well as of unconscious nature.*"—WESTMINSTER REVIEW.

Heaton.—HAPPY SPRING TIME. Illustrated by OSCAR PLETSCH. With Rhymes for Mothers and Children. By MRS. CHARLES HEATON. Crown 8vo. cloth extra, gilt edges. 3s. 6d.

"*The pictures in this book are capital.*"—ATHENÆUM.

Hervey.—DUKE ERNEST, a Tragedy; and other Poems. Fcap. 8vo. 6s.

"*Conceived in pure taste and true historic feeling, and presented with much dramatic force. . . . . Thoroughly original.*"—BRITISH QUARTERLY.

Higginson.—MALBONE: An Oldport Romance. By T. W. HIGGINSON. Fcap. 8vo. 2s. 6d.

The DAILY NEWS *says:* "*Who likes a quiet story, full of mature thought, of clear, humorous surprises, of artistic studious design? 'Malbone' is a rare work, possessing these characteristics, and replete, too, with honest literary effort.*"

Hillside Rhymes.—Extra fcap. 8vo. 5s.

Home.—BLANCHE LISLE, and other Poems. By CECIL HOME. Fcap. 8vo. 4s. 6d.

Hood (Tom).—THE PLEASANT TALE OF PUSS AND ROBIN AND THEIR FRIENDS, KITTY AND BOB. Told in Pictures by L. FRÖLICH, and in Rhymes by TOM HOOD. Crown 8vo. gilt. 3s. 6d.

> This is a pleasant little tale of wee Bob and his Sister, and their attempts to rescue poor Robin from the cruel claws of Pussy. It will be intelligible and interesting to the meanest capacity, and is illustrated by thirteen graphic cuts drawn by Frölich. "The volume is prettily got up, and is sure to be a favourite in the nursery."—SCOTSMAN. "Herr Frölich has outdone himself in his pictures of this dramatic chase."—MORNING POST.

Keary (A.)—Works by Miss A. KEARY:—

JANET'S HOME. New Edition. Globe 8vo. 2s. 6d.

> "Never did a more charming family appear upon the canvas; and most skilfully and felicitously have their characters been portrayed. Each individual of the fireside is a finished portrait, distinct and lifelike.... The future before her as a novelist is that of becoming the Miss Austin of her generation."—SUN.

CLEMENCY FRANKLYN. New Edition. Globe 8vo. 2s. 6d.

> "Full of wisdom and goodness, simple, truthful, and artistic... It is capital as a story; better still in its pure tone and wholesome influence."—GLOBE.

OLDBURY. Three vols. Crown 8vo. 31s. 6d.

> "This is a very powerfully written story."—GLOBE. "... a really excellent novel."—ILLUSTRATED LONDON NEWS. "The sketches of society in Oldbury are excellent. The pictures of child life are full of truth."—WESTMINSTER REVIEW.

Keary (A. and E.)—Works by A. and E. KEARY:—

THE LITTLE WANDERLIN, and other Fairy Tales. 18mo. 2s. 6d.

"*The tales are fanciful and well written, and they are sure to win favour amongst little readers.*"—ATHENÆUM.

THE HEROES OF ASGARD. Tales from Scandinavian Mythology. New and Revised Edition, Illustrated by HUARD. Extra fcap. 8vo. 4s. 6d.

"*Told in a light and amusing style, which, in its drollery and quaintness, reminds us of our old favourite Grimm.*"—TIMES.

Kingsley.—Works by the Rev. CHARLES KINGSLEY, M.A., Rector of Eversley, and Canon of Westminster:—

Canon Kingsley's novels, most will admit, have not only commanded for themselves a foremost place in literature, as artistic productions of a high class, but have exercised upon the age an incalculable influence in the direction of the highest Christian manliness. Mr. Kingsley has done more perhaps than almost any other writer of fiction to fashion the generation into whose hands the destinies of the world are now being committed. His works will therefore be read by all who wish to have their hearts cheered and their souls stirred to noble endeavour; they must be read by all who wish to know the influences which moulded the men of this century.

"WESTWARD HO!" or, The Voyages and Adventures of Sir Amyas Leigh. Ninth Edition. Crown 8vo. 6s.

No other work conveys a more vivid idea of the surging, adventurous, nobly inquisitive spirit of the generations which immediately followed the Reformation in England. The daring deeds of the Elizabethan heroes are told with a freshness, an enthusiasm, and a truthfulness that can belong only to one who wishes he had been their leader. His descriptions of the luxuriant scenery of the then new-found Western land are acknowledged to be unmatched. FRASER'S MAGAZINE *calls it "almost the best historical novel of the day."*

Kingsley (C.)—*continued.*

TWO YEARS AGO. Fifth Edition. Crown 8vo. 6s.

> "Mr. Kingsley has provided us all along with such pleasant incidents —such rich and brightly tinted glimpses of natural history, such suggestive remarks on mankind, society, and all sorts of topics, that amidst the pleasure of the way, the circuit to be made will be almost forgotten."—GUARDIAN.

HYPATIA; or, New Foes with an Old Face. Seventh Edition. Crown 8vo. 6s.

> The work is from beginning to end a series of fascinating pictures of strange phases of that strange primitive society; and no one portrait has yet been given of the noble-minded lady who was faithful to martyrdom in her attachment to the classical creeds. No work affords a clearer notion of the many interesting problems which agitated the minds of men in those days, and which, in various phases, are again coming up for discussion at the present time.

HEREWARD THE WAKE—LAST OF THE ENGLISH. Second Edition. Crown 8vo. 6s.

> Mr. Kingsley here tells the story of the final conflict of the two races, Saxons and Normans, as if he himself had borne a part in it. While as a work of fiction "Hereward" cannot fail to delight all readers, no better supplement to the dry history of the time could be put into the hands of the young, containing as it does so vivid a picture of the social and political life of the period.

YEAST: A Problem. Sixth Edition. Crown 8vo. 5s.

> In this production the author shows, in an interesting dramatic form, the state of fermentation in which the minds of many earnest men are with regard to some of the most important religious and social problems of the day.

ALTON LOCKE. New Edition. With a New Preface. Crown 8vo. 4s. 6d.

> This novel, which shows forth the evils arising from modern "caste," has done much to remove the unnatural barriers which existed between the various classes of society, and to establish a sympathy to some extent between the higher and lower grades of the social scale.

Kingsley (C.)—*continued.*

Though written with a purpose, it is full of character and interest, the author shows, to quote the SPECTATOR, *"what it is that constitutes the true Christian, God-fearing, man-living gentleman."*

THE WATER BABIES. A Fairy Tale for a Land Baby. New Edition, with additional Illustrations by Sir NOEL PATON, R.S.A., and P. SKELTON. Crown 8vo. cloth extra gilt. 5*s.*

"*In fun, in humour, and in innocent imagination, as a child's book we do not know its equal.*"—LONDON REVIEW. "*Mr. Kingsley must have the credit of revealing to us a new order of life. . . . There is in the 'Water Babies' an abundance of wit, fun, good humour, geniality,* élan, go.*"—*TIMES.

THE HEROES; or, Greek Fairy Tales for my Children. With Coloured Illustrations. New Edition. 18mo. 4*s.* 6*d.*

"*We do not think these heroic stories have ever been more attractively told. . . There is a deep under-current of religious feeling traceable throughout its pages which is sure to influence young readers powerfully.*"—LONDON REVIEW. "*One of the children's books that will surely become a classic.*"—NONCONFORMIST.

PHAETHON; or, Loose Thoughts for Loose Thinkers. Third Edition. Crown 8vo. 2*s.*

"*The dialogue of 'Phaethon' has striking beauties, and its suggestions may meet half-way many a latent doubt, and, like a light breeze, lift from the soul clouds that are gathering heavily, and threatening to settle down in misty gloom on the summer of many a fair and promising young life.*"—SPECTATOR.

POEMS; including The Saint's Tragedy, Andromeda, Songs, Ballads, etc. Complete Collected Edition. Extra fcap. 8vo. 6*s.*

Canon Kingsley's poetical works have gained for their author, independently of his other works, a high and enduring place in literature, and are much sought after. The publishers have here collected the whole of them in a moderately-priced and handy volume. The SPECTATOR *calls "*Andromeda*" "the finest piece of English hexameter verse that has ever been written. It is a volume which many readers will be glad to possess.*"

Kingsley (C.)—*continued.*

PROSE IDYLLS. NEW AND OLD. Second Edition. Crown 8vo. 5s.

CONTENTS:—*A Charm of Birds; Chalk; Stream Studies; The Fens; My Winter-Garden; From Ocean to Sea; North Devon.*

"*Altogether a delightful book. . . . . It exhibits the author's best traits, and cannot fail to infect the reader with a love of nature and of out-door life and its enjoyments. It is well calculated to bring a gleam of summer with its pleasant associations, into the bleak winter-time; while a better companion for a summer ramble could hardly be found.*"—BRITISH QUARTERLY REVIEW.

Kingsley (H.)—Works by HENRY KINGSLEY:—

TALES OF OLD TRAVEL. Re-narrated. With Eight full-page Illustrations by HUARD. Fourth Edition. Crown 8vo. cloth, extra gilt. 5s.

In this volume Mr. Henry Kingsley re-narrates, at the same time preserving much of the quaintness of the original, some of the most fascinating tales of travel contained in the collections of Hakluyt and others. The CONTENTS *are:*—*Marco Polo; The Shipwreck of Pelsart; The Wonderful Adventures of Andrew Battel; The Wanderings of a Capuchin; Peter Carder; The Preservation of the "Terra Nova;" Spitzbergen; D'Ermenonville's Acclimatization Adventure; The Old Slave Trade; Miles Philips; The Sufferings of Robert Everard; John Fox; Alvaro Nunez; The Foundation of an Empire.* "*We know no better book for those who want knowledge or seek to refresh it. As for the 'sensational,' most novels are tame compared with these narratives.*" ATHENÆUM. "*Exactly the book to interest and to do good to intelligent and high-spirited boys.*"—LITERARY CHURCHMAN.

THE LOST CHILD. With Eight Illustrations by FRÖLICH. Crown 4to. cloth gilt. 3s. 6d.

This is an interesting story of a little boy, the son of an Australian shepherd and his wife, who lost himself in the bush, and is, on after much searching, found dead far up a mountain-side. It contains many illustrations from the well-known pencil of Frölich. "*A pathetic story, and told so as to give children an interest in*

Kingsley (H.)—*continued*.

Australian ways and scenery."—GLOBE. *"Very charmingly and very touchingly told."*—SATURDAY REVIEW.

OAKSHOTT CASTLE. 3 Vols. Crown 8vo. 31s. 6d.

"*No one who takes up 'Oakshott Castle' will willingly put it down until the last page is turned. . . . It may fairly be considered a capital story, full of go, and abounding in word pictures of storms and wrecks."*—OBSERVER.

Knatchbull-Hugessen.—Works by E. H. KNATCHBULL-HUGESSEN, M.P. :—

Mr. Knatchbull-Hugessen has won for himself a reputation as an inimitable teller of fairy-tales. "His powers," says the TIMES, *"are of a very high order; light and brilliant narrative flows from his pen, and is fed by an invention as graceful as it is inexhaustible." "Children reading his stories," the* SCOTSMAN *says, "or hearing them read, will have their minds refreshed and invigorated as much as their bodies would be by abundance of fresh air and exercise."*

STORIES FOR MY CHILDREN. With Illustrations. Fourth Edition. Extra fcap. 8vo. 5s.

"*The stories are charming, and full of life and fun."*—STANDARD. "*The author has an imagination as fanciful as Grimm himself, while some of his stories are superior to anything that Hans Christian Andersen has written."*—NONCONFORMIST.

CRACKERS FOR CHRISTMAS. More Stories. With Illustrations by JELLICOE and ELWES. Fourth Edition. Crown 8vo. 5s.

"*A fascinating little volume, which will make him friends in every household in which there are children."*—DAILY NEWS.

MOONSHINE: Fairy Tales. With Illustrations by W. BRUNTON. Sixth Edition. Crown 8vo. cloth gilt. 5s.

Knatchbull-Hugessen (E. H.)—*continued.*

Here will be found "an Ogre, a Dwarf, a Wizard, quantities of Elves and Fairies, and several animals who speak like mortal men and women." There are twelve stories and nine irresistible illustrations. "A volume of fairy tales, written not only for younger children, but for bigger, and if you are nearly worn out, or sick, or sorry, you will find it good reading."—GRAPHIC. *"The most charming volume of fairy tales which we have ever read. . . . We cannot quit this very pleasant book without a word of praise to its illustrator. Mr. Brunton from first to last has done admirably."*—TIMES.

TALES AT TEA-TIME. Fairy Stories. With Seven Illustrations by W. BRUNTON. Fifth Edition. Crown 8vo. cloth gilt. 5s.

"Capitally illustrated by W. Brunton. . . . In frolic and fancy they are quite equal to his other books. The author knows how to write fairy stories as they should be written. The whole book is full of the most delightful drolleries."—TIMES.

QUEER FOLK. FAIRY STORIES. Illustrated by S. E. WALLER. Fourth Edition. Crown 8vo. Cloth gilt. 5s.

"Decidedly the author's happiest effort. . . . One of the best story books of the year."—HOUR.

Knatchbull-Hugessen (Louisa).—THE HISTORY OF PRINCE PERRYPETS. A Fairy Tale. By LOUISA KNATCHBULL-HUGESSEN. With Eight Illustrations by WEIGAND. New Edition. Crown 4to. cloth gilt. 3s. 6d.

"A grand and exciting fairy tale."—MORNING POST. *"A delicious piece of fairy nonsense."*—ILLUSTRATED LONDON NEWS.

Latham.—SERTUM SHAKSPERIANUM, Subnexis aliquot aliunde excerptis floribus. Latine reddidit Rev. H. LATHAM, M.A. Extra fcap. 8vo. 5s.

Besides versions of Shakespeare, this volume contains, among other pieces, Gray's "Elegy," Campbell's "Hohenlinden," Wolfe's "Burial of Sir John Moore," and selections from Cowper and George Herbert.

Lemon.—THE LEGENDS OF NUMBER NIP. By MARK LEMON. With Illustrations by C. KEENE. New Edition. Extra fcap. 8vo. *2s. 6d.*

Life and Times of Conrad the Squirrel. A Story for Children. By the Author of "Wandering Willie," "Effie's Friends," &c. With a Frontispiece by R. FARREN. Second Edition. Crown 8vo. *3s. 6d.*

> *It is sufficient to commend this story of a Squirrel to the attention of readers, that it is by the author of the beautiful stories of "Wandering Willie" and "Effie's Friends." It is well calculated to make children take an intelligent and tender interest in the lower animals.*

Little Estella, and other FAIRY TALES FOR THE YOUNG. 18mo. cloth extra. *2s. 6d.*

> "*This is a fine story, and we thank heaven for not being too wise to enjoy it.*"—DAILY NEWS.

Lowell.—Works by J. Russell LOWELL:—

AMONG MY BOOKS. Six Essays. Dryden—Witchcraft—Shakespeare once More—New England Two Centuries Ago—Lessing—Rousseau and the Sentimentalists. Crown 8vo. *7s. 6d.*

> "*We may safely say the volume is one of which our chief complaint must be that there is not more of it. There are good sense and lively feeling forcibly and tersely expressed in every page of his writing.*" —PALL MALL GAZETTE.

COMPLETE POETICAL WORKS of JAMES RUSSELL LOWELL. With Portrait, engraved by Jeens. 18mo. cloth extra. *4s. 6d.*

> *It has been generally acknowledged that Mr. Lowell is one of the most readable and most national of the American poets. The neat little volume contains the whole of his poetical works, including the famous "Biglow Papers" and "The Cathedral;" to the former, a glossary is added, and a truthful portrait of the author, engraved by Mr. Jeens, is prefixed to the volume.*

Lyttelton.—Works by LORD LYTTELTON:—

THE "COMUS" OF MILTON, rendered into Greek Verse. Extra fcap. 8vo. 5s.

THE "SAMSON AGONISTES" OF MILTON, rendered into Greek Verse. Extra fcap. 8vo. 6s. 6d.

"*Classical in spirit, full of force, and true to the original.*"—GUARDIAN.

Maclaren.—THE FAIRY FAMILY. A series of Ballads and Metrical Tales illustrating the Fairy Mythology of Europe. By ARCHIBALD MACLAREN. With Frontispiece, Illustrated Title, and Vignette. Crown 8vo. gilt. 5s.

"*A successful attempt to translate into the vernacular some of the Fairy Mythology of Europe. The verses are very good. There is no shirking difficulties of rhyme, and the ballad metre which is oftenest employed has a great deal of the kind of 'go' which we find so seldom outside the pages of Scott. The book is of permanent value.*"—GUARDIAN.

Macmillan's Magazine.—Published Monthly. Price 1s. Volumes I. to XXIX. are now ready. 7s. 6d. each.

Macmillan & Co.'s Half-crown Series of Juvenile BOOKS. Pott 8vo. cloth extra.

THE PRINCE AND THE PAGE. By the Author of "The Heir of Redclyffe." With Illustrations by Farren.

THE LITTLE DUKE. By the Author of "The Heir of Redclyffe."

RUTH AND HER FRIENDS. A Story for Girls.

DAYS OF OLD. By the Author of "Ruth and her Friends."

LITTLE ESTELLA, AND OTHER TALES FOR THE YOUNG.

LITTLE WANDERLIN, AND OTHER FAIRY TALES. By A. and E. KEARY.

Macquoid.—PATTY. By KATHARINE S. MACQUOID. Third and Cheaper Edition. Crown 8vo. 6s.

> "*A book to be read.*"—STANDARD. "*A powerful and fascinating story.*"—DAILY TELEGRAPH. *The* GLOBE *considers it* "*well-written, amusing, and interesting, and has the merit of being out of the ordinary run of novels.*"

Maguire.—YOUNG PRINCE MARIGOLD, AND OTHER FAIRY STORIES. By the late JOHN FRANCIS MAGUIRE, M.P. Illustrated by S. E. WALLER. Globe 8vo. gilt. 4s. 6d.

> "*The author has evidently studied the ways and tastes of children and got at the secret of amusing them; and has succeeded in what is not so easy a task as it may seem—in producing a really good children's book.*"—DAILY TELEGRAPH.

Marlitt (E.)—THE COUNTESS GISELA. Translated from the German of E. MARLITT. Crown 8vo. 7s. 6d.

> "*A very beautiful story of German country life.*"—LITERARY CHURCHMAN.

Masson (Professor).—Works by DAVID MASSON, M.A., Professor of Rhetoric and English Literature in the University of Edinburgh. (See also BIOGRAPHICAL and PHILOSOPHICAL CATALOGUES.)

BRITISH NOVELISTS AND THEIR STYLES. Being a Critical Sketch of the History of British Prose Fiction. Crown 8vo. 7s. 6d.

> "*Valuable for its lucid analysis of fundamental principles, its breadth of view, and sustained animation of style.*"—SPECTATOR. "*Mr. Masson sets before us with a bewitching ease and clearness which nothing but a perfect mastery of his subject could have rendered possible, a large body of both deep and sound discriminative criticism on all the most memorable of our British novelists. . . . . His brilliant and instructive book.*"—JOHN BULL.

Mazini.—IN THE GOLDEN SHELL; A Story of Palermo. By LINDA MAZINI. With Illustrations. Globe 8vo. cloth gilt. 4s. 6d.

Merivale.—KEATS' HYPERION, rendered into Latin Verse. By C. MERIVALE, B.D. Second Edition. Extra fcap. 8vo. 3s. 6d.

Milner.—THE LILY OF LUMLEY. By EDITH MILNER. Crown 8vo. 7s. 6d.

"*The novel is a good one and decidedly worth the reading.*" — EXAMINER. "*A pretty, brightly-written story.*" — LITERARY CHURCHMAN. "*A tale possessing the deepest interest.*" — COURT JOURNAL.

Milton's Poetical Works.—Edited with Text collated from the best Authorities, with Introduction and Notes by DAVID MASSON. Three vols. 8vo. With Two Portraits engraved by C. H. JEENS. (Uniform with the Cambridge Shakespeare).
[*Nearly Ready.*

Mistral (F.)—MIRELLE, a Pastoral Epic of Provence. Translated by H. CRICHTON. Extra fcap. 8vo. 6s.

"*It would be hard to overpraise the sweetness and pleasing freshness of this charming epic.*"—ATHENÆUM. "*A good translation of a poem that deserves to be known by all students of literature and friends of old-world simplicity in story-telling.*" — NONCONFORMIST.

Mitford (A. B.)—TALES OF OLD JAPAN. By A. B. MITFORD, Second Secretary to the British Legation in Japan. With Illustrations drawn and cut on Wood by Japanese Artists. Two Vols. Crown 8vo. 21s.

"*They will always be interesting as memorials of a most exceptional society; while, regarded simply as tales, they are sparkling, sensational, and dramatic, and the originality of their ideas and the quaintness of their language give them a most captivating piquancy. The illustrations are extremely interesting, and for the curious in such matters have a special and particular value.*" — PALL MALL GAZETTE.

Mr. Pisistratus Brown, M.P., IN THE HIGHLANDS. New Edition, with Illustrations. Crown 8vo. 3s. 6d.

> "The book is calculated to recall pleasant memories of holidays well spent, and scenes not easily to be forgotten. To those who have never been in the Western Highlands, or sailed along the Frith of Clyde and on the Western Coast, it will seem almost like a fairy story. There is a charm in the volume which makes it anything but easy for a reader who has opened it to put it down until the last page has been read."—SCOTSMAN.

Mrs. Jerningham's Journal. A Poem purporting to be the Journal of a newly-married Lady. Second Edition. Fcap. 8vo. 3s. 6d.

> "It is nearly a perfect gem. We have had nothing so good for a long time, and those who neglect to read it are neglecting one of the jewels of contemporary history."—EDINBURGH DAILY REVIEW. "One quality in the piece, sufficient of itself to claim a moment's attention, is that it is unique—original, indeed, is not too strong a word—in the manner of its conception and execution." —PALL MALL GAZETTE.

Mudie.—STRAY LEAVES. By C. E. MUDIE. New Edition. Extra fcap. 8vo. 3s. 6d. Contents:—"His and Mine"— "Night and Day"—"One of Many," &c.

> This little volume consists of a number of poems, mostly of a genuinely devotional character. "They are for the most part so exquisitely sweet and delicate as to be quite a marvel of composition. They are worthy of being laid up in the recesses of the heart, and recalled to memory from time to time."—ILLUSTRATED LONDON NEWS.

Myers (Ernest).—THE PURITANS. By ERNEST MYERS. Extra fcap. 8vo. cloth. 2s. 6d.

> "It is not too much to call it a really grand poem, stately and dignified, and showing not only a high poetic mind, but also great power over poetic expression."—LITERARY CHURCHMAN.

Myers (F. W. H.)—POEMS. By F. W. H. MYERS. Containing "St. Paul," "St. John," and others. Extra fcap. 8vo. 4s. 6d.

"*It is rare to find a writer who combines to such an extent the faculty of communicating feelings with the faculty of euphonious expression.*"—SPECTATOR. "'*St. Paul*' *stands without a rival as the noblest religious poem which has been written in an age which beyond any other has been prolific in this class of poetry. The sublimest conceptions are expressed in language which, for richness, taste, and purity, we have never seen excelled.*"—JOHN BULL.

Nichol.—HANNIBAL, A HISTORICAL DRAMA. By JOHN NICHOL, B.A. Oxon., Regius Professor of English Language and Literature in the University of Glasgow. Extra fcap. 8vo. 7s. 6d.

"*The poem combines in no ordinary degree firmness and workmanship. After the lapse of many centuries, an English poet is found paying to the great Carthagenian the worthiest poetical tribute which has as yet, to our knowledge, been afforded to his noble and stainless name.*"—SATURDAY REVIEW.

Nine Years Old.—By the Author of "St. Olave's," "When I was a Little Girl," &c. Illustrated by FRÖLICH. Third Edition. Extra fcap. 8vo. cloth gilt. 4s. 6d.

It is believed that this story, by the favourably known author of "*St. Olave's,*" *will be found both highly interesting and instructive to the young. The volume contains eight graphic illustrations by Mr. L. Frölich. The* EXAMINER *says:* "*Whether the readers are nine years old, or twice, or seven times as old, they must enjoy this pretty volume.*"

Noel.—BEATRICE, AND OTHER POEMS. By the Hon. RODEN NOEL. Fcap. 8vo. 6s.

"*It is impossible to read the poem through without being powerfully moved. There are passages in it which for intensity and tenderness, clear and vivid vision, spontaneous and delicate sympathy, may be compared with the best efforts of our best living writers.*"—SPECTATOR. "*It is long since we have seen a volume of poems which has seemed to us so full of the real stuff of which we are made, and uttering so freely the deepest wants of this complicated age.*"—BRITISH QUARTERLY.

Norton.—Works by the Hon. Mrs. NORTON :—

THE LADY OF LA GARAYE. With Vignette and Frontispiece. New Edition. Fcap. 8vo. 4s. 6d.

> "A poem entirely unaffected, perfectly original, so true and yet so fanciful, so strong and yet so womanly, with painting so exquisite, a pure portraiture of the highest affections and the deepest sorrows, and instilling a lesson true, simple, and sublime." — DUBLIN UNIVERSITY MAGAZINE. "Full of thought well expressed, and may be classed among her best efforts."—TIMES.

OLD SIR DOUGLAS. Cheap Edition. Globe 8vo. 2s. 6d.

> "This varied and lively novel—this clever novel so full of character, and of fine incidental remark."—SCOTSMAN. "One of the pleasantest and healthiest stories of modern fiction."—GLOBE.

Oliphant.—Works by Mrs. OLIPHANT :—

AGNES HOPETOUN'S SCHOOLS AND HOLIDAYS. New Edition with Illustrations. Royal 16mo. gilt leaves. 4s. 6d.

> "There are few books of late years more fitted to touch the heart, purify the feeling, and quicken and sustain right principles."—NONCONFORMIST. "A more gracefully written story it is impossible to desire."—DAILY NEWS.

A SON OF THE SOIL. New Edition. Globe 8vo. 2s. 6d.

> "It is a very different work from the ordinary run of novels. The whole life of a man is portrayed in it, worked out with subtlety and insight."—ATHENÆUM. "With entire freedom from any sensational plot, there is enough of incident to give keen interest to the narrative, and make us feel as we read it that we have been spending a few hours with friends who will make our own lives better by their own noble purposes and holy living."—BRITISH QUARTERLY REVIEW.

Our Year. A Child's Book, in Prose and Verse. By the Author of "John Halifax, Gentleman." Illustrated by CLARENCE DOBELL. Royal 16mo. 3s. 6d.

> "It is just the book we could wish to see in the hands of every child."—ENGLISH CHURCHMAN.

Olrig Grange. Edited by HERMANN KUNST, Philol. Professor. Extra fcap. 8vo. 6s. 6d.

> *The* NORTH BRITISH DAILY MAIL, *in reviewing the work, speak of it as affording "abounding evidence of genial and generative faculty working in self-decreed modes. A masterly and original power of impression, pouring itself forth in clear, sweet, strong rhythm. . . . Easy to cull remarkable instances of thrilling fervour, of gleaming delicacy, of scathing and trenchant scorn, to point out the fine and firm discrimination of character which prevails throughout, to dwell upon the ethical power and psychological truth which are exhibited, to note the skill with which the diverse parts of the poem are set in organic relation. . . . It is a fine poem, full of life, of music, and of clear vision."*

Oxford Spectator, The.—Reprinted. Extra fcap. 8vo. 3s. 6d.

> *These papers, after the manner of Addison's "Spectator," appeared in Oxford from November 1867 to December 1868, at intervals varying from two days to a week. They attempt to sketch several features of Oxford life from an undergraduate's point of view, and to give modern readings of books which undergraduates study.* "There is," *the* SATURDAY REVIEW *says,* "all the old fun, the old sense of social ease and brightness and freedom, the old medley of work and indolence, of jest and earnest, that made Oxford life so picturesque."

Palgrave.—Works by FRANCIS TURNER PALGRAVE, M.A., late Fellow of Exeter College, Oxford :—

THE FIVE DAYS' ENTERTAINMENTS AT WENTWORTH GRANGE. A Book for Children. With Illustrations by ARTHUR HUGHES, and Engraved Title-page by JEENS. Small 4to. cloth extra. 6s.

> "*If you want a really good book for both sexes and all ages, buy this, as handsome a volume of tales as you'll find in all the market.*"—ATHENÆUM. "*Exquisite both in form and substance.*" —GUARDIAN.

Palgrave—*continued.*

    LYRICAL POEMS. Extra fcap. 8vo. **6s.**

> "A volume of pure quiet verse, sparkling with tender melodies, and alive with thoughts of genuine poetry. . . . Turn where we will throughout the volume, we find traces of beauty, tenderness, and truth; true poet's work, touched and refined by the master-hand of a real artist, who shows his genius even in trifles."—STANDARD.

    ORIGINAL HYMNS. Third Edition, enlarged, 18mo. **1s. 6d.**

> "So choice, so perfect, and so refined, so tender in feeling, and so scholarly in expression, that we look with special interest to everything that he gives us."—LITERARY CHURCHMAN.

    GOLDEN TREASURY OF THE BEST SONGS AND LYRICS Edited by F. T. PALGRAVE. See GOLDEN TREASURY SERIES.

    SHAKESPEARE'S SONNETS AND SONGS. Edited by F. T. PALGRAVE. Gem Edition. With Vignette Title by JEENS. **3s. 6d.**

> "For minute elegance no volume could possibly excel the 'Gem Edition.'"—SCOTSMAN.

Parables.—TWELVE PARABLES OF OUR LORD. Illustrated in Colours from Sketches taken in the East by McENIRY, with Frontispiece from a Picture by JOHN JELLICOE, and Illuminated Texts and Borders. Royal 4to. in Ornamental Binding. **16s.**

> The SCOTSMAN calls this "one of the most superb books of the season." The richly and tastefully illuminated borders are from the Brevario Grimani, in St. Mark's Library, Venice. The TIMES calls it "one of the most beautiful of modern pictorial works;" while the GRAPHIC says "nothing in this style, so good, has ever before been published."

Patmore.—THE CHILDREN'S GARLAND, from the Best Poets. Selected and arranged by COVENTRY PATMORE. New Edition. With Illustrations by J. LAWSON. Crown 8vo. gilt. **6s.** Golden Treasury Edition. 18mo. **4s. 6d.**

> "The charming illustrations added to many of the poems will add greatly to their value in the eyes of children."—DAILY NEWS.

Pember.—THE TRAGEDY OF LESBOS. A Dramatic Poem. By E. H. PEMBER. Fcap. 8vo. 4s. 6d.

> *Founded upon the story of Sappho. "He tells his story with a poetic force, and in language that often rises almost to grandeur."* —ATHENÆUM.

Poole.—PICTURES OF COTTAGE LIFE IN THE WEST OF ENGLAND. By MARGARET E. POOLE. New and Cheaper Edition. With Frontispiece by R. Farren. Crown 8vo. 3s. 6d.

> *"Charming stories of peasant life, written in something of George Eliot's style. . . . Her stories could not be other than they are, as literal as truth, as romantic as fiction, full of pathetic touches and strokes of genuine humour. . . . All the stories are studies of actual life, executed with no mean art."*—TIMES.

Population of an Old Pear Tree. From the French of E. VAN BRUYSSEL. Edited by the Author of "The Heir of Redclyffe." With Illustrations by BECKER. Cheaper Edition. Crown 8vo. gilt. 4s. 6d.

> *"This is not a regular book of natural history, but a description of all the living creatures that came and went in a summer's day beneath an old pear tree, observed by eyes that had for the nonce become microscopic, recorded by a pen that finds dramas in everything, and illustrated by a dainty pencil. . . . We can hardly fancy anyone with a moderate turn for the curiosities of insect life, or for delicate French esprit, not being taken by these clever sketches."*—GUARDIAN. *"A whimsical and charming little book."*—ATHENÆUM.

Realmah.—By the Author of "Friends in Council." Crown 8vo. 6s.

Rhoades.—POEMS. By JAMES RHOADES. Fcap. 8vo. 4s. 6d.

> CONTENTS:—*Ode to Harmony; To the Spirit of Unrest; Ode to Winter; The Tunnel; To the Spirit of Beauty; Song of a Leaf; By the Rother; An Old Orchard; Love and Rest; The Flowers Surprised; On the Death of Artemus Ward; The Two Paths; The Ballad of Little Maisie; Sonnets.*

Richardson.—THE ILIAD OF THE EAST. A Selection of Legends drawn from Valmiki's Sanskrit Poem, "The Ramayana." By FREDERIKA RICHARDSON. Crown 8vo. 7s. 6d.

> "It is impossible to read it without recognizing the value and interest of the Eastern epic. It is as fascinating as a fairy tale, this romantic poem of India."—GLOBE. "A charming volume, which at once enmeshes the reader in its snares."—ATHENÆUM.

Roby.—STORY OF A HOUSEHOLD, AND OTHER POEMS. By MARY K. ROBY. Fcap. 8vo. 5s.

Rogers.—Works by J. E. ROGERS:—

RIDICULA REDIVIVA. Old Nursery Rhymes. Illustrated in Colours, with Ornamental Cover. Crown 4to. 6s.

> "The most splendid, and at the same time the most really meritorious of the books specially intended for children, that we have seen."—SPECTATOR. "These large bright pictures will attract children to really good and honest artistic work, and that ought not to be an indifferent consideration with parents who propose to educate their children."—PALL MALL GAZETTE.

MORES RIDICULI. Old Nursery Rhymes. Illustrated in Colours, with Ornamental Cover. Crown 4to. 6s.

> "These world-old rhymes have never had and need never wish for a better pictorial setting than Mr. Rogers has given them."—TIMES. "Nothing could be quainter or more absurdly comical than most of the pictures, which are all carefully executed and beautifully coloured."—GLOBE.

Rossetti.—GOBLIN MARKET, AND OTHER POEMS. By CHRISTINA ROSSETTI. With two Designs by D. G. ROSSETTI. Second Edition. Fcap. 8vo. 5s.

> "She handles her little marvel with that rare poetic discrimination which neither exhausts it of its simple wonders by pushing symbolism too far, nor keeps those wonders in the merely fabulous and capricious stage. In fact, she has produced a true children's poem, which is far more delightful to the mature than to children, though it would be delightful to all."—SPECTATOR.

BELLES LETTRES.

Runaway (The). A Story for the Young. By the Author of "Mrs. Jerningham's Journal." With Illustrations by J. LAWSON. Globe 8vo. gilt. 4s. 6d.

"This is one of the best, if not indeed the very best, of all the stories that has come before us this Christmas. The heroines are both charming, and, unlike heroines, they are as full of fun as of good. It is an admirable book to read aloud to the young folk when they are all gathered round the fire, and nurses and other apparitions are still far away."—SATURDAY REVIEW.

Ruth and her Friends. A Story for Girls. With a Frontispiece. Fourth Edition. 18mo. Cloth extra. 2s. 6d.

"We wish all the school girls and home-taught girls in the land had the opportunity of reading it."—NONCONFORMIST.

Scouring of the White Horse; or, the Long VACATION RAMBLE OF A LONDON CLERK. Illustrated by DOYLE. Imp. 16mo. Cheaper Issue. 3s. 6d.

"A glorious tale of summer joy."—FREEMAN. "There is a genial hearty life about the book."—JOHN BULL. "The execution is excellent. . . . Like 'Tom Brown's School Days,' the 'White Horse' gives the reader a feeling of gratitude and personal esteem towards the author."—SATURDAY REVIEW.

Shairp (Principal).—KILMAHOE, a Highland Pastoral, with other Poems. By JOHN CAMPBELL SHAIRP, Principal of the United College, St. Andrews. Fcap. 8vo. 5s.

"Kilmahoe is a Highland Pastoral, redolent of the warm soft air of the western lochs and moors, sketched out with remarkable grace and picturesqueness."—SATURDAY REVIEW.

Shakespeare.—The Works of WILLIAM SHAKESPEARE. Cambridge Edition. Edited by W. GEORGE CLARK, M.A. and W. ALDIS WRIGHT, M.A. Nine vols. 8vo. Cloth. 4l. 14s. 6d.

"This, now acknowledged to be the standard edition of Shakespeare, the result of many years' study and research on the part of the accomplished Editors, assisted by the suggestions of a host of Shakespearian students in all parts of the country. Two or three are the distinctive characteristics of this edition: 1. The text..."

based on a thorough collation of the four Folios, and of all the Quarto editions of the separate plays, and of subsequent editions and commentaries. 2. All the results of this collation are given in notes at the foot of the page, together with the conjectural emendations collected and suggested by the Editors, or furnished by their correspondents, so as to give the reader a complete view of the existing materials out of which the text has been constructed, or may be amended. 3. Where a quarto edition differs materially from the received text, the text of the quarto is printed literatim in a smaller type after the received text. 4. The lines in each scene are numbered separately, so as to facilitate reference. 5. At the end of each play a few notes, critical, explanatory, and illustrative, are added. 6. The Poems, edited on a similar plan, are printed at the end of the Dramatic Works. The Preface contains some notes on Shakespearian Grammar, Spelling, Metre, and Punctuation, and a history of all the chief editions from the Poet's time to the present. The GUARDIAN calls it an "excellent, and, to the student, almost indispensable edition;" and the EXAMINER calls it "an unrivalled edition."

Shakespeare's Tempest. Edited with Glossarial and Explanatory Notes, by the Rev. J. M. JEPHSON. Second Edition. 18mo. 1s.

This is an edition for use in schools. The introduction treats briefly of the value of language, the fable of the play and other points. The notes are intended to teach the student to analyse every obscure sentence and trace out the logical sequence of the poet's thoughts; to point out the rules of Shakespeare's versification; to explain obsolete words and meanings; and to guide the student's taste by directing his attention to such passages as seem especially worthy of note for their poetical beauty or truth to nature. The text is in the main founded upon that of the first collected edition of Shakespeare's plays.

Slip (A) in the Fens.—Illustrated by the Author. Crown 8vo. 6s.

Smith.—POEMS. By CATHERINE BARNARD SMITH. Fcap. 8vo. 5s.

"*Wealthy in feeling, meaning, finish, and grace; not without passion, which is suppressed, but the keener for that.*"—ATHENÆUM.

Smith (Rev. Walter).—HYMNS OF CHRIST AND THE CHRISTIAN LIFE. By the Rev. WALTER C. SMITH, M.A. Fcap. 8vo. 6s.

"These are among the sweetest sacred poems … here read … time. With no profuse imagery, expressing a ron… and expression by no means uncommon, they are true and de… and their pathos is profound and simple."—NONCONFORMIST.

Spring Songs. By a WEST HIGHLANDER. With a V… Illustration by GOURLAY STEELE. Fcap. 8vo. 1s. 6d.

"Without a trace of affectation or sentimentalism, the … tters are perfectly simple and natural, profoundly known and p… foundly true."—DAILY NEWS.

Stanley.—TRUE TO LIFE.—A SIMPLE STORY. By M… STANLEY. Crown 8vo. 10s. 6d.

"For many a long day we have not met with a more simple, l… and unpretending story."—STANDARD.

Stephen (C. E.)—THE SERVICE OF THE POOR; … an Inquiry into the Reasons for and against the Establishm… Religious Sisterhoods for Charitable Purposes. By CAROL… EMILIA STEPHEN. Crown 8vo. 6s. 6d.

"Miss Stephen devotes the first part of her volume to a brief h… of religious associations, taking as specimens—I. The Deacon… the Primitive Church; II. the Béguines; III. the Third … of S. Francis; IV. the Sisters of Charity of S. Vincent d… V. the Deaconesses of Modern Germany. In the second pa… attempts to show what are the real wants met by Sisterho… , to … extent the same wants may be effectually met by the or… ni of corresponding institutions on a secular basis, and … h… t … reasons for endeavouring to do so. "It touches incident… ly with much wisdom and tenderness on so many of the … women, particularly of single women, with society, that it … read with advantage by many who have never thought of ent… a Sisterhood."—SPECTATOR.

Stephens (J. B.)—CONVICT ONCE. A Poem. By J. Brunton Stephens. Extra fcap. 8vo. 3s. 6d.

> "It is as far more interesting than ninety-nine novels out of a hundred, as it is superior to them in power, worth, and beauty. We should most strongly advise everybody to read 'Convict Once.'"—Westminster Review.

Streets and Lanes of a City: Being the Reminiscences of Amy Dutton. With a Preface by the Bishop of Salisbury. Second and Cheaper Edition. Globe 8vo. 2s. 6d.

> This little volume records, to use the words of the Bishop of Salisbury, "a portion of the experience, selected out of overflowing materials, of two ladies, during several years of devoted work as district parochial visitors in a large population in the north of England." Every incident narrated is absolutely true, and only the names of the persons introduced have been (necessarily) changed. "One of the most really striking books that has ever come before us."—Literary Churchman.

Thring.—SCHOOL SONGS. A Collection of Songs for Schools. With the Music arranged for four Voices. Edited by the Rev. E. Thring and H. Riccius. Folio. 7s. 6d.

> The collection includes the "Agnus Dei," Tennyson's "Light Brigade," Macaulay's "Ivry," etc. among other pieces.

Tom Brown's School Days.—By An Old Boy. Golden Treasury Edition, 4s. 6d. People's Edition, 2s.

With Seven Illustrations by A. Hughes and Sydney Hall. Crown 8vo. 6s.

> "An exact picture of the bright side of a Rugby boy's experience, told with a life, a spirit, and a fond minuteness of detail and recollection which is infinitely honourable to the author."—Edinburgh Review. "The most famous boy's book in the language."—Daily News.

BELLES LETTRES. 37

Tom Brown at Oxford.—New Edition. With Illustrations. Crown 8vo. 6s.

> "*In no other work that we can call to mind are the finer qualities of the English gentleman more happily portrayed.*"—DAILY NEWS.
> "*A book of great power and truth.*"—NATIONAL REVIEW.

Trench.—Works by R. CHENEVIX TRENCH, D.D., Archbishop of Dublin. (For other Works by this Author, see THEOLOGICAL, HISTORICAL, and PHILOSOPHICAL CATALOGUES.)

POEMS. Collected and arranged anew. Fcap. 8vo. 7s. 6d.

ELEGIAC POEMS. Third Edition. Fcap. 8vo. 2s. 6d.

CALDERON'S LIFE'S A DREAM: The Great Theatre of the World. With an Essay on his Life and Genius. Fcap. 8vo. 4s. 6d.

HOUSEHOLD BOOK OF ENGLISH POETRY. Selected and arranged, with Notes, by Archbishop TRENCH. Second Edition. Extra fcap. 8vo. 5s. 6d.

> *This volume is called a "Household Book," by this name implying that it is a book for all—that there is nothing in it to prevent it from being confidently placed in the hands of every member of the household. Specimens of all classes of poetry are given, including selections from living authors. The editor has aimed to produce a book "which the emigrant, finding room for little not absolutely necessary, might yet find room for in his trunk, and the traveller in his knapsack, and that on some narrow shelves where there are few books this might be one." "The Archbishop has conferred on this delightful volume an important gift on the whole English-speaking population of the world.*"—PALL MALL GAZETTE.

SACRED LATIN POETRY, Chiefly Lyrical. Selected and arranged for Use. By Archbishop TRENCH. New Edition, Corrected and Improved. Fcap. 8vo. 7s.

> "*The aim of the present volume is to offer to members of our English Church a collection of the best sacred Latin poetry, such as they shall be able entirely and heartily to accept and approve—a collection,*

Trench (Archbishop)—*continued.*

that is, in which they shall not be evermore liable to be offended, and to have the current of their sympathies checked, by coming upon that which, however beautiful as poetry, out of higher respects they must reject and condemn—in which, too, they shall not fear that snares are being laid for them, to entangle them unawares in admiration for aught which is inconsistent with their faith and fealty to their own spiritual mother."—PREFACE.

JUSTIN MARTYR, AND OTHER POEMS. Fifth Edition. Fcap. 8vo. 6*s.*

Trollope (Anthony).—SIR HARRY HOTSPUR OF HUMBLETHWAITE. By ANTHONY TROLLOPE, Author of "Framley Parsonage," etc. Cheap Edition. Globe 8vo. 2*s.* 6*d.*

The TIMES *says:* "*In this novel we are glad to recognize a return to what we must call Mr. Trollope's old form. The characters are drawn with vigour and boldness, and the book may do good to many readers of both sexes."* *The* ATHENÆUM *remarks:* "*No reader who begins to read this book is likely to lay it down until the last page is turned. This brilliant novel appears to us decidedly more successful than any other of Mr. Trollope's shorter stories."*

Turner.—Works by the Rev. CHARLES TENNYSON TURNER:—

SONNETS. Dedicated to his Brother, the Poet Laureate. Fcap. 8vo. 4*s.* 6*d.*

SMALL TABLEAUX. Fcap. 8vo. 4*s.* 6*d.*

Vittoria Colonna.—LIFE AND POEMS. By MRS. HENRY ROSCOE. Crown 8vo. 9*s.*

"*It is written with good taste, with quick and intelligent sympathy, occasionally with a real freshness and charm of style."*—PALL MALL GAZETTE.

Volunteer's Scrap Book. By the Author of "The Cambridge Scrap Book." Crown 4to. 7*s.* 6*d.*

"*A genial and clever caricaturist, in whom we may often perceive* through small details that he has as proper a sense of the graceful as of the ludicrous. The author might be and pr... is a Volunteer himself, so kindly is the mirth he makes of ... incidents and phrases of the drill-ground."—EXAMINER.

Waller.—SIX WEEKS IN THE SADDLE: A Painter's Journal in Iceland. By S. E. WALLER. Illustrated by the Author. Crown 8vo. 6s.

"*An exceedingly pleasant and naturally written little book . . . Mr. Waller has a clever pencil, and the text is well illustrated : ... own sketches.*"—TIMES.

Wandering Willie. By the Author of "Effie's Friends," and "John Hatherton." Third Edition. Crown 8vo. 6s.

"*This is an idyll of rare truth and beauty. . . . The story is simple and touching, the style of extraordinary delicacy, precision, and picturesqueness. . . . A charming gift-book for young ladies not yet promoted to novels, and will amply repay those of their elders who may give an hour to its perusal.*"—DAILY NEWS.

Webster.—Works by AUGUSTA WEBSTER :—

"*If Mrs. Webster only remains true to herself, she will assuredly take a higher rank as a poet than any woman has yet done.*"—WESTMINSTER REVIEW.

DRAMATIC STUDIES. Extra fcap. 8vo. 5s.

"*A volume as strongly marked by perfect taste as by poetic power.*"—NONCONFORMIST.

A WOMAN SOLD, AND OTHER POEMS. Crown 8vo. 7s. 6d.

"*Mrs. Webster has shown us that she is able to draw admirably from the life; that she can observe with subtlety, and render her observations with delicacy; that she can impersonate complex conceptions and venture into which few living writers can f... to her*"—GUARDIAN.

PORTRAITS. Second Edition. Extra fcap. 8vo. 3s. 6d.

"*Mrs. Webster's poems exhibit simplicity and tenderness . . . her taste is perfect . . . This simplicity is combined with a ...*"

Webster—*continued.*

> thought, feeling, and observation which demand that attention which only real lovers of poetry are apt to bestow."—WESTMINSTER REVIEW.

PROMETHEUS BOUND OF ÆSCHYLUS. Literally translated into English Verse. Extra fcap. 8vo. 3s. 6d.

> "*Closeness and simplicity combined with literary skill.*"—ATHENÆUM. "*Mrs. Webster's 'Dramatic Studies' and 'Translation of Prometheus' have won for her an honourable place among our female poets. She writes with remarkable vigour and dramatic realization, and bids fair to be the most successful claimant of Mrs. Browning's mantle.*"—BRITISH QUARTERLY REVIEW.

MEDEA OF EURIPIDES. Literally translated into English Verse. Extra fcap. 8vo. 3s. 6d.

> "*Mrs. Webster's translation surpasses our utmost expectations. It is a photograph of the original without any of that harshness which so often accompanies a photograph.*"—WESTMINSTER REVIEW.

THE AUSPICIOUS DAY. A Dramatic Poem. Extra fcap. 8vo. 5s.

> "*The 'Auspicious Day' shows a marked advance, not only in art, but, in what is of far more importance, in breadth of thought and intellectual grasp.*"—WESTMINSTER REVIEW. "*This drama is a manifestation of high dramatic power on the part of the gifted writer, and entitled to our warmest admiration, as a worthy piece of work.*"—STANDARD.

YU-PE-YA'S LUTE. A Chinese Tale in English Verse. Extra fcap. 8vo. 3s. 6d.

Westminster Plays. Lusus Alteri Westmonasterienses, Sive Prologi et Epilogi ad Fabulas in S^{ti} Petri Collegio: actas qui Exstabant collecti et justa quoad licuit annorum serie ordinati, quibus accedit Declamationum quæ vocantur et Epigrammatum Delectus. Curantibus J. MURE, A.M., H. BULL, A.M., C. B. SCOTT, B.D. 8vo. 12s. 6d.

> IDEM.—Pars Secunda, 1820—1864. Quibus accedit Epigrammatum Delectus. 8vo. 15s.

When I was a Little Girl. STORIES FOR CHILDREN. By the Author of "St. Olave's." Fourth Edition. Extra fcap. 8vo. 4s. 6d. With Eight Illustrations by L. FRÖLICH.

> "At the head, and a long way ahead, of all books for girls, we place 'When I was a Little Girl.'"—TIMES. "It is one of the choicest morsels of child-biography which we have met with."—NONCONFORMIST.

White.—RHYMES BY WALTER WHITE. 8vo. 7s. 6d.

Whittier.—JOHN GREENLEAF WHITTIER'S POETICAL WORKS. Complete Edition, with Portrait engraved by C. H. JEENS. 18mo. 4s. 6d.

> "Mr. Whittier has all the smooth melody and the pathos of the author of 'Hiawatha,' with a greater nicety of description and a quainter fancy."—GRAPHIC.

Wolf.—THE LIFE AND HABITS OF WILD ANIMALS. Twenty Illustrations by JOSEPH WOLF, engraved by J. W. and E. WHYMPER. With descriptive Letter-press, by D. G. ELLIOT, F.L.S. Super royal 4to, cloth extra, gilt edges. 21s.

> This is the last series of drawings which will be made by Mr. Wolf, either upon wood or stone. The PALL MALL GAZETTE says: "The fierce, untameable side of brute nature has never received a more robust and vigorous interpretation, and the various incidents in which particular character is shown are set forth with rare dramatic power. For excellence that will endure, we incline to place this very near the top of the list of Christmas books." And the ART JOURNAL observes, "Rarely, if ever, have we seen animal life more forcibly and beautifully depicted than in this really splendid volume."

Wollaston.—LYRA DEVONIENSIS. By T. V. WOLLASTON, M.A. Fcap. 8vo. 3s. 6d.

> "It is the work of a man of refined taste, of deep religious sentiment, a true artist, and a good Christian."—CHURCH TIMES.

Woolner.—MY BEAUTIFUL LADY. By THOMAS WOOLNER. With a Vignette by ARTHUR HUGHES. Third Edition. Fcap. 8vo. 5s.

> "*It is clearly the product of no idle hour, but a highly-conceived and faithfully-executed task, self-imposed, and prompted by that inward yearning to utter great thoughts, and a wealth of passionate feeling, which is poetic genius. No man can read this poem without being struck by the fitness and finish of the workmanship, so to speak, as well as by the chastened and unpretending loftiness of thought which pervades the whole.*"—GLOBE.

Words from the Poets. Selected by the Editor of "Rays of Sunlight." With a Vignette and Frontispiece. 18mo. limp., 1s.

> "*The selection aims at popularity, and deserves it.*"—GUARDIAN.

Yonge (C. M.)—Works by CHARLOTTE M. YONGE. (See also CATALOGUE OF WORKS IN HISTORY, and EDUCATIONAL CATALOGUE.)

THE HEIR OF REDCLYFFE. Twentieth Edition. With Illustrations. Crown 8vo. 6s.

HEARTSEASE. Thirteenth Edition. With Illustrations. Crown 8vo. 6s.

THE DAISY CHAIN. Twelfth Edition. With Illustrations. Crown 8vo. 6s.

THE TRIAL: MORE LINKS OF THE DAISY CHAIN. Twelfth Edition. With Illustrations. Crown 8vo. 6s.

DYNEVOR TERRACE. Sixth Edition. Crown 8vo. 6s.

HOPES AND FEARS. Fourth Edition. Crown 8vo. 6s.

THE YOUNG STEPMOTHER. Fifth Edition. Crown 8vo. 6s.

CLEVER WOMAN OF THE FAMILY. Third Edition. Crown 8vo. 6s.

Yonge (C. M.)—*continued.*

THE DOVE IN THE EAGLE'S NEST. Fourth Edition. Crown 8vo. 6s.

"*We think the authoress of 'The Heir of Redclyffe' has surpassed her previous efforts in this illuminated chronicle of the olden time.*"—BRITISH QUARTERLY.

THE CAGED LION. Illustrated. Third Edition. Crown 8vo. 6s.

"*Prettily and tenderly written, and will with young people especially be a great favourite.*"—DAILY NEWS. "*Everybody should read this.*"—LITERARY CHURCHMAN.

THE CHAPLET OF PEARLS; OR, THE WHITE AND BLACK RIBAUMONT. Crown 8vo. 6s. New Edition.

"*Miss Yonge has brought a lofty aim as well as high art to the construction of a story which may claim a place among the best efforts in historical romance.*"—MORNING POST. "*The plot, in truth, is of the very first order of merit.*"—SPECTATOR. "*We have seldom read a more charming story.*"—GUARDIAN.

THE PRINCE AND THE PAGE. A Tale of the Last Crusade. Illustrated. 18mo. 2s. 6d.

"*A tale which, we are sure, will give pleasure to many others besides the young people for whom it is specially intended. . . . This extremely prettily-told story does not require the guarantee afforded by the name of the author of 'The Heir of Redclyffe' on the titlepage to ensure its becoming a universal favourite.*"—DUBLIN EVENING MAIL.

THE LANCES OF LYNWOOD. New Edition, with Coloured Illustrations. 18mo. 4s. 6d.

"*The illustrations are very spirited and rich in colour, and the story can hardly fail to charm the youthful reader.*"—MANCHESTER EXAMINER.

THE LITTLE DUKE: RICHARD THE FEARLESS. New Edition. Illustrated. 18mo. 2s. 6d.

Yonge (C. M.)—*continued.*

A STOREHOUSE OF STORIES. First and Second Series. Globe 8vo. 3*s.* 6*d.* each.

CONTENTS OF FIRST SERIES:—History of Philip Quarll—Goody Twoshoes—The Governess—Jemima Placid—The Perambulations of a Mouse—The Village School—The Little Queen—History of Little Jack.

"*Miss Yonge has done great service to the infantry of this generation by putting these eleven stories of sage simplicity within their reach.*"—BRITISH QUARTERLY REVIEW.

CONTENTS OF SECOND SERIES:—Family Stories—Elements of Morality—A Puzzle for a Curious Girl—Blossoms of Morality.

A BOOK OF GOLDEN DEEDS OF ALL TIMES AND ALL COUNTRIES. Gathered and Narrated Anew. New Edition, with Twenty Illustrations by FRÖLICH. Crown 8vo. cloth gilt. 6*s.* (See also GOLDEN TREASURY SERIES). Cheap Edition. 1*s.*

"*We have seen no prettier gift-book for a long time, and none which, both for its cheapness and the spirit in which it has been compiled, is more deserving of praise.*"—ATHENÆUM.

LITTLE LUCY'S WONDERFUL GLOBE. Pictured by FRÖLICH, and narrated by CHARLOTTE M. YONGE. Second Edition. Crown 4to. cloth gilt. 6*s.*

Miss Yonge's wonderful "knack" of instructive story-telling to children is well known. In this volume, in a manner which cannot but prove interesting to all boys and girls, she manages to convey a wonderful amount of information concerning most of the countries of the world; in this she is considerably aided by the twenty-four telling pictures of Mr. Frölich. "'Lucy's Wonderful Globe' is capital, and will give its youthful readers more idea of foreign countries and customs than any number of books of geography or travel."—GRAPHIC.

CAMEOS FROM ENGLISH HISTORY. From ROLLO to EDWARD II. Extra fcap. 8vo. 5*s.* Second Edition, enlarged. 5*s.*

A SECOND SERIES. THE WARS IN FRANCE. Extra fcap. 8vo. 5*s.*

Yonge (C. M.)—*continued.*

The endeavour has not been to chronicle facts, but to put together a series of pictures of persons and events, so as to arrest the attention, and give some individuality and distinctness to the recollection, by gathering together details at the most memorable moments. The " Cameos " are intended as a book for young people just beyond the elementary histories of England, and able to enter in some degree into the real spirit of events, and to be struck with characters and scenes presented in some relief. " Instead of dry details," says the NONCONFORMIST, *" we have living pictures, faithful, vivid, and striking."*

P's AND Q's; OR, THE QUESTION OF PUTTING UPON. With Illustrations by C. O. MURRAY. Second Edition. Globe 8vo. cloth gilt. 4s. 6d.

" *One of her most successful little pieces . . . . just what a narrative should be, each incident simply and naturally related, no preaching or moralizing, and yet the moral coming out most powerfully, and the whole story not too long, or with the least appearance of being spun out.*"—LITERARY CHURCHMAN.

THE PILLARS OF THE HOUSE; OR, UNDER WODE, UNDER RODE. Second Edition. Four vols. crown 8vo. 20s.

" *A domestic story of English professional life, which for sweetness of tone and absorbing interest from first to last has never been rivalled.*"—STANDARD. " *Miss Yonge has certainly added to her already high reputation by this charming book, which, although in four volumes, is not a single page too long, but keeps the reader's attention fixed to the end. Indeed we are only sorry there is not another volume to come, and part with the Underwood family with sincere regret.*"—COURT CIRCULAR.

LADY HESTER; OR, URSULA'S NARRATIVE. Second Edition. Crown 8vo. 6s.

" *We shall not anticipate the interest by epitomizing the plot, but we shall only say that readers will find in it all the gracefulness, right feeling, and delicate perception which they have been long accustomed to look for in Miss Yonge's writings.*"—GUARDIAN.

MACMILLAN'S
GOLDEN TREASURY SERIES.

UNIFORMLY printed in 18mo., with Vignette Titles by Sir NOEL PATON, T. WOOLNER, W. HOLMAN HUNT, J. E. MILLAIS, ARTHUR HUGHES, &c. Engraved on Steel by JEENS. Bound in extra cloth, 4s. 6d. each volume. Also kept in morocco and calf bindings.

> "*Messrs. Macmillan have, in their Golden Treasury Series, especially provided editions of standard works, volumes of selected poetry, and original compositions, which entitle this series to be called classical. Nothing can be better than the literary execution, nothing more elegant than the material workmanship.*"—BRITISH QUARTERLY REVIEW.

The Golden Treasury of the Best Songs and LYRICAL POEMS IN THE ENGLISH LANGUAGE. Selected and arranged, with Notes, by FRANCIS TURNER PALGRAVE.

> "*This delightful little volume, the Golden Treasury, which contains many of the best original lyrical pieces and songs in our language, grouped with care and skill, so as to illustrate each other like the pictures in a well-arranged gallery.*"—QUARTERLY REVIEW.

The Children's Garland from the best Poets. Selected and arranged by COVENTRY PATMORE.

> "*It includes specimens of all the great masters in the art of poetry, selected with the matured judgment of a man concentrated on obtaining insight into the feelings and tastes of childhood, and*

desirous to awaken its finest impulses, to cultivate its keenest sensibilities."—MORNING POST.

The Book of Praise. From the Best English Hymn Writers. Selected and arranged by Sir ROUNDELL PALMER. *A New and Enlarged Edition.*

"*All previous compilations of this kind must undeniably for the present give place to the Book of Praise. . . . The selection has been made throughout with sound judgment and critical taste. The pains involved in this compilation must have been immense, embracing, as it does, every writer of note in this special province of English literature, and ranging over the most widely divergent tracks of religious thought.*"—SATURDAY REVIEW.

The Fairy Book; the Best Popular Fairy Stories. Selected and rendered anew by the Author of "JOHN HALIFAX, GENTLEMAN."

"*A delightful selection, in a delightful external form; full of the physical splendour and vast opulence of proper fairy tales.*"—SPECTATOR.

The Ballad Book. A Selection of the Choicest British Ballads. Edited by WILLIAM ALLINGHAM.

"*His taste as a judge of old poetry will be found, by all acquainted with the various readings of old English ballads, true enough to justify his undertaking so critical a task.*"—SATURDAY REVIEW.

The Jest Book. The Choicest Anecdotes and Sayings. Selected and arranged by MARK LEMON.

"*The fullest and best jest book that has yet appeared.*"—SATURDAY REVIEW.

Bacon's Essays and Colours of Good and Evil. With Notes and Glossarial Index. By W. ALDIS WRIGHT, M.A.

"*The beautiful little edition of Bacon's Essays, now before us, does credit to the taste and scholarship of Mr. Aldis Wright. . . . It puts the reader in possession of all the essential literary facts and chronology necessary for reading the Essays in connection with Bacon's life and times.*"—SPECTATOR. "*By far the most complete as well as the most elegant edition we possess.*"—WESTMINSTER REVIEW.

The Pilgrim's Progress from this World to that which is to come. By JOHN BUNYAN.

"*A beautiful and scholarly reprint.*"—SPECTATOR.

The Sunday Book of Poetry for the Young. Selected and arranged by C. F. ALEXANDER.

"*A well-selected volume of Sacred Poetry.*"—SPECTATOR.

A Book of Golden Deeds of All Times and All Countries. Gathered and narrated anew. By the Author of "THE HEIR OF REDCLYFFE."

"*... To the young, for whom it is especially intended, as a most interesting collection of thrilling tales well told; and to their elders, as a useful handbook of reference, and a pleasant one to take up when their wish is to while away a weary half-hour. We have seen no prettier gift-book for a long time.*"—ATHENÆUM.

The Poetical Works of Robert Burns. Edited, with Biographical Memoir, Notes, and Glossary, by ALEXANDER SMITH. Two Vols.

"*Beyond all question this is the most beautiful edition of Burns yet out.*"—EDINBURGH DAILY REVIEW.

The Adventures of Robinson Crusoe. Edited from the Original Edition by J. W. CLARK, M.A., Fellow of Trinity College, Cambridge.

"*Mutilated and modified editions of this English classic are so much the rule, that a cheap and pretty copy of it, rigidly exact to the original, will be a prize to many book-buyers.*"—EXAMINER.

The Republic of Plato. TRANSLATED into ENGLISH, with Notes by J. Ll. DAVIES, M.A. and D. J. VAUGHAN, M.A.

"*A dainty and cheap little edition.*"—EXAMINER.

The Song Book. Words and Tunes from the best Poets and Musicians. Selected and arranged by JOHN HULLAH, Professor of Vocal Music in King's College, London.

"*A choice collection of the sterling songs of England, Scotland, and Ireland, with the music of each prefixed to the Words. How much true wholesome pleasure such a book can diffuse, and must diffuse, we trust through many thousand families.*"—EXAMINER.

La Lyre Française. Selected and arranged, with Notes, by GUSTAVE MASSON, French Master in Harrow School.

A selection of the best French songs and lyrical pieces.

Tom Brown's School Days. By AN OLD BOY.

"*A perfect gem of a book. The best and most healthy book about boys for boys that ever was written.*"—ILLUSTRATED TIMES.

A Book of Worthies. Gathered from the Old Histories and written anew by the Author of "THE HEIR OF REDCLYFFE." With Vignette.

"*An admirable addition to an admirable series.*"—WESTMINSTER REVIEW.

A Book of Golden Thoughts. By HENRY ATTWELL, Knight of the Order of the Oak Crown.

"*Mr. Attwell has produced a book of rare value. . . . Happily it is small enough to be carried about in the pocket, and of such a companion it would be difficult to weary.*"—PALL MALL GAZETTE.

Guesses at Truth. By TWO BROTHERS. New Edition.

The Cavalier and his Lady. Selections from the Works of the First Duke and Duchess of Newcastle. With an Introductory Essay by EDWARD JENKINS, Author of "Ginx's Baby," &c. 18mo. 4s. 6d.

"*A charming little volume.*"—STANDARD.

Theologia Germanica.—Translated from the German, by SUSANNA WINKWORTH. With a Preface by the REV. CHARLES KINGSLEY, and a letter to the Translator from the Chevalier Bunsen.

Milton's Poetical Works.—Edited, with Notes, &c., by PROFESSOR MASSON. Two vols. 18mo. 9s. [*Shortly.*

D

MACMILLAN'S

GLOBE LIBRARY.

Beautifully printed on toned paper and bound in cloth extra, gilt edges, price 4s. 6d. each; in cloth plain, 3s. 6d. Also kept in a variety of calf and morocco bindings at moderate prices.

BOOKS, Wordsworth says, are
"the spirit breathed
By dead men to their kind;"
and the aim of the publishers of the Globe Library has been to make it possible for the universal kin of English-speaking men to hold communion with the loftiest "spirits of the mighty dead;" to put within the reach of all classes *complete* and *accurate* editions, carefully and clearly printed upon the best paper, in a convenient form, at a moderate price, of the works of the MASTER-MINDS OF ENGLISH LITERATURE, and occasionally of foreign literature in an attractive English dress.

The Editors, by their scholarship and special study of their authors, are competent to afford every assistance to readers of all kinds: this assistance is rendered by original biographies, glossaries of unusual or obsolete words, and critical and explanatory notes.

The publishers hope, therefore, that these Globe Editions may prove worthy of acceptance by all classes wherever the English Language is spoken, and by their universal circulation justify their distinctive epithet; while at the same time they spread and nourish a common sympathy with nature's most "finely touched" spirits, and thus help a little to "make the whole world kin."

> *The* SATURDAY REVIEW *says:* "*The Globe Editions are admirable for their scholarly editing, their typographical excellence, their compendious form, and their cheapness.*" *The* BRITISH QUARTERLY REVIEW *says:* "*In compendiousness, elegance, and scholarliness, the Globe Editions of Messrs. Macmillan surpass any popular series of our classics hitherto given to the public. As near an approach to miniature perfection as has ever been made.*"

Shakespeare's Complete Works. Edited by W. G. CLARK, M.A., and W. ALDIS WRIGHT, M.A., of Trinity College, Cambridge, Editors of the "Cambridge Shakespeare." With Glossary. pp. 1,075.

> *This edition aims at presenting a perfectly reliable text of the complete works of "the foremost man in all literature." The text is essentially the same as that of the "Cambridge Shakespeare." Appended is a Glossary containing the meaning of every word in the text which is either obsolete or is used in an antiquated or unusual sense. This, combined with the method used to indicate corrupted readings, serves to a great extent the purpose of notes. The* ATHENÆUM *says this edition is "a marvel of beauty, cheapness, and compactness. . . . For the busy man, above all for the working student, this is the best of all existing Shakespeares." And the* PALL MALL GAZETTE *observes:* "*To have produced the complete works of the world's greatest poet in such a form, and at a price within the reach of every one, is of itself almost sufficient to give the publishers a claim to be considered public benefactors.*"

Spenser's Complete Works. Edited from the Original Editions and Manuscripts, by R. MORRIS, with a Memoir by J. W. HALES, M.A. With Glossary. pp. lv., 736.

> *The text of the poems has been reprinted from the earliest known editions, carefully collated with subsequent ones, most of which were published in the poet's lifetime. Spenser's only prose work, his sagacious and interesting "View of the State of Ireland," has been re-edited from three manuscripts belonging to the British Museum. A complete Glossary and a list of all the most important various*

readings serve to a large extent the purpose of notes explanatory and critical. An exhaustive general Index and a useful " Index of first lines" precede the poems; and in an Appendix are given Spenser's Letters to Gabriel Harvey. "Worthy—and higher praise it needs not—of the beautiful 'Globe Series.' The work is edited with all the care so noble a poet deserves."—DAILY NEWS.

Sir Walter Scott's Poetical Works.

Edited with a Biographical and Critical Memoir by FRANCIS TURNER PALGRAVE, and copious Notes. pp. xliii., 559.

" Scott," says Heine, " in his every book, gladdens, tranquillizes, and strengthens my heart." This edition contains the whole of Scott's poetical works, with the exception of one or two short poems. While most of Scott's own notes have been retained, others have been added explaining many historical and topographical allusions; and original introductions from the pen of a gentleman familiar with Scotch literature and scenery, containing much interesting information, antiquarian, historical, and biographical, are prefixed to the principal poems. "We can almost sympathise with a middle-aged grumbler, who, after reading Mr. Palgrave's memoir and introduction, should exclaim—' Why was there not such an edition of Scott when I was a schoolboy?'"—GUARDIAN.

Complete Works of Robert Burns.—THE POEMS, SONGS, AND LETTERS,

edited from the best Printed and Manuscript Authorities, with Glossarial Index, Notes, and a Biographical Memoir by ALEXANDER SMITH. pp. lxii., 636.

Burns's poems and songs need not circulate exclusively among Scotchmen, but should be read by all who wish to know the multitudinous capabilities of the Scotch language, and who have the capacity of appreciating the exquisite expression of all kinds of human feeling—rich pawky humour, keen wit, withering satire, genuine pathos, pure passionate love. The exhaustive glossarial index and the copious notes will make all the purely Scotch poems intelligible even to an Englishman. Burns's letters must be read by all who desire fully to appreciate the poet's character, to see it on all its many sides. Explanatory notes are prefixed to most of these letters, and Burns's Journals kept during his Border and Highland Tours, are appended. Following the prefixed biography by the editor, is a Chronological Table of Burns's Life and Works. "Admirable in all respects." Set Taylor. *"The cheapest, the most perfect, and the most interesting edition that has ever been published."*—BELL'S MESSENGER.

Robinson Crusoe. Edited after the Original Edition, with a Biographical Introduction by HENRY KINGSLEY. [pp. xxxi, 607.]

Of this matchless truth-like story, it is scarcely possible to put an unabridged edition. This edition may be relied upon as containing the whole of "Robinson Crusoe" as it came from the pen of its author, without mutilation, and with all peculiarities religiously preserved. These points, combined with its handsome paper, large clear type, and moderate price, ought to render this par excellence the "Globe," the Universal edition of Defoe's fascinating narrative. "A most excellent and in every way desirable edition."—COURT CIRCULAR. *"Macmillan's 'Globe' Robinson Crusoe is a book to have and to keep."*—MORNING STAR.

Goldsmith's Miscellaneous Works. Edited, with Biographical Introduction, by Professor MASSON. pp. lx., 695.

This volume comprehends the whole of the prose and poetical works of this most genial of English authors, those only being excluded which are mere compilations. They are all accurately reprinted from the most reliable editions. The faithfulness, fulness, and literary merit of the biography are sufficiently attested by the name of its author, Professor Masson. It contains many interesting anecdotes which will give the reader an insight into Goldsmith's character, and many graphic pictures of the literary life of London during the middle of last century. "Such an admirable compendium of the facts of Goldsmith's life, and so careful and minute a delineation of the mixed traits of his peculiar character as to be a very model of a literary biography in little." SCOTSMAN.

Pope's Poetical Works. Edited, with Notes and Introductory Memoir, by ADOLPHUS WILLIAM WARD, M.A., Fellow of St. Peter's College, Cambridge, and Professor of History in Owens College, Manchester. pp. lii., 508.

This edition contains all Pope's poems, translations, and adaptations, —his now superseded Homeric translations alone being omitted. The text, carefully revised, is taken from the best editions. Pope's own use of capital letters and apostrophied syllables, wherever necessary to an understanding of his meaning, has been preserved;

while his uncertain spelling and his frequently perplexing interpunctuation have been judiciously amended. Abundant notes are added, including Pope's own, the best of those of previous editors, and many which are the result of the study and research of the present editor. The introductory Memoir will be found to shed considerable light on the political, social, and literary life of the period in which Pope filled so large a space. The LITERARY CHURCHMAN *remarks: "The editor's own notes and introductory memoir are excellent, the memoir alone would be cheap and well worth buying at the price of the whole volume."*

Dryden's Poetical Works. Edited, with a Memoir, Revised Text, and Notes, by W. D. CHRISTIE, M.A., of Trinity College, Cambridge. pp. lxxxvii., 662.

A study of Dryden's works is absolutely necessary to anyone who wishes to understand thoroughly, not only the literature, but also the political and religious history of the eventful period when he lived and reigned as literary dictator. In this edition of his works, which comprises several specimens of his vigorous prose, the text has been thoroughly corrected and purified from many misprints and small changes often materially affecting the sense, which had been allowed to slip in by previous editors. The old spelling has been retained where it is not altogether strange or repulsive. Besides an exhaustive Glossary, there are copious Notes, critical, historical, biographical, and explanatory: and the biography contains the results of considerable original research, which has served to shed light on several hitherto obscure circumstances connected with the life and parentage of the poet. "An admirable edition, the result of great research and of a careful revision of the text. The memoir prefixed contains, within less than ninety pages, as much sound criticism and as comprehensive a biography as the student of Dryden need desire."—PALL MALL GAZETTE.

Cowper's Poetical Works. Edited, with Notes and Biographical Introduction, by WILLIAM BENHAM, Vicar of Addington and Professor of Modern History in Queen's College, London. pp. lxxiii., 536.

This volume contains, arranged under seven heads, the whole of Cowper's own poems, including several never before published, and all his translations except that of Homer's "Iliad." The text is taken from the original editions, and Cowper's own notes are given at the foot of the page, while many explanatory notes by the editor himself are appended to the volume. In th[e] very [full ...] it will be found that much new light has been thr[own on many] of the most difficult passages of Cowper's spiritual[ly ... life]. "Mr. Benham's edition of Cowper is one [of permanent value]. The biographical introduction is excellent, f[ull of information], singularly neat and readable and modest in[deed to ... in] its comments. The notes are concise and accurate, and th[e editor] has been able to discover and introduce some hitherto u[nprinted] matter. Altogether the book is a very excellent on[e]." SATURDAY REVIEW.

Morte d'Arthur.—SIR THOMAS MALORY'S BOOK OF KING ARTHUR AND OF HIS NOBLE KNIGHTS OF THE ROUND TABLE. The original Edition of CAXTON, revised for Modern Use. With an Introduction by Sir EDWARD STRACHEY, Bart. pp. xxxvii., 509.

This volume contains the cream of the legends of chivalry which have gathered round the shadowy King Arthur and his Knights of the Round Table. Tennyson has drawn largely on them in his cycle of Arthurian Idylls. The language is simple and quaint as that of the Bible, and the many stories of knightly adventure of which the book is made up, are fascinating as those of the "Arabian Nights." The great moral of the book is to "do after the good, and leave the evil." There was a want of an edition of the work at a moderate price, suitable for ordinary readers, and especially for boys: such an edition the present professes to be. The Introduction contains an account of the Origin and Matter of the book, the Text and its several Editions, and an Essay on Chivalry, tracing its history from its origin to its decay. Notes are appended, and a Glossary of such words as require explanation. "It is with perfect confidence that we recommend this edition of the old romance to every class of readers."—PALL MALL GAZETTE.

The Works of Virgil. Rendered into English Prose, with Introductions, Notes, Running Analysis, and an Index. By JAMES LONSDALE, M.A., late Fellow and Tutor of Balliol College, Oxford, and Classical Professor in King's College, London; and SAMUEL LEE, M.A., Latin Lecturer at University College, London. pp. 288.

The publishers believe that an accurate and readable translation of all the works of Virgil is perfectly in accordance with the object of the

"*Globe Library.*" *A new prose-translation has therefore been made by two competent scholars, who have rendered the original faithfully into simple Bible-English, without paraphrase; and at the same time endeavoured to maintain as far as possible the rhythm and majestic flow of the original. On this latter point the* DAILY TELEGRAPH *says,* "*The endeavour to preserve in some degree a rhythm in the prose rendering is almost invariably successful and pleasing in its effect;" and the* EDUCATIONAL TIMES, *that it* "*may be readily recommended as a model for young students for rendering the poet into English." The General Introduction will be found full of interesting information as to the life of Virgil, the history of opinion concerning his writings, the notions entertained of him during the Middle Ages, editions of his works, his influence on modern poets and on education. To each of his works is prefixed a critical and explanatory introduction, and important aid is afforded to the thorough comprehension of each production by the running Analysis. Appended is an Index of all the proper names and the most important subjects occurring throughout the poems and introductions.* "*A more complete edition of Virgil in English it is scarcely possible to conceive than the scholarly work before us.*" —GLOBE.

The Works of Horace. Rendered into English Prose, with Introductions, Running Analysis, Notes, and Index. By JOHN LONSDALE, M.A., and SAMUEL LEE, M.A.

This version of Horace is a literal rendering of the original, the translators having kept in view the same objects as they had before them in their edition of Virgil in "Globe Series." As in the case of Virgil, the original has been faithfully rendered into simple English, without paraphrase; and at the same time the translators have endeavoured to maintain as far as possible the rhythm and flow of the original. The general and particular Introductions and the Notes will afford the ordinary English reader all needful information as to Horace and his time, and the allusions in his works. The STANDARD *says,* "*To classical and non-classical readers it will be invaluable as a faithful interpretation of the mind and meaning of the poet, enriched as it is with notes and dissertations of the highest value in the way of criticism, illustration, and explanation.*"